Montana
Off the Beaten Path®

Help Us Keep This Guide Up to Date

Every effort has been made by the author and editors to make this guide as accurate and useful as possible. However, many things can change after a guide is published—establishments close, phone numbers change, facilities come under new management, etc.

We would love to hear from you concerning your experiences with this guide and how you feel it could be improved and be kept up to date. While we may not be able to respond to all comments and suggestions, we'll take them to heart and we'll also make certain to share them with the author. Please send your comments and suggestions to the following address:

The Globe Pequot Press
Reader Response/Editorial Department
P.O. Box 480
Guilford, CT 06437

Or you may e-mail us at:

editorial@globe-pequot.com

Thanks for your input, and happy travels!

OFF THE BEATEN PATH® SERIES

Montana

FOURTH EDITION

Off the Beaten Path®

by Michael McCoy

The Globe Pequot Press

Guilford, Connecticut

The prices and rates listed in this guidebook were confirmed at press time. We recommend, however, that you call establishments before traveling to obtain current information.

Maps created by Equator Graphics © The Globe Pequot Press
Cover and text design: Laura Augustine
Illustrations by Carole Drong
Cover photo by Gay Bumgarner/Index Stock

Library of Congress Cataloging-in-Publication Data Is Available

McCoy, Michael, 1951-
    Montana : off the beaten path / by Michael McCoy. —4th ed.
    p. cm. —(Off the beaten path series)
  Includes index.
  ISBN 0-7627-0760-7
  1. Montana—Guidebooks. I. Title. II. Series.
  F729.3.M36   2000
  917.8604'34—dc21   00-041707
                            CIP

Manufactured in the United States of America
Fourth Edition/Second Printing

*For Boone, a remarkable town,
and all of its boys and girls . . .
young and old, there and gone*

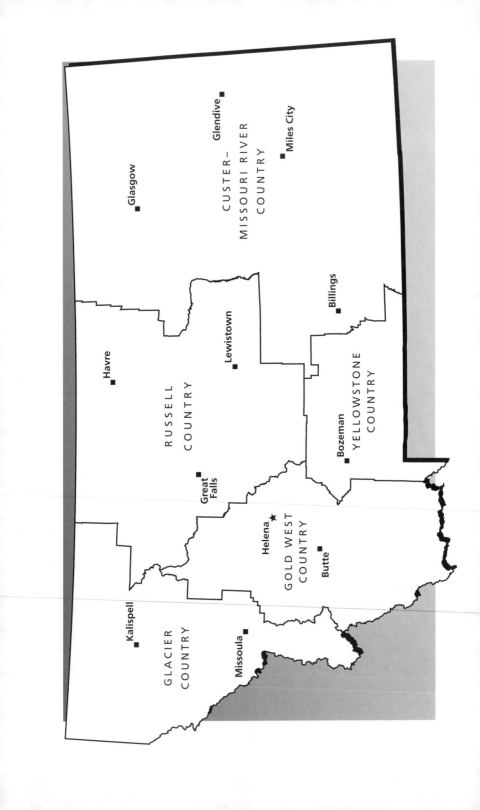

Contents

Introduction ix

Glacier Country.. 1

Gold West Country 41

Yellowstone Country..................................... 73

Custer–Missouri River Country 103

Russell Country... 139

Index.. 165

About the Author....................................... 171

Introduction

My wife and I lived for several years in Troy, a timber town squeezed into a tight, tree-filled valley so far west in Montana that from there you can almost spit into Idaho, and so far north that half its residents speak with a Canadian accent. Having already lived in Montana for several years, I knew, theoretically, that it was big. But it wasn't until living in its extreme northwest corner that I came to appreciate just how big.

Early on a July morning in 1981, Nancy and I packed our Mazda sedan with more gear than it was meant to hold and took off to visit family in the Midwest. After driving for fifteen hours and covering more than 800 long, hot miles, we were disappointed at nightfall to find ourselves still in Montana. We were relieved, however, and honestly surprised to learn that we were more than halfway to where we were going.

Yes, Montana is spacious. Inside its 145,388 square miles you could fit Maine, New Hampshire, Vermont, Delaware, Rhode Island, New York, and Pennsylvania and have room to spare. Here's the clincher: Fewer people live in Montana than in Rhode Island alone. While the typical Rhode Island square mile holds 930 people, an average of a little more than 6 occupy that space in Montana.

Montana is big, and it's a melting pot. During the short, 140-year history of white settlement, the state has been a magnet for the restless and intrepid, the displaced and persecuted—those willing or forced to take a chance with their lives. The result is an eclectic mix of people who settled in the state's mountains and valleys and on its windswept, arid plains: the Hi-Line Scandinavians. The faithful of Park County's controversial Church Universal and Triumphant. The many Germans, including the communal Hutterites of the north-central plains. The Butte Irish, the Butte Chinese, the Butte Polish, the Butte almost-any-thing-you-can-name. And the American Indians, a glance at whose family trees will prove everyone else newcomers by a large measure.

So here in the immensity of Montana we have a wide cast of characters populating a land vibrant and beautiful, a country also cursed (or blessed, depending on your perspective) with a climate of extremes. These factors coalesce to create an atmosphere ripe for the fashioning of unorthodox ways to make ends meet. As a result, a fascinating mix of attractions—some strange, some wonderful, some strange and wonderful—awaits the traveler in Montana.

Montana, the setting for countless western novels and movies, has been subjected to endless romanticizing and dealt more than its share of nicknames: The Bonanza State, Big Sky Country, The Treasure State, and—overused and overstated—The Last Best Place. Of all the descriptive phrases I've heard, far and away my favorite is *Montana: High, Wide, and Handsome*, the title of the 1943 book by Joseph Kinsey Howard. Unpretentious, honest, and unerringly accurate, it fits Montana like a well-worn pair of cowboy boots.

Speaking of which, as you might expect, you'll still find plenty of working cowboys, miners, and loggers in Montana, and you can still experience no-holds-barred Wild West celebrations (try Butte on St. Patrick's Day or the World Famous Bucking Horse Sale in Miles City). But you also can find gourmet restaurants employing Paris-trained chefs and surroundings that whisper rather than scream. You can bed down at night in a dude-ranch bunkhouse or under a down comforter at a bed-and-breakfast inn as elegant as any found in New England or California's wine country. You might dine on buffalo-hump roast one night and Greek cuisine the next. You're bound to tour spectacular and highly touted Yellowstone and Glacier National Parks, but the lands beyond the park boundaries—some subdued and others of national park quality themselves—may catch you off guard.

The House committee charged with splitting the Montana Territory from the Idaho Territory in 1864 was leaning toward designating the Continental Divide as the boundary between the two. A group led by Sidney Edgerton, chief justice of the Idaho Territory, however, persuaded the committee to include in the Montana portion those lands west of the Divide and east of the Bitterroot Range. Consequently, cities including Missoula, Butte, and Kalispell today are in Montana rather than Idaho; likewise all of Glacier National Park ended up in Montana, rather than the majority of it residing in Idaho. Edgerton may not have won new friends among the Idaho delegation, but he did win the subsequent governorship of the newly created and larger for his efforts Montana Territory.

Sidney Edgerton and fate were responsible for the boundaries Montana claimed when it finally became a state in 1889, and this book dishes out a sample of what's contained within them 111 years later. My goal is to showcase a spicy mixture of the state's diverse attractions, while emphasizing lesser known places of both the natural and human-made varieties. Where well-known destinations, such as Glacier National Park, are included, I've highlighted features overlooked by the majority of visitors.

If an attraction in this broad and wide state seems too far removed and isolated to bother traveling to, know this: As you stray off the beaten path to visit some of my favorite places in Montana, you're bound to find others just as interesting and worthy of mention. Attempting to include them all would have been a Herculean task, and the data collected would fill a dozen volumes of this size.

To complement this guide, carry a state road map for getting an overall picture of where you are, and where you're headed. To verify that the hours of operation listed are still in effect, call ahead to attractions you absolutely do not want to miss.

With regard to restaurants, I've used a three-tiered scale for the prices of entrees: inexpensive, less than $8.00; moderate, $8.00–$15.00; and expensive, more than $15.00.

The state promotion bureau has done a logical job of dividing Montana into six travel regions, and I've borrowed them for the book's chapters. However, I've covered the two easternmost regions—Custer Country and Missouri River Country—in a single chapter. Although the two "countries" comprise a staggeringly vast expanse of terrain, it's a wide-open, largely empty region, where services and attractions are relatively few and far between.

In closing, permit me to share a little background. I came into the world in this part of the country—Wyoming, actually—but when I was still an infant, my folks packed up and moved the family to Iowa, and there I sprouted, alongside the corn, soybeans, and piglets.

After napping through high school in Boone, a great little farm town originally known as "Montana," believe it or not, I returned to my birthright region in 1970 to attend college. Here I found myself confronted, confounded, and a little scared by the electrifying heights of the northern Rocky Mountain ranges—where mighty rivers come to life, conceived in winter and born in spring—and the impossible spaces of the plains between. Both were so different from my familiar surroundings that they shook me, unexpectedly, from an adolescent stupor. For the first time in nineteen years I was truly awake . . . and awakened to the power of landscape and the possibilities provided by strange faces and new ways of thinking. And I've rarely slept since.

If you're a resident of Montana or a return visitor, here's hoping this volume will lead you to some new favorite places. If it's your first time to the state that is high, wide, and ever so handsome, welcome! May the endless stretch of prairie, the magic of the mountains, and the smile of Montana's friendly citizens energize you as they did, and do, me.

P.S. I've omitted a few of my very favorite, hard-to-find and hard-to-get-to places. My friends would never forgive me for publicizing them!

Tourist Information

Travel Montana offers free vacation guides and accommodations listings.

Address: 1424 9th Avenue, P.O. Box 200533, Helena, MT 59620–0533

Telephone: (800) 847–4868

Web site: www.visitmt.com

About Montana

The following is a list of information and resources an off-the-beaten-path traveler like yourself might find useful.

Major Newspapers: *Missoulian, Helena Independent Record, Butte Standard, Billings Gazette, Great Falls Tribune*

Capital: Helena (pronounced HEL-uh-nuh)

Cities and Counties: Montana is divided into 56 counties, with 126 incorporated cities and towns and two consolidated city-county governments.

Population: 880,000 plus

Schools: 900 schools serving nearly 120,000 elementary and secondary students. The State University System of Higher Education consists of The University of Montana in Missoula, Western Montana College of The University of Montana in Dillon, Montana State University–Bozeman, Montana State University–Billings, Montana State University–Northern (in Havre), and the College of Mineral Science and Technology in Butte. The state also boasts three community colleges and three private colleges.

Average Daily High and Low Temperatures

	January		July	
	High	Low	High	Low
Billings	32.0	13.3	87.0	58.4
Bozeman	30.2	7.8	75.7	40.5
Butte	28.4	4.2	80.1	45.1
Great Falls	30.9	12.3	83.6	54.9
Missoula	29.8	14.0	84.8	50.4

Average Annual Precipitation: Ranges from 12.16 inches on the north-central plains to 16.14 inches in the northwest valleys. The high mountains often receive much more than this (as much as 100 inches per year in parts of the northwest mountains).

Famous People from Montana: Gary Cooper, Myrna Loy, Chet Huntley, Plenty Coups, and Jeanette Rankin, the first woman to serve in the U.S. House of Representatives

Recommended Reading for Children:

Montana in Words and Pictures, Dennis Fradin, Children's Press, 1981. (2nd grade, nonfiction)

Montana, Allan Carpenter, Children's Press, 1979. (4th grade, nonfiction)

One Summer in Montana, Dayton O. Hyde, Atheneum, 1985. (6th grade, fiction)

Recommended Reading for Adults:

The Big Sky, A. B. Guthrie Jr., Houghton-Mifflin, 1947

Out West: American Journey Along the Lewis and Clark Trail, Dayton Duncan, Penguin Books, 1987

A River Runs Through It and Other Stories, Norman Maclean, University of Chicago Press, 1976

Tough Trip Through Paradise, Andrew Garcia, Houghton-Mifflin, 1967

About Montana

State Animal: Grizzly bear

State Flower: Bitterroot

State Tree: Ponderosa pine

State Fish: Cutthroat trout

State Fossil: Anatosaurus *(Maiasaura peeblesorum)*

State Song: "Montana Melody"

A Sampling of Radio Stations:

KBLG, 910 kHz, Billings

KBOZ, 1090 kHz, Bozeman

KMMS-FM, 95.1 MHz, Bozeman

KBOW, 500 kHz, Butte

KMON, 560 kHz, Great Falls

KOFI, 1180 kHz, Kalispell

KGRZ, 1450 kHz, Missoula

KUFM-FM, 89.1 MHz, Missoula (National Public Radio)

Area Code

The area code for the entire state of Montana is 406.

Glacier Country

oasting the terrific city of Missoula, world-famous Glacier National Park, and the skiing-golfing-boating mecca of Flathead Valley, it is no surprise that Glacier Country is Montana's preeminent tourism region. It is an area of stunning natural beauty, graced with forested mountains and lush valleys teeming with fish-filled lakes and streams.

Although you can jump in and join it at any point, the best place to begin is in the timbered fastness of the Yaak River Valley, nestled in the extreme northwest corner of Montana. From there forest roads wind their way to Eureka, from which point State Highway 37 leads to Libby and U.S. Highway 2. You'll then follow State Highway 56 as it snakes through the memorable Bull River Valley, a tangle of wild terrain that would not appear out of place in Alaska, to the valley of the Clark Fork River and State Highway 200. After going through Thompson Falls and Paradise, you'll travel to the Mission Valley and along the shores of massive Flathead Lake. From there it is on to Kalispell and Whitefish, jumping-off point for Glacier National Park and the Blackfeet Indian Reservation. Finally, State Highway 83 takes you through the forested, lake-adorned Seeley-Swan Valley to a juncture with State Highway 200, which leads west to Missoula. From Montana's unofficial capital of art and recreation and undisputed bastion of liberalism, U.S. Highway 93 leads south up the Bitterroot Valley to Lost Trail Pass, where you'll descend into Gold West Country.

Kootenai Timberlands

he remote Yaak River Valley, occupying the northwest notch of Montana, is home to the settlement of Yaak, a tiny island of enterprise set amid a rolling sea of timber. If you make your way to Yaak, you can't miss the **Dirty Shame Saloon**, a funky bar and eatery with a decor to match the kicked-back and independent character of the majority of local residents. The town is situated along Highway 508,

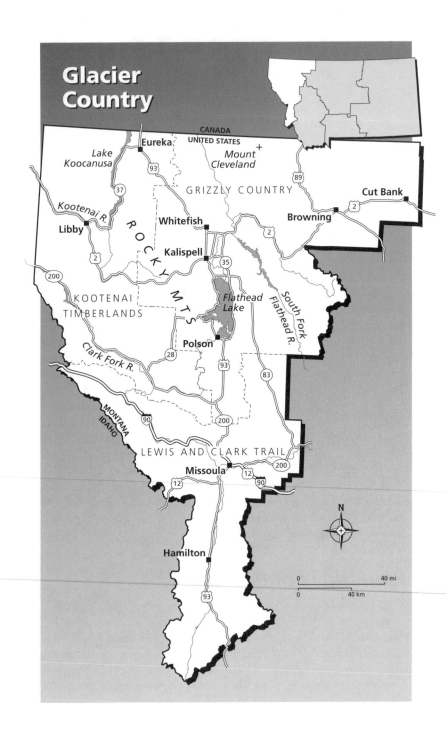

Glacier Country

CANADA
UNITED STATES

Lake Koocanusa

Eureka

Mount Cleveland

GRIZZLY COUNTRY

Cut Bank

Browning

Kootenai R.

Whitefish

Libby

Kalispell

KOOTENAI TIMBERLANDS

R O C K Y   M T S

Flathead Lake

South Fork Flathead R.

Polson

Clark Fork R.

MONTANA
IDAHO

LEWIS AND CLARK TRAIL

Missoula

Hamilton

N

| 0 | 40 mi |
| 0 | 40 km |

Dirty Shame Saloon, Yaak

30 miles northeast of Highway 2 (beginning $3^{1}/_{2}$ miles southeast of the point where Highway 2 crosses the Montana-Idaho state line). The Dirty Shame's phone number is 295–5439.

While "up the Yaak," as the locals say, consider also following Pete Creek to Hawkins Lakes and the *Northwest Peak Scenic Area*, a spectacular setting of rocky peaks and sparkling lakes. The area is like a miniature and little-visited version of Glacier National Park, and it's ideal for hiking, picnicking, and car camping. Getting there is a journey unto itself, for from the already remote outpost of Yaak, it is 3 miles west on Highway 508, then 22 miles north and west on Forest Road 338 (12 miles paved and 10 dirt). Call the Troy Ranger District at 295–4693 for maps and information.

Also worth the trip is *West Fork Falls*, gracing the West Fork of the Yaak River. The falls are located at the end of a short trail that begins in a parking area near the 39-mile marker on the Yaak River Road. The falls and the deep, amazingly clear pool they feed can be viewed from a wooden observation deck, built courtesy the Kootenai National Forest.

In the town of Eureka, just east of the Yaak area, is the *Tobacco Valley Historical Village*. The Peltier log home (Eureka's first residence) and the Rexford train depot are located here, as are a vintage hand-hewn log ranger cabin, a one-room school, the old Fewkes Store—with works by local artists on sale—and several other buildings, all connected by a stout boardwalk. The museum houses artifacts and interpretive displays illustrating the Kootenai Indians' movement through the region and the Eureka area's logging heritage. There's no charge to visit the historical village, open daily from 1:00 to 5:00 P.M. Memorial Day through Labor Day.

One mile west of Highway 93 on the Fortine Creek Road, 12 miles south of Eureka, is the *Ant Flat Natural Resource Education Center and Historic Site*. Location of the first Forest Service administrative activities in the area, Ant Flat features two historic buildings, a picnic grounds, and a mile-long nature trail. The first portion of the trail is wheelchair accessible, ending at a boardwalk and observation deck that extend out over a vibrant wetland. It's a great spot for bird-watching . . . and mosquito-slapping! Contact the Murphy Lake Ranger District at 882–4451 for more information on the site, open in summer only.

It's thought that only approximately 200 pairs of common loons nest in Montana, and most are in the northwestern reaches of the state. Almost as hard to locate as the bird it's named after is the **Loon's Echo**, nestled at the base of Stryker Peak on the banks of forty-acre Fish Lake and completely surrounded by Stillwater State Forest lands. Several pairs of loons reside on the waters here, providing guests with a special

The Yaak

*R*oad warriors who enjoy visiting places seen by relatively few travelers should not miss venturing into the Yaak River country. Not many places remaining in the contiguous 48 states can claim to be more off the beaten path than this remote valley nestled in the extreme northwest corner of the Big Sky State.

The Yaak River drains a large portion of the Purcell Mountains, a range teeming with ancient coniferous forests and not-so-ancient clear-cuts. "The Yaak," as the surrounding countryside is typically referred to, is a backwoodsy backwaters that has attracted an eclectic mix of human residents, including back-to-the-land Mother Earth types, artists and writers, tree fellers, tree huggers, and plain old hermits. As diverse as the homesteaders are, though, all share this trait: They enjoy getting away from it all and being left alone. Either that or they don't last long in the isolated Yaak River country.

For two years in the very early 1980s, I worked as a wildlife assistant for the Kootenai National Forest, stationed at the Sylvanite Ranger Station, which is located several miles up the Yaak River from U.S. Highway 2. I found staying dry to be just about the biggest challenge while working outdoors in the Yaak because the weather there is often more akin to that of the Pacific Northwest than to that of the high Rocky Mountains.

Although trying to stay dry was nearly a constant, my duties were varied—from the unexciting and ignoble task of counting piles of elk droppings (to determine relatively how many of the critters were using a given area) to the almost too-exciting job of assisting in the release of a recently orphaned grizzly-bear cub. The cub's mother had been a "trouble bear" and was killed in nearby Glacier National Park. The young bear was captured in Glacier, transported to the Yaak in a culvert trap, then released to start a new life. Wildlife biologists hoped that he, like his human neighbors, would find that folks simply left him alone in the vast spread of wild country known as the Yaak.

treat in the mornings and evenings, with their haunting yodels, wails, and echoing tremolos.

The Loon's Echo features a new lodge with five cozy rooms, as well as several rental homes, ranging from rustic to luxurious, all with kitchen facilities included and available year-round. The establishment is also a working trout farm, and guests can fish for trophy-size brookies in the Loon's Echo fourteen-acre pond. Also at hand are world-class opportunities for hiking, mountain biking, photography, and—if you can find the time—relaxing. Popular winter activities include cross-country skiing, snowmobiling, and dog-sledding (arranged through Dog Sled Adventures, 881–BARK).

To find the Loon's Echo, travel 22 miles south of Eureka on Highway 93 to Stryker, and then turn east onto Forest Road 900 and continue for 4 miles to Fish Lake. Rates range from $144 to $431 per night in summer, $113 to $328 in winter, and $98 to $276 during the spring and fall shoulder seasons. For more details call 882–4791 or tap into the establishment's Web site at www. loonsecho.com.

Libby Logger Days, the premier summerfest in Lincoln County, celebrates the heritage of Lincoln County's most important industry. Professional and amateur loggers alike test their skills—or lack thereof—as woodsmen and woodswomen in competitions such as the double-buck saw and the Bull of the Woods boxing challenge. Nonloggers needn't feel left out, for also on tap are a parade, foot and bicycle races, water fights, a rafting competition, a carnival, and more. Logger Days are held Thursday through Sunday during the second full week in July. Call the Libby Area Chamber of Commerce at 293–4167 or E-mail them at LACC@Libby.org to request further information. On the Web you can find information at www.libby.org/libbyacc.

Libby townsfolk have suffered tremendously in recent years, with the discovery that many of those associated with the venerable vermiculite-mining industry were exposed to and poisoned by asbestos. But this is a town filled with survivors; Libby has a legacy of dealing with

---

Best Attractions

Dirty Shame Saloon,
Yaak; (406) 295-5439

Loon's Echo, *Stryker;*
(406) 882-4791

Wildhorse Island,
Big Arm; (406) 752-5501;
www.fwp.state.mt.us

Garden Wall Inn,
Whitefish; (406) 862-3440;
www.wpt.net./go/gardenwall
(888) 530-1700

Hornet Peak Fire Lookout,
Polebridge; (406) 387-3800

Clearwater Canoe Trail,
Seeley Lake;
(406) 677-2233

Stringed Instrument
Division, *Missoula;*
(406) 549-1502

The Schoolhouse and
Teacherage Bed
and Breakfast,
Ninemile; (406) 626-5879

Montana Valley Bookstore,
Alberton; (406) 722-4950

Lee Metcalf National
Wildlife Refuge,
Stevensville;
(406) 777-5552

Bull River Ranger Station

One of Granny and Pauline Gordon's three daughters, Blanche Gordon Claxton, recalled that during the conflagration of 1910 the family stationed buckets of water filled with soaking gunny sacks on the porch of their Bull River Ranger Station. Mrs. Gordon advised the girls that if the fire advanced toward the house, they should wrap the gunny sacks around their bodies and run for their lives to the river.

The station endured, and through the ensuing years it was used off and on as a residence for teachers, rangers, and forest work crews. Eventually it fell into disrepair, and in 1989 volunteers from the Cabinet Wilderness Historical Society joined with the Forest Service to begin renovating the old building—fighting continuously, it was written, "incessant rain storms, blistering heat, enraged pack rats, and annoyed bats." The station now sits atop a sound foundation and sports a new roof, window panes, and porches.

adversity, facing as it has the on-again off-again nature of the timber industry. Don't hurry through town; take some time to mosey around the side streets and have a look. One treasure you may come across is the **Hidden Chapel Restaurant,** located at 1207 Utah Avenue, inside a picturesque old church. At the Hidden Chapel you'll dine while sitting in old pews and gazing at a painting of the Last Supper hanging over the door. All in all, a peaceful Victorian-style dining experience, featuring fresh, delicious foods. The restaurant is open for lunch weekdays from 11:00 A.M. to 2:00 P.M. and for supper seven nights a week, from 5:00 to 10:00 P.M. (in summer until 11:00 P.M. Friday and Saturday). For reservations or additional information, call 293–2928.

Between Troy and Libby, just below Highway 2, the broad Kootenai River flows through clefts and over cliffs, resulting in a stunning stretch of foaming white water known as **Kootenai Falls.** The protected site is sacred to the Confederated Salish and Kootenai tribes, who have joined with the state and county to build a park adjacent to the falls. The park includes a picnic grounds and a mile-long hiking trail to the falls, which splashed across the wide screen in the 1994 production *The River Wild*, starring Meryl Streep and a particularly dastardly Kevin Bacon.

A pair of monumental fires raged through the forests of northwest Montana and northern Idaho in 1890 and then 1910, taking with them a large share of the old-growth timber. But for a fortuitous location, the giant cedars at the **Ross Creek Scenic Area** would have gone up in smoke, too. A visit to the enchanting grove, situated above the scenic Bull River Valley and in one of the wettest spots in Montana, might make you wonder for a moment if you've unknowingly been whisked to a Northwest coastal rain forest. The mile-long interpretive trail through the shade of the robust, tall trees—some more than 175 feet high and 500 years old—is perfect for an easy hike on a hot summer's day or for a mystical cross-country skiing experience come winter. The trail is wheelchair-accessible.

From Troy, the Ross Creek Scenic Area is 3 miles east on Highway 2, 16 miles south on Highway 56, and then 3 miles up Forest Road 398. Call Kootenai National Forest headquarters at 293–6211 for information.

Also barely surviving the 1910 fire was the **Bull River Ranger Station**, a relatively recent addition to the National Register of Historic Places. The high and jagged peaks of the Cabinet Mountains Wilderness form a stirring backdrop for the two-story log structure, which rests in a tranquil meadow above the East Fork of the Bull River.

The station was built in 1908 by District Ranger Granville "Granny" Gordon and served for years as his headquarters and family home. Before going to work for the Forest Service, Granville was a guide for "Buffalo Bill" Cody, and his wife, Pauline, had been Cody's pastry maker. The spirited couple's dances and home cooking made the ranger station and its grounds a popular and sometimes rompin', stompin' stop for those living in or traveling through the Bull River country.

To get there, go 9 miles south on Highway 56 from the turnoff to the Ross Creek Scenic Area; at the 8-mile marker turn east onto Forest Road 407. Proceed for $1^{1}/_{2}$ miles, then go right onto gravel at the fork, and in another $^{1}/_{2}$ mile you'll arrive at the ranger station. For more information call 293–6211.

Trout Creek calls itself the Huckleberry Capital of Montana, and the community underscores the nickname each August by hosting its **Huckleberry Festival**. Closely related to the blueberry, the fruit has never been successfully domesticated, but in a good year millions, some as big as marbles, ponderously hang from their greenery high in the mountains of northwest Montana. Both the black and the grizzly bear also are common in these mountains, and huckleberries constitute a large part of their diets in the late summer; hence the Huckleberry Festival's slogan, "Celebrating One of the Bear Necessities." Fun runs, huckleberry-pancake breakfasts, a parade, horseshoe-tossing competitions, a Little Miss Huckleberry Pageant, and other events round out the huckleberry happenings.

In Thompson Falls the unusual **Old Jail Museum** houses relics from the town's past, including the jail itself, which operated from about 1908 until 1980. A quick peek inside one of the claustrophobic cells will make you thankful you never ran afoul of the law in Thompson Falls during those years. The facility also includes revolving and permanent displays, such as an exhibit detailing the involvement of local men and women in World War II. The museum, located just south of Main Street behind the present-day Sheriff's Office, is open daily Mother's Day through Labor Day, from noon to 4:00 P.M., and is free of charge to enter.

Twenty-five miles southeast of Thompson Falls on Highway 200 is the village of Plains, home to the **Old Log Schoolhouse** and its collection of locally created crafts and artwork for sale. The solid old Wild Horse Plains schoolhouse was completed in the mid-1880s (until 1884 Plains was called "Horse Plains") and used for its intended purpose until about 1898. It subsequently served various other functions for many years thereafter. In 1976 it was moved from its original site to town.

Four miles farther southeast along Highway 200 is the community of Paradise, whose founders obviously found to be quite a special place. Maybe the naturally hot waters that now fill the pools at **Quinn's Paradise Resort** had something to do with their choice in town names. From Paradise, the resort is 3 miles southeast on Highway 200, then 2 miles southwest on Highway 135. Year-round the large pool is maintained at or near 96 degrees and the smaller Jacuzzi pool at a toasty 105 degrees; private Jacuzzi rentals are also available. For $5.00 on weekends and $4.00 week days adults can soak away any worries they might still have after spending a few days touring northwest Montana. It's $3.75 weekends/$3.00 weekdays for kids over twelve, and free for those twelve and under.

Good Medicine

*B*ig Medicine was a bison born on the National Bison Range outside Moiese, Montana, in 1933. Although white in color, Big Medicine was not a true albino for his eyes were light blue (not pink), his hooves were tan rather than white, and his topknot was of dark-brown hair. In his prime Big Medicine weighed just a few pounds under a ton, stood 6 feet high at the hump, and measured nearly 12 feet long from the tip of his tail to his nose. He became one of the monarchs of the National Bison Range, fathering many offspring—including Little Medicine, a true albino bison born deaf and blind in 1937. Little Medicine was transported to the National Zoological Gardens in Washington, D.C., where he survived for twelve years.

White bison are an exceedingly rare phenomenon, and to Plains Indians, such as the Blackfeet, they are believed to carry potent good medicine tied to the power of the sun. Such was the case with Big Medicine, who was highly revered by the Native Americans. On his death in 1959 his hide was sent for tanning to the renowned Jonas Brothers in Denver, then shipped to Browning, Montana, where sculptor-taxidermist Bob Scriver molded a mannequin on which he mounted Big Medicine's hide. On July 13, 1961, Governor Donald G. Hutter dedicated the Big Medicine mount at the Montana Historical Society's museum in Helena, where hundreds of thousands of travelers have since paid him visits.

The resort also includes a spacious campground ($18 for a partial hookup and $22 for a full hookup), rooms ($45 to $65 per night), a sometimes raucous dance hall, and a supper club featuring moderately priced dinners and breakfasts on weekends. For information and reservations call 826–3150.

Grizzly Country

ake County is named after massive Flathead Lake—at 27 miles long, 8 to 15 miles wide, and with 124 miles of shoreline, the largest body of fresh water west of the Mississippi. The lake, in turn, was named for the Flathead Indians, whose reservation, home to the Confederated Salish and Kootenai tribes, takes in most of Lake County. The reservation also covers a sizable portion of Sanders County, as well as smaller parts of Missoula and Flathead counties.

Both humans and nature have the capacity to create wondrous works of beauty. These potentials coalesce at the **St. Ignatius Mission**, where the stunning Mission Mountains form the backdrop for the house of worship that gave the range its name. The St. Ignatius Mission, originally established by Father Pierre DeSmet along the Pend d'Oreille River in Washington State, was moved to the Mission Valley in 1854 at the request of the Flathead Indians. The resplendent church you walk through today was built in 1891 under the direction of Jesuit missionaries by Native American workers, using local materials to fire bricks on the spot. Inside, the walls and ceilings are adorned with dramatic murals de-picting the biblical history of humankind. Brother Joseph Carignano, a mission cook with no formal art training, created the masterpieces in his spare time.

The St. Ignatius Mission, open free of charge daily from 9:00 A.M. to 5:00 P.M., is immediately off Highway 93 in St. Ignatius, a town also known locally as "Mission." Call 745–2768 for information.

Stop in at the **Four Winds Indian Trading Post**, located 3 miles north of St. Ignatius on Highway 93. It's open daily in summer—from Memorial Day to Labor Day—from 9:00 A.M. to 7:00 P.M., and from 10:00 A.M. to 5:00 P.M. the remainder of the year. Several prestatehood log structures have been moved to the site over the years, lending the post an authentic feel. Owners Preston Miller and Carolyn Corey maintain their living quarters in the old Ravalli Depot, built in 1885, where they've also developed a museum of toy trains and railroad memorabilia. In other buildings you'll discover a fantastic selection of American Indian material goods, old and new—tools, quillwork,

St. Ignatius Mission, Mission Valley

traditional dress, weapons, tobacco twists, medicine pouches, and much more. Some of Four Winds' inventory is so uncommon that it has appeared in the movies: The proprietors have supplied artifacts to the producers of *Dances With Wolves*, *Far and Away*, *Son of the Morning Star*, and other films. Call 745–4336 for more information on this unusual enterprise that's been in business for more than a quarter of a century. You can also check them out on the Internet at www.4winds.com/.

Approximately 5 miles north of Four Winds, immediately opposite the Ninepipe National Wildlife Refuge, you'll encounter a beautiful new museum overflowing with Native America artifacts, historic items relating to Anglo exploration and settlement of the Mission Valley, western art, and wildlife mounts. *The Ninepipes Museum of Early Montana* is a dream fulfilled of the Cheff family, longtime residents and ranchers of the area. Admission is $4.00 for adults, $3.00 for students, and $2.00 for children ages six to twelve (kids younger than that are admitted free of charge). There's also an associated restaurant and motel next door. You can learn more at www.ninepipes.com or by calling 644–3435.

The People's Center, located south of Polson in Pablo, celebrates the unique cultural heritages of the Native Americans who call the Flathead Indian Reservation home—the Salish, Kootenai, and Pend d'Oreille peoples. Visit here and, as they say, you'll gain an altogether new perspective on the phrase "Made in Montana." More than a simple museum filled with displays and artwork, The People's Center offers dynamic opportunities to become intimately acquainted with the life-ways of the tribes through classes, plays, demonstrations, and interpretive tours. The center is open daily from 9:00 A.M. to 7:00 P.M., April 1 through September 30; and Monday through Friday from 9:00 A.M. to 5:00 P.M. the rest of the year. Admission is free. Call 675–0160 or (800) 883–5344, or visit the Web site www.peoplescenter.org for additional information.

A mile south of Polson on Highway 93 is the *Miracle of America Museum*, an eclectic collection of memorabilia and artifacts, ranging from the ordinary to the preposterous. More than 100,000 objects are displayed; for beginners: early-day farm implements, World War I and World War II poster art and troop-transport vehicles, vintage motorcycles and musical instruments, and a horse-drawn hearse from the 1880s. Also residing at the museum is the land-stranded *Paul Bunyan*, a 65-foot logging tow listed on the International Register of Historic Large Vessels. For years the *Paul Bunyan* transported felled logs across Flathead Lake to the mills. The Miracle of America Museum is

For more than a decade, after being covered with ash from the 1980 eruption of Washington's Mount St. Helens, Grinnell Glacier in Glacier National Park absorbed, rather than reflected, most of the available summertime sunlight—thereby greatly accelerating the pace of its melting.

open daily from 8:00 A.M. to 8:00 P.M., April through September; between October and March it opens daily for shorter hours. Expect to pay a $3.00 admission fee ($1.00 for kids three to twelve). For more information call 883–6804 or visit www.cyberport. net/museum.

While in town, stop by **Richwine's Burgerville**, a Polson institution since the 1950s. The meat for the burgers—reputed to be the best in Montana—is ground on-site in a meat room behind the restaurant. Try a Royal Burger (a single, double, or triple cheeseburger), their most popular item, named after Royal Morrison, the Polson football coach who founded Burgerville in the early 1950s before moving on to coach in Missoula.

Burgerville (883–2620) ordinarily opens sometime in February and closes again in the late fall. It's hard to miss: Just watch for the orange windmill and the neon cow wearing a police uniform.

Is there an establishment anywhere, other than **Three Dog Down,** with a shingle on the door reading, SORRY: WE'RE OPEN? Owner Bob Ricketts has parlayed his zany sense of humor, sharp acumen for marketing, and strong belief in customer service into one of the most popular businesses in Montana.

Ricketts, a music-business dropout who sang with the Cincinnati Opera and the Chicago Lyric Opera, is still an entertainer. It's not uncommon to see him strolling about the store, accordion in hands, singing off-the-wall tunes in a rich tenor. Customers can also sing—and for discounts. A sign near the cash register reads, SING YOUR NATIONAL ANTHEM. The quality of the singing determines the discount, which can range from $1.00 to $10.00. Countless renditions of "The Star Spangled Banner," as well as the anthems of countries far beyond America have been heard resounding through the display rooms at Three Dog Down.

At Three Dog Down, actually a factory outlet for the Ohio-based Down Lite International, you'll find comforters, jackets, and other down products at prices well below those you might find elsewhere. The business is located, as the ad goes, "a bridge and a bump north of Polson on 93," and it's open seven days a week (9:00 A.M. to 9:00 P.M. in summer; 9:00 A.M. to 7:00 P.M. the rest of the year). Just watch for the three dogs, in howling-at-the-moon posture, sitting in a carriage by the side of the road. You can call (800) DOG–DOWN (364–3696) or visit www.cache.net/3dogdown for more information and to request "Montana's only FREE $2.00 catalog."

Also in Polson is the lavish *KwaTaqNuk Resort*. Unveiled in 1992, KwaTaqNuk represents a landmark effort by the Confederated Salish and Kootenai tribes to enhance their role in the region's burgeoning tourist trade. The large resort, staffed primarily by tribe members, features a full-service marina, a 112-room hotel, restaurants, and a centerpiece gallery brimming with a collection of fine western and American Indian art and photography.

KwaTaqNuk, which translates to "where the water leaves the lake," is situated on the shores of Flathead Lake. Call 883–3636 or (800) 882–6363 or find them on the Web at www.kwataqnuk.com for more information.

The 2,163-acre mountain of timbered ridges and slopeside meadows rising high above the waters of Big Arm Bay is *Wildhorse Island State Park*. On the island, purchased by the state in 1978, one can still spot an abandoned resort hotel and old homestead around the shoreline, and, in fact, approximately fifty private lots remain. The island is home to a growing bighorn sheep population, now numbering more than one hundred, as well as bald eagles, numerous songbirds, and, fittingly, several wild horses captured and relocated here through the Bureau of Land Management's adopt-a-horse program.

Open for day use only, Wildhorse Island is one state park not likely to become overcrowded soon because the only way to get there is by watercraft. Call Pointer Scenic Cruises (837–5617) to arrange transportation to the island; alternatively, captain-it-yourselfers can rent a boat at Big Arm Resort and Marina (849–5622). For more information on Wildhorse Island, call the Montana Department of Fish, Wildlife, and Parks in Kalispell at 752–5501.

Montana Trivia

The **Mission Mountain Winery**, situated just outside Dayton, produces award-winning wines, a feat not expected at these northern reaches. It seems the climate and soils of the Dayton area are ideal for growing the grapes used in making Mission Mountain's Pinot Noir and Pale Ruby champagnes. As relatively mild as the weather is here in Montana's "banana belt," however, the growing season is a couple of weeks too short for most grape varieties, so the majority of their fruits are imported from Washington State. Still, they fashion great wines, and the bottles feature splendid labels created by Missoula artist Monte Dolack. The Mission Mountain Winery is open for tours and tasting from 10:00 A.M. to 5:00 P.M., May 1 through October 31. Call 849–5524 for information.

The Nature Conservancy's Dancing Prairie Preserve, located outside Eureka, is one of the Mountain West's few remaining leks, or dancing and mating grounds, of the formerly abundant Columbian sharp-tailed grouse. The birds are unable to thrive in grasslands that have been altered by the plow or grazed by cattle.

After choosing your wine, drive north on Highway 93 for 5 miles to **M & S Meats**, renowned for its selection of buffalo meats, sausages, and jerky. The store is open 8:00 A.M. to 7:00 P.M. in summer, and 7:30 A.M. to 6:00 P.M. the rest of the year. There you can also pick up a loaf of French bread, then head out for an unforgettable picnic along the shore of sparkling Flathead Lake. Contact them at 844–3414 or (800) 454–3414 or at www.msmeats.com/.

Continuing north along the west shore of Flathead Lake, pass through Lakeside, and in another 3 miles turn left into **The Osprey Nest Antiques**. The should-be-a-country-lodge structure claims 6,000 square feet of floor space, an area jam-packed with western memorabilia, riding tack, oak furniture, old books, Indian artifacts, and much more. Bargains may be as hard to find as osprey's teeth, but stop anyway, if only to browse and savor the view of Somers Bay and the Mission Mountains beyond.

An active osprey nest sits atop a power pole just across the highway from the antiques shop. The obvious question: Which came first—the nest or the name of the business? The Osprey Nest is open year-round, Monday through Saturday from 10:00 A.M. to 5:00 P.M., Sunday from 11:00 A.M. to 4:00 P.M.; call 857–3714 for more information.

Plan on devoting a day and an evening to gadding about the tastefully decked-out tourist town of Bigfork, located at the north end of Flathead Lake. Here you can attend a performance at the **Bigfork Summer Playhouse**, which is enjoying its fourth decade of Broadway-style shows. The theater runs from late May until Labor Day, during which time plays are staged Monday through Saturday. The playhouse is at 526 Electric Avenue, and the box office number is 837–4886.

Eva Gates Homemade Preserves have been cooked down and put up in the Bigfork area since 1949, a year when—so the story goes—the Gateses' strawberry patch produced more than the family could eat on its own. So, man of the house George designed a label and started selling pint jars filled with the delectables cooked up by Eva on her wood-burning range to neighbors.

Today the preserves and wild huckleberry and chokecherry syrups are still a family tradition, concocted by Eva's granddaughter, Pamela Gates Siess. The Gateses have maintained their products' consistency by adhering to the "why fix it if it ain't broke" philosophy: Just as when Eva was at the kitchen helm, the preserves are cooked atop a stove, five pints at a time, with no additives or preservatives used.

The shop is in downtown Bigfork. Visitors are also welcome to watch the preserves being made in the cookhouse, which is open seven days a week and evenings from mid-June through August, and from 9:00 A.M. to 5:00 P.M. the remainder of the year. Call (800) 682–4283 to order a jar for your breakfast table.

Immediately south of Bigfork on Highway 35 watch for the unassuming sign marking the entrance to the not-so-unassuming **Averill's Flathead Lake Lodge and Dude Ranch.** If you have a few spare days on your hands—and a spare $2,063 (per adult) in your pocket—consider a week at this first-class lodge and dude ranch. Even if a lack of time or money precludes a layover, drive out and have a look, for a grander scene is hard to envision. It belongs in a 1930s Cary Grant–Katharine Hepburn movie.

The enterprise includes over 2,000 acres of mountain timberland and meadow. At the core of the ranch are two log lodges and several smaller cabins, a large corral and rodeo grounds, several acres of lawn, a swimming pool, tennis courts, and a long stretch of sandy Flathead Lake beach.

The Averills, who opened the ranch in 1945 as a getaway for folks from the world over, are intent on keeping their dudes busy: Fishing, swimming (pool or lake), tennis, golf, barbecues, trail rides, sailing, waterskiing, mountain biking, river-raft trips, horse games and rodeo training, breakfast rides, and volleyball are but a few of the diversions at hand. Some guests even help with the chores. Others, somehow, find time to just lie around, resting.

The lodge operates on the American Plan (all meals and recreational options included), and a full week's worth of guests arrive and depart simultaneously. For additional information call 837–4391 or log on to www.averills.com.

For digs that are less pretentious and more reasonably priced, make your way to the *O'Duachain Country Inn*, nestled outside Bigfork in a mellow rural setting of meadows and towering conifers. Five rooms are available to rent, with prices ranging from $120 for shared-bath accommodations to $195 for a two-bedroom suite. Your hosts, Bill Knoll and Mary Corcoran Knoll, are so affable and unassuming that you'd swear they must be lifelong Montanans (truth be told, they're relatively recent transplants from Washington, D.C.). Tempt him, and Bill might bring out the hilarious cartoon book on seaside humor he wrote while living back east, entitled *Beach Rap*; Mary, meantime, may share her stories of magical experiences with bald eagles and ravens. To find the O'Duachain (*O-dew-cane*), go south from Bigfork on Highway 35 then turn east onto Highway 209; go 3.5 miles and turn left (north) onto Ferndale Drive, following it as it curves right toward the mountains in about a mile. You'll see the inn at 675 Ferndale Drive. To make reservations, call (800) 837–7460 or E-mail innbigfork@aol.com.

Not far from the O'Duachain is the *Coyote Roadhouse Restaurant,* owned and operated by master chef and successful restaurateur Gary Hastings. Considered one of Montana's finest restaurants—in fact, *Travel & Leisure* magazine once called it the state's very best—the establishment specializes in gourmet Mayan, Southwestern, Sicilian, and Cajun delectables. Call 837–4250 for requisite reservations.

The *Jewel Basin Hiking Area,* located 10 miles north of Bigfork, resides at the northern end of the sweeping Swan Range. The 15,000-acre preserve is designated by the Forest Service as a hikers-only area—no pack stock, motorized vehicles, or bicycles permitted. The hiking area offers good fishing in many of its twenty-eight lakes, and includes 35 miles of trails, many suitable for neophyte hikers and kids.

To find the trailhead, travel 2 miles north from Bigfork on Highway 35 and turn right onto Highway 83. In about $2^1/_2$ miles, turn left onto Echo Lake Road, and after another $2^1/_2$ miles, follow the Noisy Creek Road east to the parking area (a high-clearance vehicle is recommended for the last couple of miles). For more information call the Flathead National Forest at 755–5401.

Keep your nose peeled for the heady scent of mint, one of the Flathead Valley's newer cash crops, as you continue north from Bigfork toward the

Montana Trivia

wide spot in the road called Creston. Lovers of gardening and flowers may be rendered speechless at the **Gatiss Gardens**, just south of Creston along State Highway 35. The resident families—until recently the Gatisses, and now the Sibleruds—have spent thousands of hours working the four-acre grounds. Hundreds drive by the spot gaping in disbelief, wondering how anyone could grow such extraordinary gardens, and not knowing that they're open to the public.

A mile-long, self-guided trail winds through the profusion of color provided largely by a vast assortment of perennials. The gardens are open daily, 9:00 A.M. to dusk, and there's also a small gift shop on the premises. The guest register and trailhead are adjacent to the free parking area, a hundred yards west of the houses, just off Broeder Loop Road. For more information call 755–2418.

Immediately across the road from Gatiss Gardens is Fish Hatchery Road. Follow it to the north for a mile and you'll come to the **Creston Fish Hatchery**, the rearing grounds for thousands of FLMs (Future Lunkers of Montana). You can take a walk around the grounds and watch swarms of rainbow and cutthroat trout breeding stock and their offspring swimming about in raceways. Spawning, a fascinating procedure to watch, takes place between January and March, with maximum fish populations generally attained in April.

No dummies they, numerous fish-eating birds also live in the vicinity and will be spotted by the observant: kingfishers, ospreys, and great blue herons, to name three. There's also a picnic grounds adjacent to the hatchery. Staff are on duty weekdays from 7:30 A.M. to 4:00 P.M. For more information call 758–6868.

Kalispell's quiet eastside historic district includes what is arguably the most resplendent bed-and-breakfast in all of Big Sky Country: **The Keith House.** The old beauty has served numerous functions since it was built to house the family of Kalispell's first mercantile owner early in the twentieth century, and the present owners were compelled to scrub off years of tarnish to bring the residence to its current state of grace.

The five guest rooms are exquisite. Take the English country–style Valerie's Room: Embellished in shades of coral and sage green, it features a king-size, iron-rail-frame bed, wide enough to sleep in sideways, and positively smothered in comforters, pillows, and lace. A heavy 8-foot door and polished hardwood wainscoting yield to a bright wallpaper of bold stripes and floral patterns. Antique chests, a mahogany writing desk, a bamboo armoire, an irresistible, down-stuffed sofa, and an aroma of spices add the finishing touches.

Outside the guest rooms on both the main and upper floor hang large works by Russell Chatham (see Yellowstone Country, Livingston), bringing indoors the moods of the Montana outdoors. Hosts Rebecca and Don Bauder are top-notch endurance athletes and, given the chance, one or the other might lead you on a running tour of Kalispell. The warm and hospitable Bauders have thought of countless unusual, delightful touches; on returning from supper, for instance, you may find your blinds pulled, the windows cracked, your bed turned down, and a card containing tomorrow's weather forecast. Room rates range from $135 per night for Sarah's Room to $220 for the elaborate Rebecca's

Best Annual Events

1. **OSCR Cross-Country Ski Race,**
   Seeley Lake; late January;
   (406) 677-2343

2. **Foresters' Ball,**
   Missoula; early February;
   (406) 243-0211

3. **Winter Carnival,**
   Whitefish; early February;
   (406) 862-3501

4. **Montana Storytelling Roundup,**
   Cut Bank; early April;
   (406) 873-2039

5. **International Wildlife Film Festival,**
   Missoula; mid-April; (406) 728-9380

6. **Bigfork Whitewater Festival,**
   Bigfork; mid-May; (406) 837-9914

7. **Lake to Lake Canoe Race,**
   Whitefish; late June; (406) 862-3501

8. **Libby Logger Days,**
   Libby; mid-July; (406) 293-4167

9. **North American Indian Days,**
   Browning; early July;
   (406) 338-7179

10. **Standing Arrow Powwow,**
    Elmo; late July; (406) 849-5798

11. **Rocky Muntain Accordion Celebration,** Philipsburg; early
    August; (406) 859-3388

12. **Montana State Fiddlers Contest,**
    Polson; late July; (406) 323-1198

13. **Cycle Montana**
    (route of week-long ride changes yearly); early August;
    (406) 721-1776

14. **Huckleberry Festival,**
    Trout Creek; early August;
    (406) 827-4091

15. **Western Montana Fair & Rodeo,**
    Missoula; mid-August;
    (406) 721-3247

16. **Northwest Montana Fair,**
    Kalispell; late August;
    (406) 758-5810

17. **Whitefish Summer Games,**
    Whitefish; mid-September;
    (406) 862-4035

18. **First Night Missoula,**
    Missoula; New Year's Eve;
    (406) 549-4755

Suite. The inn is located at 538 Fifth Avenue East. Call for reservations at (800) 972–7913 or E-mail the inn at keithbb@digisys.net. You can visit their Web site at www.keithhousebb.com.

Forty-two miles west of Kalispell on Highway 2, tucked away in the upper Thompson River Valley, is a very different, but no less appealing Montana getaway. The **Hargrave Cattle & Guest Ranch** is a real working ranch; fact is, they added "Guest" to their name only a few years back. Leo and Ellen Hargrave are true pieces of work, authentic westerners, as you'll realize the moment you meet them. (Guests arriving at the Kalispell airport are picked up by Leo and Ellen in their Lincoln stretch limousine outfitted with a bull-horn hood ornament.) A weekly stay (Sunday arrival, Saturday departure) at the big spread costs between $1,120 to $1,640 per adult, depending on the season and choice of accommodations—main house, cabin, or deluxe log lodge. The price includes three meals per day and the use of all ranch facilities. You can become as involved—or stay as uninvolved—in the cattle-ranching activities as you choose. When the dinner bell clangs, hearty meals are served at a long farm table in the dining room, with Leo presiding over one end and Ellen over the other. Riding lessons, skeet shooting, horseshoes, fishing, and sneaking across the meadow to sample the suds at Lang Creek Brewery are all possibilities here. Call the Hargraves at 858–2284 to learn more, or visit their Web site at www.hargraveranch.com.

Eight miles north of Whitefish, a resort town located 14 miles north of Kalispell, is the **Big Mountain Ski and Summer Resort,** Montana's most popular ski area. During the warm months you can ride the chairlift to the summit ($9.50 for adults). En route, keep an eye out for wildlife—bears, moose, deer, mountain lions, coyotes, and any number of smaller animals can be seen on the slopes at one time or another.

At the basement level of the Summit House Restaurant, you'll find the **Big Mountain Environmental Education Center**. The Flathead National Forest and Winter Sports, Inc., joined together to develop this illuminating, hands-on interpretive center, where kids of all ages can run their hands through a coyote or wolf pelt, inspect a variety of western Montana's owls (they're stuffed), or borrow a pair of binoculars to get a close-up view of the ice-clad peaks of Glacier National Park, looming to the east.

Knowledgeable Forest Service personnel are on hand to answer questions and aid in helping visitors better understand and appreciate the natural history of Glacier Country. At scheduled times, staffers present lectures on topics such as endangered species, wetlands and fisheries, and the bears of Montana. The Big Mountain Environmental Education Center is open from June 1 through September 30, daily from 10:00 A.M. to 5:00 P.M. For further information call 862–1972.

After enjoying the nature center and savoring the 360-degree view earned at the summit, some visitors forgo the chairlift and opt to hike back to the base area, through timber stands and "gardens" of wildflowers, on the 5.6-mile *Danny On Memorial Trail*. (A much smaller number of visitors hike up the challenging but well-graded trail to reach the summit, an elevation gain of more than 2,000 feet.) The Big Mountain also maintains an extensive network of mountain-biking trails, and full-suspension mountain bikes can be rented on-site.

The trail was dedicated to the memory of a man who touched the lives of hundreds of Flathead Valley residents and visitors. Danny On was a Forest Service silviculturist, acclaimed nature photographer, and ardent skier who died here in 1979, skiing on the slopes that he loved. On was known for taking novices under his wing and showing them the ropes, whether they be the ropes of downhill skiing, natural history, or photography.

Back down below, along the Whitefish Lake Road at a point 1 mile north of the Big Mountain junction, you'll see a left-hand turn onto a gravel road that leads down to the parking area for *Les Mason Park*. From the parking area a short trail leads to a brush-embraced beach. This quiet lakeside spot can be deserted even when sunbathers are lying nose-to-toes at the very popular City Beach. Les Mason Park (862–7633) is supported by donation.

Unlike many alpine ski resorts, Whitefish was a town long before it became a destination for schussers. At the newly renovated 1927 *Burlington Northern Depot*, the Stumptown Historical Society maintains a museum exploring the old days, with exhibits on the area's Native Americans, early logging practices, the Great Northern Railroad, and more. An exquisitely restored 1940s Pullman car guards the museum, situated at the north end of Central Avenue and open daily from 10:00 A.M. to 2:00 P.M.

The *Garden Wall Inn*, located at 504 Spokane Avenue, is Whitefish's original bed-and-breakfast inn. Several others have sprung up in recent years, but the Garden Wall remains the friendliest. A choice of five antiques appointed rooms provides intimate and comfortable quarters just two blocks from downtown. Afternoon/evening sherry in front of the fireplace is one Garden Wall tradition; another is an incredible, multicourse breakfast. Skiing is spoken here—both cross-country and alpine—and owner-hostess Rhonda Fitzgerald has collected an impressive and entertaining library of skiing-related books. Rooms start at $85 and range up to $175 for a two-bedroom suite; for additional information call 862–3440 or (888) 530–1700, or visit www.wtp.net/go/gardenwall.

If you prefer your breakfasts on the lighter side, or if the Garden Wall's "No Vacancy" sign is hanging, try the light and airy **Good Medicine Lodge,** located in Whitefish at 537 Wisconsin Avenue, on the way to the Big Mountain. The nine-bedroom lodge features a western ambience of dark-stained cedar beams, banisters, and loft railings, highlighted with Native American–inspired textiles and accessories. All rooms have private bath, telephone, and air conditioning, and most feature balconies with mountain views. There's also a television/videotape machine with a great movie selection in the smaller of the inn's two sitting rooms. Rates for double occupancy range from $85 to $145. Call for reservations at 862– 5288 or E-mail at goodrx@digisys.net. Good Medicine also maintains a Web site at www.wtp.net/go/goodrx.

Leading north from Columbia Falls is Highway 486, a secondary road paralleling the west shore of the wild and scenic North Fork of the Flathead River. The road soon turns into Forest Road 210 and becomes gravel before leading to the town of Polebridge, 35 miles north of Columbia Falls. Check out the historic **Polebridge Mercantile** and the funky **Northern Lights Saloon,** where you're bound to hear more than one bear story, or other north-country tall tale, from a local. (Much like the Yaak, we're talking way off the beaten path here, so it's a good idea to pick up a detailed map for navigational purposes. Stop by the Glacier View Ranger Station in Columbia Falls and ask for the visitor map of the North Half of the Flathead National Forest.)

Another 10 miles north of Polebridge along Forest Road 210 is the Ford Work Center. To visit the **Hornet Peak Fire Lookout**—the last D-1 Standard fire-lookout tower remaining in its original location—from Ford proceed $3^1/_2$ miles up Forest Road 318, and then go 5 miles on Forest Road 9805. The forest roads are generally passenger-car friendly. From the obvious turnoff, it's a steep mile-plus climb to the historic lookout tower. But the effort spent is not wasted. The lookout is intriguing, and from atop Hornet Mountain you'll admire one of the best views in northwest Montana. From the peak, elevation 6,744 feet, you can see far to the east into Glacier National Park and pick out many of its jagged, high peaks.

The lookout was constructed in 1922, largely with native, on-site materials. U.S. Forest Service employees cut timber with crosscut saws, squared the logs and fit the corners with broad axes, and split roofing shingles with froes. More recently, members of the North Fork Preservation Association have contributed hundreds of hours of free labor to restore the old structure to near-new condition. For more information call the Hungry Horse–Glacier View Ranger Station at 387–3800.

Once back in Polebridge, consider driving the narrow and winding 14-mile road that leads to sparkling **Kintla Lake**. The long body of water fills one of the deep, glacier-carved clefts striating the relatively little-visited western reaches of Glacier National Park. The view is stunning from the lakeshore campground.

Highway 2 between Columbia Falls and West Glacier is one of those free-enterprise-gone-berserk stretches of road that seem to spring up near the entrances to our national parks, featuring the sorts of attractions parents may shun but kids inevitably love: water slides, go-kart tracks, mazes, caged bears, T-shirt shops, chainsaw-art galleries. . . . You'll encounter all of these and much more.

One of the most curiously named towns in Montana is Hungry Horse, which is situated along this section of Highway 2 and includes its share of the tacky and wacky. Among its more subdued, yet impressive attractions is the **Hungry Horse Dam Visitor Center**.

Hungry Horse Dam impounds the lower stretches of the South Fork of the Flathead, a river that runs wild for mile after mile through the Bob Marshall Wilderness before being tamed. The visitor center, operated by the Bureau of Reclamation, explains the history and functions of the dam and also contains displays on the Flathead National Forest and area natural history. The visitor center is open Memorial Day through Labor Day, 9:30 A.M. to 6:00 P.M. every day, with guided tours offered on the hour between 10:00 A.M. and 5:00 P.M. The dam and visitor center are 4 miles southeast of town. Call 387–5241 for information.

There's a great new/old find in West Glacier, near the west entrance of Glacier National Park: the **Belton Chalet,** built in 1910 as the first of James J. Hill's Swiss-style Great Northern Railroad hotels. This Rip Van Winkle of a lodge slept for half a century; now, newly renovated and listed as a National Historic Landmark, in the summer of 2000 it again began receiving guests. The chalet's thirty period rooms (no television or phones) go for between $95 and $125, while an adjacent cottage sleeping up to six costs $200 per night. Call Belton Chalet, which is located next to the Belton Station Amtrak depot, at 888–5000, or check out their Web site at www.beltonchalet.com.

The Great Northern Railroad's isolated line over Marias Pass is subject to heavy snows and strong winds in the winter, and the task of keeping the tracks open is a mighty one. The *Izaak Walton Inn* in Essex is another inn with ties to the area's railroading past. It was built in the late 1930s to house the men servicing the line, and their numbers grew rapidly as winter strengthened its icy north-country grip. Still, the inn was built larger than needed for even the largest of crews, for Essex once was slated to become the central entrance into Glacier National Park—an idea eventually erased from the drawing board.

Even lacking a nearby park entrance, the Izaak Walton has become a

Winning an Oscar

*M*y first cross-country ski marathon was a dilly. Known as OSCR—pronounced "Oscar" and standing for Ovando to Seeley Citizens Race—the February 1985 race was slated to start at the Whitetail Ranch near Ovando and end 50 kilometers, or 31 miles, later in the town of Seeley Lake.

The temperature at the supposed start time of 9:00 A.M. was an Arctic-like 27 degrees below zero. Nervous conversations rattled like tinkling ice in the frozen morning air. Still, we racers-to-be knew in our hearts that the event would be canceled, and that inside a couple of hours we'd be back in the warm comfort of our homes.

But after an hour the temperature had warmed all the way to minus 20 degrees, and suddenly the race director fired the starting gun. We were off, thirty-one strong, our skis gliding across the cold, humidity-free snow about as readily as rubber-soled gym shoes slide across a basketball court

covered in sandpaper. Everyone, even the eventual winner, would be out at least four hours, so keeping noses and digits from freezing was of more concern than the finishing order. The warmest temperature recorded along the course that day was minus 14 degrees. Still, it was a brilliant day, filled with deep-blue sky, snow-smothered mountain slopes, and bright winter sunshine.

As I reached the third of three aid stations, each of which was manned by two or three volunteers from the Seeley Lake snowmobile club, I blurted, "How much farther?" I remember being pleased to find that my mouth still moved. "Ten kilometers," said one of the men. "No—10 miles!" contended the other. They couldn't reach an agreement, so they offered me a blast of warmth from their bottle of Jack Daniels as a consolation. I thanked them but declined and skied off, not knowing if I had 6 miles or 10 miles of bitter, frozen Montana wilderness still to contend with.

popular tourist stop. Its railroading legacy continues: Essex is a flag stop on Amtrak's *Empire Builder* line, and passengers can load or unload literally at the Izaak Walton's front door. Railroading memorabilia hang from the walls, and groups of up to four can opt to spend the night in refurbished historic cabooses, replete with modern plumbing and cooking facilities.

The inn is a popular summer spot for hikers, mountain bikers, and fly-fishers, who cast in the spirit of the celebrated angler after whom the inn is named. The Izaak Walton Inn's long winters and well-groomed trails also make it one of the most popular spots for cross-country skiing in Montana. Rooms go for $98 to $160, and cabooses for $525 for three nights, the minimum stay. For reservations and

The Man Who Talks Not

*T*ucked away in a small structure on the main street of East Glacier is the **John L. Clarke Western Art Gallery and Memorial Museum.** *John L. Clarke, whose Blackfeet name was Cutapuis, "The Man Who Talks Not," was a Blackfeet Indian born in Highwood in 1881. Epidemics of smallpox and scarlet fever swept through the area in the early 1880s, killing five of Clarke's brothers and leaving him, at age two and one half, deaf and unable to speak.*

After his father moved what remained of the family to Midvale, near the present site of East Glacier, Clarke was sent away at age thirteen to a school for deaf children. There he learned the skill of wood carving, and his obvious abilities led to a budding career in art. His first big break came in 1917, when the Academy of Fine Arts in Philadelphia began regularly exhibiting his work. Then, a year later at age thirty-seven, he met and married Mamie Peters Simon, an astute businesswoman who became Clarke's promoter, interpreter, and secretary-manager. With their combined talents, Clarke soon became known as one of the world's best portrayers of Western wildlife.

Clarke's specialty was detailed cottonwood carvings of bears, mountain goats, and other wildlife thriving in his home territory. After he died in 1970, his friend J. W. Tschache, an avid collector of Clarke's works, said about a carving of a big grizzly bear freeing itself from a trap that "the real significance of this work is that J. L. Clarke created it when he was approaching ninety years old, when his eyes were so clouded with cataracts that he could barely see. He created this sculpture almost entirely by feel."

In addition to his intricate wildlife carvings, Clarke also modeled in clay, painted in watercolors and oils, and sketched in charcoal and crayon. At the memorial museum in East Glacier—which his adopted daughter, Joyce Clark Turvey, started in 1977—limited editions of Clarke's works are for sale, along with the creations of numerous other Western artists.

more information call 888–5700 or E-mail the inn at izaakw@digisys.net.

Browning is the social, economic, and administrative headquarters for those Blackfeet Indians living south of the international border. Here you'll find the **Museum of the Plains Indian**, home to a comprehensive collection of Blackfeet artifacts. The museum also showcases arts and crafts—not only the Blackfeet's, but also those of the Crow, Northern Cheyenne, Sioux, and other Plains tribes, all traditional enemies of the Blackfeet. A highlight in the permanent display area is an exhibit of traditional costumes, while "Winds of Change," a multimedia show narrated by the late Vincent Price and produced by Montana State University, illuminates the continuing evolution of Indian cultures.

In the changing-exhibits area the works of modern-day sculptors, carvers, painters, and other artists and craftspeople are highlighted. The sales shop, offering a wide variety of contemporary products, is operated by the Indian-owned Northern Plains Indian Crafts Association.

The museum, founded in 1941, is administered by the Indian Arts and Crafts Board, operating under the Department of the Interior. The Museum of the Plains Indian, located at the junction of Highways 2 and 89 just west of town, is open daily June through September from 9:00 A.M. to 4:45 P.M. and, during the rest of the year, Monday through Friday from 10:00 A.M. to 4:30 P.M. Admission is free in winter and $4.00 for adults and $1.00 for children six to twelve in summer. For more information call 338–2230.

North American Indian Days is held each July in Browning at the Blackfeet Tribal Fairgrounds, next to the Museum of the Plains Indian. The four-day celebration brings together Indians from throughout the United States and Canada, as well as non-Indian visitors, for dancing, games, sporting events, and more. For details call 338–7179 or check out the Web site at blackfeet.3rivers.net/powwow.htm.

Van tours along the legendary Going-to-the-Sun Road in Glacier National Park, guided by Native Americans from the Browning area, are available through **Going-to-the-Sun (Natos'i At'apoo) Sun Tours**. On these informative outings you'll have the opportunity to listen to the Blackfeet Indians' interpretation of the sacred landscape of Glacier National Park, a philosophy markedly different from the often impersonal, scientific outlook common among those of European descent.

Arrangements can also be made to be picked up in either East Glacier or St. Mary. Sun Tours is an authorized concessioner of the National Park Service. Call 226-9220 for more information.

Lewis and Clark Trail

As you motor along Highway 83 in the sleepy Seeley-Swan Valley, that's the **Bob Marshall Wilderness** straddling the Continental Divide to the east. "The Bob," named in honor of a pioneer in the American wilderness movement, joins together with the Great Bear and Scapegoat wilderness areas to form one of the largest wilderness complexes in the lower forty-eight states. More than 1½ million acres of protected forest are accessible only by trails—nearly 2,000 miles of them.

Approximately 7 miles south of the turn to picturesque *Holland Lake Lodge,* watch for Forest Road 4370 going northeast. After roughly 5 miles the gravel road bends southward, leading in 2½ more miles to the ½-mile-long foot trail that will take you to sparkling and little-visited *Clearwater Lake.* A better place for a summer's picnic and cooling dip is tough to envision. Don't be surprised if you encounter a

Rocky Mountain Oysters

The **Rock Creek Testicle Festival**, *held annually in late September at the Rock Creek Lodge (22 miles east of Missoula), has been described as the "last best party in the last best place." The raucous event's highlight—outshining the dancing, cowpie tossing, and constant beer swilling—is the munching of Rocky Mountain oysters, a euphemistic label for the testicles of bulls, calves, sheep, and/or lambs. Nearly 10,000 pilgrims have come in recent years to the festival to sample the beer-marinated, breaded, and deep-fried bull testicles, whose flavor ranges— depending on who's eating them and on the age of the animal when neutered—from a taste described as*

similar to chicken, to that of liver, to that of bungee cords sauteed in cod-liver oil.

For another out-of-the-ordinary culinary experience—this one available twenty-four hours a day any day—the epicurious can head for downtown Missoula to **The Oxford** *and try the house specialty of brains and eggs. Sampling them once is considered a right of passage to becoming a Missoulian; to try them more than once is, well . . . . The Oxford, a popular drinking and poker-gaming establishment, is located at 337 North Higgins. Arguably, it's also the best place in Missoula to view a parade of the city's astoundingly diverse array of humanity.*

party or two of loaded-down mountain bikers while prowling these backroads: Forest Road 4370 is part of the 2,470-mile Great Divide Mountain Bike Route, a project of the Missoula-based Adventure Cycling Association.

When Lolo National Forest recreation planners were looking for a peaceful stretch of river that novice and solo paddlers could manage without getting in over their heads, they couldn't have done better than the *Clearwater Canoe Trail*. The river trail, beginning 5 miles north of the town of Seeley Lake off Highway 83, peacefully meanders to the south for 4 miles before reaching the open and often more turbulent waters of Seeley Lake.

The canoe trail is one of the best bird-watching locales in western Montana. Large raptors, such as bald eagles and ospreys, can be seen fishing for dinner, the sounds of warblers and other songbirds are abundant in the spring, and common loons nest along the shores of Seeley Lake not far from the river trail's inlet.

The Clearwater Canoe Trail enjoys protection under the Wild and Scenic Rivers Act. For information and maps call the Seeley Lake Ranger District at 677–2233.

The *Emily A Bed and Breakfast*, which opened its doors in 1992, is a sumptuous, 11,000-square-foot structure built of larch logs felled in the surrounding forest. The lodge and property, 160 acres of prime Montana woodland and meadow, are 5 miles north of Seeley Lake on Highway 83, near the 20-mile marker (just south of the turnoff to the Clearwater Canoe Trail).

Marilyn Shope Peterson, who owns and operates the inn with her husband, Keith (a renowned sports-medicine physician who runs Montana Sports Medicine from the lodge), named the Emily A in honor of her grandmother, Emily Alvis Stinson Shope. In a sense, Marilyn is carrying on a family tradition: To help support the raising of her seven children, her grandmother, who moved to Montana in 1893, operated one of the first boardinghouses in Missoula.

The Emily A features five guest rooms, two with private bath; a family suite with two bedrooms and a kitchen; and an original homestead cabin. Rates range from $95 to $150 per night. Hiking and cross-country ski trails radiate out from the spacious inn. Moose and deer are common on the surrounding lands, and large trout regularly are pulled from the private, eight-acre pond. How seriously is fishing fun taken at the Emily A? Consider its phone number: 677–FISH. You can also learn more at the inn's Web site, www.The EmilyA.com.

At the **Double Arrow Lodge**, traditional western fare—spelled beef and trout—is found at its best. The Double Arrow offers food and lodging all year long, golf in summer, and groomed cross-country ski trails and horse-drawn sleigh rides in winter. The log lodge, with its massive rock fireplace, was built in 1929 by international financier and Dutch cavalry officer Jan Boissevain. Following his tour of America after World War I,

On a Carousel

*T*he Missoulian at the forefront of the creation of the marvelous Carousel for Missoula was Chuck Kaparich, who as a child played on the carousel at Butte's Columbia Gardens, a now-defunct amusement park that shone like a diamond in the rough copper-mining town.

It began innocently enough when, a few years ago, Kaparich and his wife happened across the turn-of-the-century carousel at Riverfront Park in Spokane, Washington. Kaparich, a life-long woodworker, was simultaneously transported back to his childhood and smitten by the beauty of the carved wooden horses. It occurred to him that an antique carousel horse might look good in the front room of his home. Soon, however, that relatively modest thought sprouted into a vision that captured the collective imagination of Missoula's citizens and rapidly blossomed into one of the most unifying movements ever to hit a Montana town. "I will deliver to you a carousel and sign it over to the city as a gift," Kaparich proclaimed to the Missoula Redevelopment Agency in the summer of 1991. "In return, I would like the city to give it a good home."

In its fine home at Caras Park the carousel stands out as a captivating work of art, yet some of its brightest beauty is found in the dozens of stories telling of its creation. Hundreds of hands-on volunteers were involved, and thousands of others donated money to the effort. Grade-school classes held a "Pennies for Ponies" competition to see who could raise the most money. By the end of 1994 the not-for-profit A Carousel for Missoula Foundation had raised three-quarters of a million dollars.

Now, for 50 cents children of any age can mount one of the carousel's thirty-eight ponies—each of which took volunteers under Kaparich's tutelage several hundred hours to carve in his garage/workshop—and spin around, at up to eleven miles per hour, to musical accompaniment provided by America's largest military band organ. (The foundation purchased the 400-pipe music machine for $65,000.) Leading all the horses, whose tails are fashioned from actual horsehair, is the stately, patriotically bedecked "Columbia Belle," named in honor of the Columbia Gardens in Butte, which Chuck Kaparich so enjoyed as a boy and which burned to the ground in 1973.

A Carousel for Missoula celebrates the beauty of horses and wood, the history and spirit of a city, and the difference one man can make . . . with a thousand volunteers at his side.

Boissevain labeled the American West a "wasteland." But he radically changed his thinking after accepting an invitation from Allen Toole, son of Anaconda Company executive John H. Toole, to stay at his family's cabin in the Seeley-Swan Valley. Boissevain was captivated by the area's beauty, and he set out with partner Colonel George Weisel to build a private retreat where he could share his new-found love of the West with others.

It's interesting to note that the Double Arrow brand came to Montana, by way of Holland, from Montana. Boissevain first saw the brand on a horse given to him by his father; that particular horse had come to Holland from the Spears brothers' Double Arrow Ranch in Drummond, Montana.

Meals at the Double Arrow range from moderate to expensive in price. Call 677–2777 or visit their Web site at www.doublearrowresort.com for reservations and information.

Garnet Ghost Town, one of Montana's best preserved pioneer settlements, celebrated its 100th birthday on the Fourth of July weekend in 1995. Although placer gold miners had been active in the Garnet Range as early as the 1860s, it wasn't until the mid-1890s, when thousands of miners were suddenly unemployed as a result of the repeal of the Sherman Silver Purchase Act, that activity in the Garnet area shifted into high gear. In 1895, Dr. Armistad Mitchell built an ore-crushing mill at the head of First Chance Gulch, around which grew a town—first called Mitchell, but by 1897 known as Garnet, named after the semiprecious, ruby-colored stones found in the nearby hills.

By 1898, when a rich vein was struck at the Nancy Hanks mine, nearly 1,000 people called Garnet home. It consisted of numerous cabins, a doctor's office, an assay building, a union hall (boasting what was regarded as one of the best dance floors in Montana), thirteen saloons, two barber shops, four stores, four hotels, and more. Many miners brought families with them to Garnet, so, not surprisingly, the social life here was more civilized than in many of the Montana gold camps.

As in most boomtowns, buildings were built quickly and bereft of sound foundations. Most have collapsed, although several of the 1800s buildings remain intact a century after being constructed. The Bureau of Land Management is working with the nonprofit Garnet Preservation Association to save and stabilize the remaining structures, including the impressive, three-story J. K. Wells Hotel, built in the winter of 1897 on a wooden-post foundation.

You'll also find several newer buildings. Two 1930s-vintage cabins are available for rent during the winter, making the ghost town a popular destination for cross-country skiers and snowmobilers. Another fun time to come is during the preservation association's annual fundraiser, the Hard Times Dinner and Dance, held sometime during the summer (the date changes).

To get to Garnet, which some old-timers claim is a ghost town actually

Ninemile Station

*E*arly in the twentieth century, vast stands of timber in northern Idaho and northwest Montana were destroyed by a series of huge wildfires—including the infamous fire of 1910, which took more than three million acres and eighty-two lives. The year 1929 brought another particularly dry summer, and the available fire-fighting resources rapidly dwindled. Inadequately trained emergency crews and stock were sent out, resulting in inefficient efforts.

This gave regional forester Evan Kelley the impetus to create a centralized depot at Ninemile to serve as a training and dispatching center for mules and work crews. Wanting it to be a showplace and not just another rustic, backwoods ranger station, Kelley built the depot to resemble a well-maintained Kentucky horse farm, with Cape Cod–style buildings, sporting green-shake roofs, erected by the Civilian Conservation Corps.

For the next two decades the depot served as a major hub of backcountry activities. Two factors combined to bring the center's role as a remount depot to an end: the introduction of aerial fire fighting (one of the first USFS smokejumper centers was estab-

lished near Ninemile), and the post-World War II demand for lumber to build new houses. The latter resulted in an ever-growing network of roads, making access to the backcountry easier and mules no longer vital. The remount depot closed in 1953.

In 1962 the buildings and grounds became the Ninemile Ranger Station. More recently, the Forest Service established the Arthur Carhart National Wilderness Training Center at Ninemile, where they conduct clinics in packing, backcountry skills, and the use of primitive tools. Such "lost skills" are again becoming important, especially for crews working in the wilderness areas where motorized vehicles and power tools are prohibited.

The station also is home to the Forest Service mule pack train, which can be seen in parades and celebrations throughout the West (they marched in the 1991 Tournament of Roses Parade and also have appeared on the Today Show). No one can say these irresistible critters are all show and no go, however, for they'll be found packing workers into the wilds or packing garbage out just as often as they're seen performing in parades.

inhabited by spectres, from near the 22-mile marker on Highway 200 east of Potomac, turn onto the well-signed Garnet Range Road and travel approximately 11 miles. The road is closed to wheeled vehicles between January 1 and April 30, when it turns into an over-snow route for snowmobilers and skiers. For information call the Bureau of Land Management at 329–3914.

Missoula, best known for the University of Montana, is considered by many to be the state's cultural center and most progressive city, although some residents of Billings, Helena, and other towns are quick to disagree. Missoula's attractions range from quaint to sophisticated to off the wall.

Several national organizations are headquartered in Missoula, including the Boone and Crockett Club, the Adventure Cycling Association, the Outdoor Writers Association of America, and the Rocky Mountain Elk Foundation, a group dedicated to enhancing and increasing elk habitat throughout the West. The foundation's *Wildlife Visitor Center,* located at 2291 West Broadway, provides a glimpse of the ways of the wild wapiti and also features collections of wildlife art and outstanding taxidermy, including mounted grizzly bears and mountain goats. The center is open daily, Memorial Day through Labor Day, from 8:00 A.M. to 6:00 P.M., and on a shortened schedule during the winter. For information call 523–4545.

The *U.S. Forest Service Smokejumpers Visitor Center* is adjacent to Johnson-Bell Airport, 7 miles west of town. The facility is the largest active smokejumper base and training center in the United States.

Here the visitor will come to appreciate the "ups and downs" encountered by the Forest Service's elite corps of air-delivered firefighters. Murals, videos, and displays detail the sixty-year history of these men and women who risk their lives by parachuting from planes into remote wildfires. The visitor center features tours on the hour from Memorial Day through Labor Day; call 329–4934 for information on special group tours and tours during the off-season.

The prices are reasonable and the coffee strong at *The Shack* (a.k.a. Cafe 222), which claims—not without some justification—to serve the best breakfasts in Montana. They're so good, in fact, that you can get them for lunch or dinner, as well as at the more conventional time of day.

Considering the upscale surroundings, you may wonder what the term *shack* has to do with anything, but until a few years ago the restaurant truly did occupy hovel-like quarters. The name and great food remain the same—only the place has changed. The Shack (549–9903) is located downtown at 222 West Main.

Those who enjoy lusting over high-quality guitars should not miss visiting the **Stringed Instrument Division,** located at 541 South Higgins Avenue. The enterprise sells new and vintage acoustic and electric guitars from makers that include Guild, Dobro, and Bozeman-based Gibson, as well as banjoes, fiddles, and other stringed instruments. Call 549–1502 to find out more.

The earthy settlement of Hot Springs, located 30 miles southwest of Flathead Lake off State Highway 28, boasts several commercial enterprises where visitors can soak in mineral-water baths. Free-to-enjoy plunges and mud baths can be found by traveling up Spring Street.

The golden age of logging, the day-to-day affairs of a young Missoula, and much more are recalled at the **Historical Museum at Fort Missoula.** The museum features more than 15,000 exhibits and twelve structures—including a relocated fire-lookout tower—on a thirty-two-acre parcel of grassy land adjacent to the Bitterroot River.

Fort Missoula was constructed in 1877 in response to the demands of a growing citizenry that wanted protection from Indians and other perceived frontier threats. One of the most compelling events in the fort's history occurred in 1897, when Lt. James Moss and his 25th Infantry, made up entirely of black soldiers, mounted a bicycle expedition from Fort Missoula to St. Louis, Missouri. The corps pedaled their chain-driven, single-speed bicycles for 1,900 miles over dirt tracks and muddy roads, making St. Louis in a respectable forty-five days. The Army never did warm up to Moss's idea of utilizing the bicycle for large-scale troop transportation, but the 25th Infantry's feat was remarkable all the same. (Perhaps Moss is enjoying the last laugh, for today Missoula is heralded as one of the major cycling cities in America and is home to the nation's largest bicycling organization, the Adventure Cycling Association.)

To find the Historical Museum at Fort Missoula, go west on South Avenue past Reserve, then watch for the sign on your left. The free museum is open year-round, Tuesday through Sunday. For more information call 728–3476 or visit the museum's Web site: www. montana/ftms/amuseum.com.

Out to Lunch is one of two exceedingly popular celebrations taking place regularly throughout the summer in Missoula. The food-and-music bash begins at noon at Caras Park, along the Clark Fork River in downtown Missoula, every Wednesday from June through August.

Montana Trivia

Out to Lunch began in 1986, when crowds averaging one or two hundred ventured out for the lunchtime live tunes; now the event draws upward of 3,000 to listen to top regional bands and sample the goods of dozens of food vendors. Out to Lunch has become *the* midweek social event in Missoula, and its enviable success has spawned similar lunch-fests in Hamilton, Butte, Helena, and other communities.

After enjoying the tastes and tunes of Out to Lunch, saunter across the Caras Park grounds to have a look at the trotting, cantering, and bucking horses that grace *A Carousel for Missoula*. The carousel operates daily from noon to 7:00 P.M., Memorial Day through Labor Day, and noon to 4:00 P.M. the rest of the year.

The community's other popular gathering is the *Missoula Farmers' Market*. Boasting humble origins like Out to Lunch—it began in 1972 with only seven sellers—in twenty-eight years the market has blossomed and fruited into a biweekly extravaganza, with more than one hundred booths and thousands of shoppers each Saturday morning. A large share of the sellers are Hmong, a Laotian mountain people, several hundred of whom settled in Missoula after the Vietnam War. Theirs are known consistently to be among the tastiest and most beautifully displayed vegetables.

Sensory overload is a real danger: You'll behold seasonal bouquets of cut flowers and colorful displays of yellow, red, green, and orange vegetables; you'll smell newly cut herbs and fresh-baked breads; and you'll hear live music and the chatter of friends meeting friends. The Saturday market runs from 9:00 to 11:00 A.M., and the smaller Tuesday version begins at 6:30 P.M. To find the market, go north through downtown on Higgins Street until you can't go any farther. Now, if only you can find a parking space.

From the town of Lolo, go 26 miles southwest on Highway 12 to find *Lolo Hot Springs Resort*, where the Lewis and Clark party camped and enjoyed hot baths in a natural pool. Amenities not found when the explorers visited include a recently remodeled bar and restaurant, RV campground, motel, and clean concrete pools open year-round. Call 273–2290 to learn more.

Lolo Hot Springs is an especially popular spot for snowmobilers and cross-country skiers, who flock by the hundreds between November and April to play on the snowy trails at the *Lolo Pass Winter Sports Area*.

GLACIER COUNTRY

Montana Trivia

Fifteen owl species live in or occasionally visit Montana: the snowy, eastern screech, western screech, northern pygmy, northern saw-whet, long-eared, short-eared, great gray, burrowing, flammulated, barred, boreal, northern hawk-owl, the rarely seen barn owl, and the most common of all, the great horned owl.

The warming hut at the pass, 7 miles southwest of Lolo Hot Springs on Highway 12, is open Friday through Monday 10:00 A.M. to 4:30 P.M., December through March. For information call the Powell Ranger District at (208) 942–3113.

In 1975, Les and Hanneke Ippisch purchased an old schoolhouse and adjacent outbuildings in the Ninemile Valley, west of Missoula near Huson. Today it's both their home and unique business enterprise, *The Schoolhouse and Teacherage Bed and Breakfast.*

The original schoolhouse was built in the early 1900s by the Anaconda Company for the children of loggers cutting timber to stoke the fires at the smelters in Butte and Anaconda. Later, the larger schoolhouse was built, and the smaller building was converted into a teacherage. When logging activities dwindled in the 1930s, many families moved on, and by 1936 school no longer was in session. The building served for years as a community center for residents of the lower Ninemile Valley.

The Ippisches opened the bed-and-breakfast relatively recently, after already garnering a regional reputation for their popular Christmas Market. The market, open only on weekends between Thanksgiving and Christmas, features handmade toys, ornaments, and nativities. More recently they've added an Easter Market to their schedule.

The Amish, Swedish, Montana, and Dutch rooms are appointed with featherbeds, down comforters and pillows, and handmade quilts. Folk art abounds, rounding out the atmosphere unique to each of the ethnic rooms. Room rates are $45 to $65.

To find The Schoolhouse and Teacherage, go 20 miles west from Missoula along Interstate 90 and take exit 82. After traveling $1\frac{1}{2}$ miles along the road winding to the north, turn right onto Remount Road and go another $1\frac{1}{2}$ miles. Watch for the distinctive wrought-iron gates and yellow-and-gold-colored buildings on the left. For information call 626–5879.

The *Ninemile Remount Depot and Ranger Station* is a mile beyond The Schoolhouse and Teacherage on Remount Road. The visitor center, open since 1989, details the intriguing history of the outpost. The center is open Memorial Day through Labor Day only; however, enjoy self-guided tours of the depot at any time of the year. The entire, intriguing remount depot—classic weathervanes and all—is listed on the National Register of Historic Places. For information call the Ninemile Ranger District of the Lolo National Forest at 626–5201.

If you've run short on reading material, head to tiny Alberton, located a few miles west of the Ninemile exit along Interstate 90. Here, in a 1910 building on Railroad Street, the **Montana Valley Bookstore** stocks some 100,000 used books for sale.

Store owner-operator Keren Wales is understandingly comfortable in the bookselling business, for she's been working in bookstores since age eight. Her father opened the Alberton store in 1978, with 30,000 volumes on the shelves, another 50,000 in storage awaiting pricing, and 15,000 enroute from the "East Coast branch." (Her family also owns Chester Valley Old Books in Chester County, Pennsylvania.) Wales, who like all independent booksellers must compete with remainder bookstores, megachains, and mail-order outlets, has found her special niche in stocking plenty of Western novels, out-of-print and tough-to-find books, poetry—six shelves full of it—and even a few rare books.

A question regularly asked of Wales by customers is, "Do you really have 100,000 used books?" Her stock answer, "Let me know when you're done counting." The Montana Valley Bookstore opens for browsing and book-counting 365 days a year from 8:00 A.M. to 7:00 P.M. Call 722–4950 for more information.

Ravalli County is rich in history, wildlife, scenery, and opportunities to soak in naturally heated waters. At Stevensville, Montana's oldest town and original capital, you can see the **St. Mary's Mission**, established by Father Pierre DeSmet in 1841, only thirty-six years after the Lewis and Clark expedition first passed through the Bitterroot Valley.

Montana Trivia

The Bitterroot Valley is one of many namesakes of Montana's official state flower, the bitterroot. The first Anglo to collect the beautiful flower was Captain Meriwether Lewis, which he did in 1806 in the Bitterroot Valley. Botanist Frederick Pursh later named it Lewisia rediviva, *in honor of the explorer.*

The arrival of the Jesuits, or "black robes" as the American Indians called them, marked the opening of the western frontier to white settlement. Ironically, although their arrival ultimately signaled the undoing of many native cultural traditions, the missionaries came west at the urging of Indians. It is told that Shining Shirt, a prophet and medicine man, predicted the coming of the black robes even before Lewis and Clark arrived. Shining Shirt learned through visions that the men with long black robes would give the Indians a new strength.

In 1831 a delegation of four braves traveled to St. Louis in an attempt to persuade priests to come back west with them. The first recruiting trip was unsuccessful, as were at least two subsequent ones. Finally, however, a group of Indians that traveled east in 1839 and met with Father DeSmet in Council Bluffs, Iowa, convinced him to come west. Soon afterward DeSmet was guided to the Bitterroot Valley, where he supervised construction of the St. Mary's Mission and was joined by Father Anthony Ravalli.

Today at the site you can see the mission building, as well as Father Ravalli's log house, the cabin of Chief Victor, and an old Indian cemetery. Admission is $3.00 ($1.00 for students) and tours are conducted daily between April 15 and November 15 from 10:15 A.M. to 4:15 P.M. Call 777–5734 for further information.

Stevensville is also your base for *The Watchable Wildlife Triangle*, which includes the Lee Metcalf National Wildlife Refuge, the Willoughby Environmental Education Area, and the Charles Waters Nature Trail. Designated by the U.S. Forest Service and U.S. Fish and Wildlife Service, the triangle presents the opportunity to view an impressive array of animals native to numerous habitats, all inside a 30-mile drive. You'll visit streamsides, old-growth forest, sagebrush benchlands, forested bottomlands, meadows, and wetlands. For maps and additional information call 777–5552.

As you pass through the bustling Bitterroot Valley burg of Hamilton, find your way downtown then up the stairs at 217 Main Street to *Maggie's Wild Oats Café & Coffee House* (363–4567). Exceptional breakfasts, deli lunches, and high-octane coffee are served daily at this out-of-the-way eatery. And, speaking of out-of-the-way, here's how to find the *Deer Crossing Bed & Breakfast,* situated on a 25-acre spread of pines and pasture at 396 Hayes Creek Road: South of Hamilton, turn west onto Camas Creek Loop adjacent to Rocky Mountain Log Homes; go three-

Montana Trivia

Marcus Daly, who made his fortune in Butte copper, established Hamilton in 1890 and built his 24,000-square-foot mansion outside of town in 1897. It encompasses more than 40 rooms, including 24 bedrooms and 15 bathrooms.

quarters of a mile then turn left onto Hayes Creek Road and continue until you see the inn. A pair of private rooms and two suites are available, along with a wonderful old bunkhouse dating to when the place was homesteaded. In the main house the Charlie Russell Suite is a favorite, with its sitting area, soaking tub, western-eclectic decor, and expansive cathedral ceiling. Rates begin at $45 and top out at $115, based on single or double occupancy. Host Mary Lynch provides a breakfast you'll long remember, served in her light-filled Sun Room. Call the Deer Crossing at 363–2232 for reservations or visit their Web site at www.wtp.net/go/deercrossing.

Trail of the Great Beer

*T*he Trail of the Great Bear is a well-promoted tourist route linking the Rocky Mountains of Montana and Alberta, Canada. With a great deal of help from the Glacier Country regional tourism commission, in March 2000 I discovered a route entirely within northwest Montana that I fondly refer to as the "Trail of the Great Beer."

Like many areas of the country, in recent years western Montana has experienced a boom in microbreweries. These can make a nice addition to, or even the focus of, a journey through the region; sort of like cowboy country's version of a California wine-country tour. Just be sure you have a designated driver along! The breweries differ vastly in scope, in the taste of their products, and in the names they employ to brand their brews: from the understated (Bayern Amber) to the outrageous (Moose Drool). At the more laidback end of the microbrewery spectrum is the Whitefish Brewing Company, owned by former beer hobbyist Gary Hutchinson and operated out of the garage of a house just south of Whitefish. At the other end is Bayern Brewery of Missoula, the big baby of Master Brewer Jürgen Knöller, who studied and apprenticed long and hard in his native Germany to learn to make beer the Old Country way. (Here's Jürgen's take on the American custom of serving green beer on St. Patrick's Day: "Over my dead body

would I allow anyone to put green dye in my beer.") As disparate as their operations are, though, Gary and Jürgen are very much alike in some basic ways: outspoken, gregarious, fiercely independent, and proud of their beers.

Here's a list of the breweries our tour group visited, along with the vital facts:

Whitefish Brewing Company, 5650 Highway 93 South, Whitefish; 862–2684; www.WhitefishBrewing.com

Great Northern Brewing Company, 2 Central Avenue, downtown Whitefish; 863–1000; www.blackstarbeer.com

Lang Creek Brewery, 655 Lang Creek Road, west of Marion; 858–2000; www.langcreekbrewery.com

Raven Brewing, south of Bigfork at 25999 Highway 35 (Eastside Highway); 837–6096

Big Sky Brewing Company, 120 Hickory, Missoula; 549–2777; www.bigskybrew.com

Kettlehouse Brewing Co., 602 Myrtle Street, Missoula; 728–1660; www.kettlehouse.com

Bayern Brewing, Inc., 2600 South 3rd Street West, Missoula; 721–1482; www.bayernbrewery.com

Bitter Root Brewing, 101 Marcus, Hamilton; 363–7468

The *Historic Darby Ranger Station*, located along the highway at the north end of the Old West–flavored settlement of Darby on the way to Lost Trail Pass, focuses on the U.S. Forest Service's wildlife management practices during the Great Depression and World War II eras. The museum is open to visitors daily May 1 through November from 9:00 A.M. to 5:00 P.M. Call 821–3913 for more information.

PLACES TO STAY IN GLACIER COUNTRY

TROY-LIBBY-EUREKA

Bull Lake Guest Ranch, 15303 Bull Lake Road; (800) 995–4228

Libby Super 8, 448 U.S. Highway 2 West; (800) 800–8000

Kootenai Country Inn, 264 Mack Road (outside Libby); (406) 293–7878

Ksanka Motor Inn, Jct. U.S. Highway 93 and State Highway 37 in Eureka; (406) 296–3127

POLSON

Port Polson Inn, U.S. Highway 93; (800) 654–0682

Best Western KwaTaqNuk Resort, U.S. Highway 93; (800) 882–6363

Hawthorne House Bed & Breakfast, 304 3rd Avenue East; (800) 290–1345

NORTHERN FLATHEAD LAKE

Osprey Inn Bed & Breakfast, 5557 Highway 93 South in Somers; (800) 258–2042

O'Duachain Country Inn, outside Bigfork near Ferndale; (800) 837–7460

Marina Cay Resort, 180 Vista Lane in Bigfork; (800) 433–6516

Eagle Bend Rental, on Bigfork's Eagle Bend Golf Course; (800) 239–9933

Woods Bay Motel, 26481 East Shore near Bigfork; (406) 837–3333

KALISPELL-WHITEFISH

Best Western Outlaw Inn, 1701 Highway 93 South in Kalispell; (800) 237–7445

Cavanaugh's, 20 North Main at Kalispell Center; (800) 843–4667

Keith House B&B, 538 5th Avenue East in Kalispell; (800) 972–7913

Garden Wall Inn, 504 Spokane Avenue in Whitefish; (406) 862–3440

Grouse Mountain Lodge, 1205 Highway 93 West in Whitefish; (800) 321–8822

Good Medicine Lodge, 537 Wisconsin Avenue in Whitefish; (406) 862–5288

Whitefish Super 8, 800 Spokane Avenue; (800) 800–8000

ST. MARY-EAST GLACIER

Glacier Park Lodge, East Glacier; (602) 207–6000 (Glacier National Park central reservations)

Mountain Pine Motel, East Glacier; (406) 226–4403

Bear Creek Guest Ranch, outside East Glacier; (800) 445–7379

SEELEY-SWAN VALLEY

Holland Lake Lodge, between Swan Lake and Seeley Lake; (800) 648–8859

Montana Pines Hideaway, outside Seeley Lake; (800) 867–5678

The Lodges at Seeley Lake, Boy Scout Road; (800) 900–9016

The Tamaracks Resort, Seeley Lake; (800) 477–7216

MISSOULA

Holiday Inn Parkside, 200 South Pattee; (800) 399–0408

Hubbard's Ponderosa Lodge, 800 East Broadway; (800) 341–8000

Creekside Inn, 630 East Broadway; (800) 551–2387

BITTERROOT VALLEY
Best Western Hamilton Inn, 409 South 1st Street; (800) 426–4586

Hamilton Comfort Inn, 1113 North 1st Street; (800) 442–4667

Deer Crossing Bed & Breakfast, 396 Hayes Creek Road; (800) 763–2232

Starfire Farm Lodge, 401 Fleet Road outside Hamilton (close to the Deer Crossing); (406) 363–6240

PLACES TO EAT IN GLACIER COUNTRY

TROY-LIBBY
Silver Spur, in Troy at 120 Highway 2 North; (406) 295–9937

M-K Steak House, in Libby at 9948 Highway 2 South; (406) 293–5686

4-B's, in Libby at 442 Highway 2 West; (406) 293–8751

Hidden Chapel, in Libby at 1207 Utah Avenue; (406) 293–2928

POLSON
4-B's, south of town at Jct. Highway 93 and 35; (406) 883–6180

Watusi Cafe, 318 Main Street; (406) 883–6200

Best Western KwaTaqNuk Resort, U.S. Highway 93; (406) 883–3636

NORTHERN FLATHEAD LAKE
Bridge Street Gallery Restaurant, Bigfork; (406) 837–5825

Bigfork Inn, Bigfork; (406) 837–6680

Swan River Cafe and Dinner House; Bigfork, (406) 837–2220

Showthyme (gourmet), downtown Bigfork; (406) 837–0707

KALISPELL
Cafe Max ("Quintessential Cuisine"), 121 Main Street; (406) 755–7687

WHITEFISH
Cafe Kandahar, located above town at The Big Mountain; (406) 862–6247

Hellroaring Saloon (Mexican), located in the Chalet at The Big Mountain; (406) 862–6364

Diamond K Chuckwagon, south of Whitefish off Highway 93; (406) 862–8828 (summer only)

Truby's (gourmet pizza), 115 Central Avenue; (406) 862–4979

Tupelo Grille (Cajun), 17 Central Avenue; (406) 862–6136

Whitefish Lake Restaurant (fine dining), at the Whitefish Lake Golf Course; (406) 862–5285

ST. MARY-EAST GLACIER
Snowgoose Grille, St. Mary Lodge & Resort; (406) 732–4431

Great Northern Steak and Rib House, Glacier Park Lodge in East Glacier; (406) 226–5593

SEELEY-SWAN VALLEY
Elkhorn Cafe, Seeley Lake; (406) 677–9211

Lindey's Prime Steak House, Seeley Lake; (406) 677–9229

The Filling Station, Seeley Lake; (406) 677–2080

MISSOULA
MacKenzie River Pizza Co., 137 West Front Street; (406) 721–0077

Hob Nob Cafe, located in the Union Club at 208 East Main; (406) 542–3188

Marianne's at the Wilma, downstairs at 131 South Higgins; (406) 728–8543

Shadows Keep (fine dining),
102 Ben Hogan Drive;
(406) 728–5132

The Bridge (eclectic
gourmet), upstairs at 515
South Higgins;
(406) 542–0002

Bagels on Broadway,
223 West Broadway;
(406) 728–8900

BITTERROOT VALLEY
Cantina la Cocina, U.S.
Highway 93 in Victor;
(406) 642–3192

The Hamilton, A Public
House, 104 Main Street,
Victor; (406) 642–6644

Morning Glory Coffee
House, 111 South 4th
Street, Hamilton;
(406) 363–7500

Maggie's Wild Oats
Café & Coffee House,
217 Main Street, Hamilton;
(406) 363–4567

Gold West Country

Perhaps more than any other region, Gold West Country embodies the Montana of the imagination, reflecting the image of the state held by thousands of curious folks who have yet to visit. It is a broad expanse of majestic mountains, basins filled with haystacks and Herefords, old mining camps, and big, blue sky. As you travel through some areas—such as the remote country penetrated by the Big Sheep Creek Back Country Byway—you may be convinced that you've been transported back in time fifty or a hundred years.

From Lost Trail Pass the narrative leads you past the Big Hole Battlefield National Monument, a major regional attraction, then through a string of one-horse cow towns including Wisdom, Wise River, and Jackson. From the Big Hole Valley it is on to the ghost town of Bannack, then to the very much alive town of Dillon. After following a dirt road through the Red Rock Lakes National Wildlife Refuge, you'll travel through a small corner of Idaho and back into Montana via the Madison River Valley. From Ennis it's on to Virginia City, from which point State Highways 287, 41, and 69 wind north to Boulder, where a left turn onto Interstate 15 leads to Butte. From Butte, a loop around Interstate 90 and State Highway 1 will take you through Anaconda, Philipsburg, Drummond, and Deer Lodge. Finally, there's historic Helena and several small towns lying to the north and west of the capital city.

Montana's Birthplace

The Continental Divide serves as the western and northern boundaries for the vast sweep of meadow and mountain country known as Beaverhead County. It's obvious that a lot of people have tried to make a living here at one time or another, for in Beaverhead County (and all of southwest Montana) ghost towns are abundant. This is where the 1860s gold rush started, first as a trickle, then as a flood.

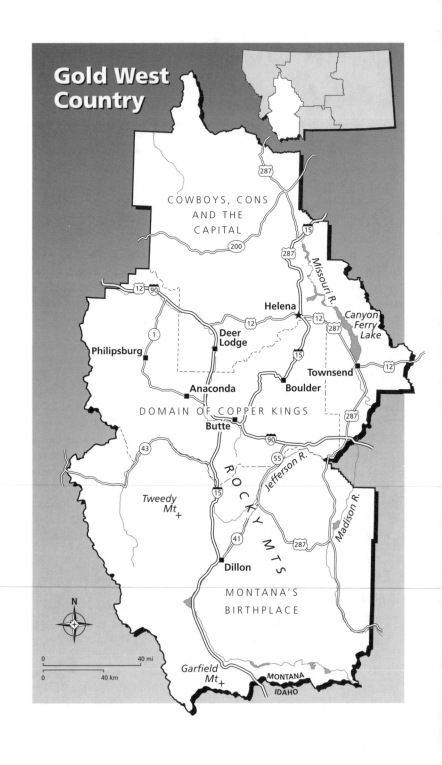

Gold West
Country

COWBOYS, CONS
AND THE
CAPITAL

287

15

200

287

Missouri R.

12 90

Helena

12

Canyon
Ferry
Lake

Deer
Lodge

1

12

287

Philipsburg

15

Townsend

287

12

Anaconda

Boulder

DOMAIN OF COPPER KINGS

287

Butte

90

43

55

Jefferson R.

R O C K Y   M T S

Tweedy
Mt +

15

Madison R.

41

287

N

Dillon

MONTANA'S
BIRTHPLACE

0   40 mi

0   40 km

Garfield
Mt +

MONTANA

IDAHO

GOLD WEST COUNTRY

The rigorous weather and rough terrain have precluded dense settlement, however, and Beaverhead remains among the most sparsely populated counties in the state.

If you've come to enjoy the winter wonders of southwest Montana, consider contacting the Beaverhead National Forest to inquire about overnighting at rustic **Hogan Cabin**. Skiers reach the cabin via one of two trails, while snowmobilers follow a separate route. The cabin sleeps four in relative comfort and comes equipped with firewood and a stove, beds, and cooking utensils. Campers haul in their own sleeping bags and food.

Hogan Cabin is available by reservation only between December 1 and March 31. During the summer it becomes a working Forest Service outpost, but the drive up Trail Creek Road to the cabin still comes highly recommended for the sensational display of wildflowers that often fills the surrounding Trail Creek Meadows. Call the Wisdom Ranger District at 689–3243 for information.

Continue east into the Big Hole River Valley, also known as "the land of 10,000 haystacks." The basin's rich soil is ideal for growing hay, which in recent years Montana ranchers have begun exporting in large quantities to other regions of the country. Throughout the Big Hole you'll see numerous "beaver slide" haystackers standing about the valley like so many tilted monuments. First developed in the Big Hole, and patented in 1910 as the Sunny Slope Slide Hay Stacker, this clever contraption allowed ranchers to stack hay much higher than previously was possible, utilizing horses to run the belts that hauled hay to the top of the inclined slide before depositing it on the stack. Many beaver slides are still in use, although in most cases motors have replaced horse power.

In the town of Wisdom, it's hard to miss **Conover's Trading Post.** Country music typically blares into the streets from loudspeakers mounted on the garishly painted building, which features a likeness of an Indian maiden reclining above the entrance. What all you'll find available for sale inside is anybody's guess. (If your sense of humor leans toward the weird, don't miss having a peek at the "rearwolf" taxidermy mount.)

BEST ATTRACTIONS

Jackson Hot Springs,
Jackson; (406) 834–3151

Bannack State Park,
Bannack; (406) 834–3413

Yesterday's Calf-A,
Dell; (406) 276–3308

Big Sheep Creek Back Country Byway,
Dell; (406) 494–5059

Red Rock Lakes National Wildlife Refuge,
Lakeview; (406) 276–3536

World Museum of Mining on Hell Roarin' Gulch,
Butte; (406) 723–7211

Lost Creek State Park,
Anaconda; (406) 542–5500

Old Works Golf Course,
Anaconda; (406) 563–5989

The Parrot Confectionery,
Helena; (406) 442–1470

The Bungalow, Wolf Creek;
(406) 235–4276

From Wisdom continue following Highway 43 and the Big Hole River. In 39 miles you'll arrive at the blink-and-miss-it town of Wise River. Here you'll find the northern terminus of the **Pioneer Mountains National Scenic Byway**, which wends its way south through the grand backcountry separating the East and West Pioneer Mountains. The ribbon of blacktop skirts a selection of exceptionally pleasant Forest Service campgrounds with names like **Lodgepole Campground**, **Willow Campground**, and **Little Joe Campground**. Any one of these comes highly recommended if you're outfitted for camping.

Approximately 29 miles from Wise River the Pioneer Mountains National Scenic Byway skirts **Crystal Park**, where the Butte Mineral & Gem Club maintains mining claims. In partnership with the Forest Service, the club keeps the claims open to the public, which is permitted to dig crystals, using hand tools only. A first-rate picnic area, featuring hard-surfaced sites, picnic tables, and fire grates sits adjacent to the digging grounds. For a map of the area and a list of rules and regulations, call the Beaverhead National Forest at 683–3900.

Just south of Crystal Park the paved road turns to gravel. At the bottom of a 4-mile hill, you'll encounter the first of two nearby, natural hotwater fun spots, **Elkhorn Hot Springs**. The Anaconda Standard in 1921

Taking the High Road

*T*he Pioneer Mountains National Scenic Byway, paved for the northernmost 29 of its 46 miles, runs between the east and west subranges of the Pioneer Mountains. The byway begins at an elevation of 5,600 feet above sea level at Wise River and climbs to 7,782 feet before dropping again into the valley of Grasshopper Creek.

As you will see, the two components of the Pioneers appear dramatically different from one another. Some 70 million years ago the western mountains subsided about ¹/₂ mile in relation to the eastern range, along the fault running through the valley separating them. The higher and more rugged East Pioneers have

therefore endured far more erosion, exposing the underlying granites. By comparison, the West Pioneers are rolling, subdued mountains, blanketed in dark timber.

Much of the terrain penetrated by the byway, although surrounded by the imposing Pioneers, is surprisingly flat. In Harrison and Moose Parks you'll see thousands of rocks and boulders littering the ground, ranging in size from tiny to huge. The rocks, called glacial erratics, are composed of the same rock as the high East Pioneer Mountains. The erratics broke off thousands of years ago and were transported to the open meadows by glaciers and mudflows.

MAJOR ATTRACTIONS WORTH SEEING

Big Hole Battlefield
National Monument,
Wisdom

Virginia City

Lewis and Clark Caverns
State Park

Grant-Kohrs Ranch
National Historic Site,
Deer Lodge

reported, "It is possible that within the next two years Montana will have another national park, to be known as the Elkhorn national park . . . which will contain scenery second to none of the national parks now in existence."

The overzealous prediction didn't prove out. Still, although the accommodations found at the resort range from rustic to extremely rustic, Elkhorn does occupy a beautiful spot. At its timbered setting in the Grasshopper Valley you can soak in an outdoor hot pool or a cedar-lined Grecian wet sauna, and order a meal in the Trail Creek Lodge. The pools and restaurant, open seven days a week all year, are particularly inviting after a day of downhill skiing at nearby Maverick Mountain. Call 834–3434 or visit www.elkhornhotsprings.com for information and reservations.

Turn right on reaching Highway 278 and in 15 miles you'll arrive at the town of Jackson, home to *Jackson Hot Springs.* The resort made the national news in the wake of the August 1992 Hurricane Andrew, when the proprietors rounded up volunteers to help fill thousands of gallon jugs with the pure water bubbling from the ground here. The drinking water then was shipped on trucks to Florida to aid in recovery efforts.

The Jackson Hot Springs lodge sports a large bar and an oak dance floor of gymnasium proportions. The full-service restaurant with moderately priced meals and the outdoor, 30-foot-by-75-foot hot pool round out the scene. Year-round you can overnight in cabins, which go for around $65 a night. For more information call 834–3151 or go to the Web site www.jacksonhotsprings.com.

On July 28, 1862, John White and a group of fellow Coloradans discovered placer-gold deposits in the waters of Grasshopper Creek. The "White's Bar" discovery was the first recorded mining claim in the region, and it triggered a gold rush. People flocked to the area in droves, and the town of *Bannack,* now a well-preserved ghost town, sprang up almost overnight.

Within a year, some 3,000 persons lived in Bannack. Most were prospectors, but arriving also were the tradespeople who inevitably follow to offer those who strike it rich somewhere to spend their money. Saloons, bakeries, doctors' offices, a brewery, barber shops, general stores, blacksmith shops, a bowling alley, and more quickly graced the streets of the burgeoning town.

The population boom was short-lived, though, and within two years most had moved on to golder pastures, at Virginia City and elsewhere along Alder Gulch. But a stable population of miners and service providers remained, and Bannack began to mature. When in 1864 the Montana Territory was split and created from the year-old Idaho Territory, Abraham Lincoln appointed Sidney Edgerton as governor. He, in turn, named Bannack the capital, and the first Territorial Legislature met here on December 12, 1864.

Bannack's reign as capital also was short-lived: Along with the hundreds of prospectors, the territorial capital moved to Virginia City in 1865. But the town endured until the 1940s, by which time most mine-milling activity had ceased, and Bannack was virtually deserted.

More than fifty structures remain at Bannack, many in excellent condition, and the fascinating walking tour of the town can easily steal half a day. Among the highlights are the Graves House, built in the mid-1860s, the first frame house in the Montana Territory; the Masonic Temple, the first floor of which served for years as the Bannack school; and the Meade Hotel, originally the Beaverhead County courthouse.

Bannack Days, held during the third weekend in July, celebrates the past with buffalo barbecues, horse-and-buggy rides, a muzzle-loader shooting competition, old-time crafts and music, a "Henry Plummer hanging," and more. The town is located 4 miles south off Highway 278 from midway between Jackson and Dillon. For more information on Bannack ghost town, Bannack Days, and the state park campground, call 834–3413 or E-mail the park at bannack@montana.com.

The Plummer Gang

*T*he life of one Henry Plummer shed some notoriety on Bannack in the early 1860s. The territorial court determined that Bannack and Virginia City, 70 miles apart, needed only one sheriff, and Plummer managed to get himself elected to the post. During his eight-month tenure—the purpose of which allegedly was to protect the public—Plummer and his gang of road agents terrorized those traveling the road connecting the two settlements. It's estimated that they killed no fewer than 102 individuals, while relieving countless others of their heavy burdens of gold.

Late in 1863 justice prevailed when the Vigilantes Committee formed; they hanged or banished all known members of Plummer's crew. Plummer was hanged early in 1864 from the gallows he himself had erected only a year earlier. Today a replica of the gallows stands at the approximate site of the hanging.

GOLD WEST COUNTRY

In the county seat of Dillon, enjoy the historic walk through town and visit the **Beaverhead County Museum**, since 1947 one of Montana's finest small-town museums. Housed in a historic log building downtown on Montana Street, among its many displays are Indian artifacts and exhibits on the area's natural history and rich record of mining and ranching. Recently added to the complex are the renovated, 1909 brick depot of the Utah and Northern Railroad (now the Union Pacific) and a pioneer's log cabin. The museum is open daily during summer from 8:00 A.M. to 7:00 P.M. and on an abbreviated schedule the rest of the year. Call 683–5027 for more information.

You might be surprised also to find in Dillon the **Patagonia Outlet** store. Lovers of the rugged outdoor apparel make the pilgrimage here from all over western Montana and beyond to find deals on their favorite clothes. The outlet is located at 34 North Idaho Street, and the phone number is 683–2580. Summer hours are Monday through Saturday 10:00 A.M. to 6:00 P.M. and Sunday 11:00 A.M. to 5:00 P.M. (Hint: On special weekends, such as those around Labor Day, President's Day, and Memorial Day, the outlet runs blow-out sales.)

Words can't do justice to **Yesterday's Calf-A**, located in Dell, just off Interstate 15 at exit 23. Stop in for some home cookin' and you'll see for yourself why it's one of Montana's most unusual eateries . . . and why people come literally from hundreds of miles away to sample the homemade pies.

The old school it's housed in *was* a school from 1903 until 1963, with an average enrollment of twenty kids, and then opened as a restaurant in 1978. Its walls, shelves, and bare pine floor are blanketed with memorabilia: fur-bearing trout, piles of old *Life* magazines, vintage rifles, an old piano with yellowed sheet music, rocks and fossils, a bedpan banjo, well-worn school desks, pull-down maps, spurs, kerosene lanterns, a ceramic water cooler, and a whole lot more.

Best Annual Events

1. **Winternational Sports Festival,** Butte; February through March; (406) 723-3177

2. **Race to the Sky Sled Dog Race,** Helena and points beyond; mid-February; (406) 442-4008

3. **St. Patrick's Day Festival,** Butte; March 17; (406) 494-5595

4. **Governor's Cup Road Runs,** Helena; early June; (406) 447-3414

5. **Gold Rush Fever Day,** Virginia City; mid-June; (406) 843-5555

6. **Mineral & Gem Show,** Butte; mid-July; (406) 496-4395

7. **Bannack Days,** Bannack State Park; late July; (406) 834-3413

8. **Southwest Montana Fair,** Butte; early August; (406) 723-8262

9. **Bald Eagle Migration,** Helena; mid-November through mid-December; (406) 475-3128

Yesterday's Calf-A, Dell

The past flows through the entryway and spills into the yard, where you'll find a veritable museum of life on the western frontier. It's worth stopping to browse around the grounds even if the restaurant is closed. Crosscut saws, farm equipment, elk antlers, wagon wheels, bison skulls, windmills, and dozens of other items are scattered about.

The cowboy coffee pot is always on at Calf-A, where you'll sit on press-back chairs at a large oak table and, likely as not, join a local stock grower and his family as you dine. Don't look for a printed menu; the information is written in chalk on a blackboard. The restaurant opens daily at 7:00 A.M. year-round for breakfast, lunch, and dinner. Prices are inexpensive to moderate.

If you're a fan of truly wide-open spaces, consider tackling the rough-and-tumble **Big Sheep Creek Back Country Byway**. Beginning near Dell, the rugged road is one of several Back Country Byways designated throughout the West by the Bureau of Land Management. These tend to be unpaved and rougher than the U.S. Forest Service-designated National Scenic Byways that also are common throughout the West (such as the Pioneer Mountains National Scenic Byway described earlier). To find the road, from Dell, pass under Interstate 15 and take the first left. For information on road conditions, which can change daily, call the Butte District Office of the Bureau of Land Management at 494–5059.

The near ghost town of Monida sits beside Interstate 15 at exit 0, immediately north of the Continental Divide and the state of Idaho. (Mon-Ida—get it?) Although never a metropolis by anyone's measure, the town did boast 125 residents in the mid-1920s, when it served as one of the most active stock-shipping railheads in the state. The railroad has long since pulled out, the U.S. Post Office closed shop in 1970, and the last business in Monida was boarded up more than ten years ago. Only four or five residents remain.

During its heyday the town also served another several hundred people who ranched in the Centennial Valley to the east. Today, the starkly beautiful valley is almost deserted; old-timers will tell you that's because of the **Red Rock Lakes National Wildlife Refuge**, which removed some of the most productive land in the area from use by ranchers when it was established in 1935.

At the refuge, the shallow waters of Upper and Lower Red Rock Lakes and Swan Lake and adjacent marshlands provide a home for a proliferation of birds and wildlife. The preserve is nestled between the spectacular Centennial Mountains on the south and the equally impressive Gravelly Range to the north.

The 40,000-acre refuge was created primarily to provide sanctuary for the rare trumpeter swan. The bird's population had dwindled to fewer than 100 in the tri-state area by the end of the Great Depression, while

Big Sheep Creek

*T*he Big Sheep Creek Back Country Byway loops through a sweep of some of the emptiest country in the West. This area is not only way off the beaten path, much of it is devoid of paths altogether. It makes a great day (or longer) trip if your vehicle and spirit of adventure are up to the challenge.

The byway leaves Interstate 15 at Dell, rejoining pavement 60 miles to the northwest, where a turn east leads back to Interstate 15. Or, by turning left rather than right at the junction with pavement, you can follow paved, gravel, and rough dirt roads up and over 7,373-foot Lemhi Pass, where the Lewis and Clark expedition first crested the Continental Divide.

Anglers in particular will find the bubbling waters of Big Sheep Creek inviting, while history buffs will relish tracing portions of the 1860s wagon supply road that joined the Bannack mining camp with the Union Pacific railhead in Corinne, Utah. Pronghorn antelope, mule deer, and eagles are common to the environs, and bighorn sheep can often be spotted at dusk in the tight portions of the Big Sheep Creek canyon. Undeveloped camping sites abound, particularly along the first 20 miles of the route. After leaving the relatively narrow canyon of Big Sheep Creek, the road shoots through a broad swath of open country bordered on the west by the barren Beaverhead Mountains, whose ridgeline forms the Continental Divide and the Montana-Idaho state line. In some locations you'll drive through grassy meadows where, if you listen carefully, you may be treated to the delightful melody of a western meadowlark or two.

You'll find the Big Sheep Creek Back Country Byway to be rough and muddy in places—possibly even impassable—so a high-clearance vehicle is advised. Also be sure you're equipped with a spare tire and tire-changing tools, a full tank of gas, a good map, and an adequate supply of food and water.

only a few other remnant populations remained in Canada and Alaska. Happily, today in the Greater Yellowstone Ecosystem there are nearly 500 resident swans, and the influx of migratory birds from the north brings the number closer to 2,500 in winter.

The refuge received additional protection in 1976, when three-quarters of it was designated a federal wilderness area, meaning that motorboats and other mechanized equipment are prohibited. Also, through the acquisition of private properties, the refuge has grown since being created.

Moose are year-round residents, and deer, elk, and pronghorn antelope are common in the snowless months. The bird life rivals that of nearly any place in the Rocky Mountain region: No fewer than 258 species can be seen at one time of the year or another, including bald eagles, avocets, long-billed curlews, great blue herons, sandhill cranes, white pelicans, tundra swans, and twenty-three species of ducks and geese. Migratory birds by the thousands appear during the spring and fall.

The impressive, snow-white trumpeters, which visitors are urged to view from no closer than 400 yards, are immense birds, measuring up to 4 feet from beak to toe and 8 feet from wing tip to wing tip, and weighing as much as thirty pounds. And they're hungry big birds with phenomenal metabolisms: It's common for an adult to eat up to twenty pounds of wet herbage in a day's time.

To experience this isolated piece of country occupying the extreme southwest corner of the state is well worth the trouble of getting there. The outpost of Lakeview—population ten—stands sentinel over the wetlands, and the refuge headquarters are found there. Lakeview is midway along the 60-mile gravel road connecting Interstate 15 at Monida and Highway 87 west of West Yellowstone. The road is generally not passable by automobile until mid-May and is usually snowed in again by early November. For more information on Red Rock Lakes National Wildlife Refuge, call 276–3536.

From Red Rock Lakes, continue east on gravel over Red Rock Pass to Highway 87, where you'll want to turn north. In 12 miles, turn east onto Highway 287, and soon you'll arrive at the *Madison Canyon Earthquake Area*. Displays at the visitor center explain the geologic and human stories of the fateful night of August 17, 1959, when at 11:37 P.M. a 7.1-magnitude earthquake rocked the area, causing a large portion of a mountain to slide. Twenty-eight of the 250 campers in the canyon below were killed, and the Madison River was dammed by rocks and debris (enough to fill the Rose Bowl ten times), forming Earthquake Lake.

Dead, skeletal trees rise above the lake's surface, and the gash on the mountainside and the rocks and rubble scattering the countryside below remain as testimony to the violence of the recent geologic past. The Madison Canyon Earthquake Area visitor center opens daily Memorial Day through Labor Day. For more information call 646–7369.

You'll know the minute you pull into Ennis, 42 miles north of the earthquake center, that it's a sporting town. In autumn huge elk racks, still attached to their recently deceased owners, sprout from pick-up truck beds. In winter snowmobiles parked along Main Street await their owners, who are in drinking coffee to warm up. And in summer drift boats and rafts on trailers line the street, and storefronts connected by a boardwalk advertise fly-fishing gear, guided trips, and fishermen's specials.

An unexpected find here is *The Continental Divide* gourmet restaurant. Owner and chef Jay Bentley, first drawn to the area because of its world-class fly-fishing opportunities, describes the menu as "nouvelle eclectic" and warns that he might never prepare a dish exactly the same.

Quiet by Nature

*A*wakening at Upper Lake Campground in Red Rock Lakes National Wildlife Refuge in mid-June, we found, is a bit like greeting the day on Montana's version of a Tarzan movie set, considering all the noise the local critters make.

It started when it was still dark and starry with the resonant hoot of a great gray owl and two choruses of coyotes yipping, yammering, and squealing back and forth. From our tent it sounded like a demonstration of stereo speakers: One bunch of coyotes was over there to the west; the other was clearly off in another direction, somewhere to the southeast in the foothills of the Centennial Range.

With the first hint of light in the eastern sky, the Canada geese began honking, followed by the deeper and louder honking of trumpeter swans. Then ducks—hundreds of them, maybe thousands—began chiming in with their variously timbred quacking. And then the singing of dozens of songbirds. It all coalesced into a cacophony that was terribly dissonant if we tried to separate the sounds, but marvelously musical if we just took it in as a whole. I've never heard anything quite like it anywhere else.

Upper Lake Campground, on the shore of shallow Upper Red Rock Lake, is a primitive campground with few services other than a pair of outhouses, several tent sites, and a spring delivering cold, tasty water. Canoeing (after July 15 on Upper Lake, and after mid-September on the lower lake), mountain biking, hiking, and wildlife-viewing opportunities are all right at hand, and the sunrises and sunsets are out of this world.

The Continental Divide's Cajun-style seafood and 2-inch-thick, marinated steaks are celebrated far and wide, but you're just as apt to find Thai or Vietnamese dishes on the menu or Bentley's "Italian soul food." The restaurant usually opens in mid-June and closes in late October. For more information and requisite reservations, call 682–7600.

The **Ennis National Fish Hatchery**, located in the Madison River Valley since 1931, rears some 300,000 trout in an average year in the consistently cold waters of Blaine Springs. One of eighty hatcheries in America operated by the U.S. Fish and Wildlife Service, this one is found 12 miles southwest of Ennis at the foot of the sensational Gravelly Range, making the drive worth the trip even if no trout waited at the end of the line.

But they do. Humans—through logging, mining, drawing down water for agricultural use, and too much sport fishing—have radically altered the fish habitat in Montana's waters. It's the job of the Ennis facility to stock trout where they're needed in many parts of the state, in order to bring the numbers closer to what might have existed had people not intervened. The manipulations workers perform to bring the male and female trout together and to raise adults from eggs to fry to fish make a fascinating story.

Most trout leave for waters beyond when they're from 5 to 8 inches long, via insulated tank trucks holding up to a ton of wiggling fish. But each year the hatchery also releases a number of 2-foot-plus lunkers that have played out their roles as breeding machines.

From Ennis, go 2 miles west on State Highway 287 toward Virginia City, and then turn south onto the Gravelly Range Road/Varney Road. Eight miles after leaving Highway 287, bear right at the fork, following the sign to the hatchery. For more information call 682–4847.

Perhaps your visit to the hatchery has you hankering to wet a line in wild waters and catch a wily trout? Back at the earlier-mentioned fork, by turning to the east you'll arrive at the door of the **9T9 Ranch Bed and Breakfast**, a small inn just a short stroll away from the Madison River. The guest floor of the 9T9 ranch house features a private living room (with TV, stereo, and telephone), two bedrooms that share a bath, and one bedroom with a private bath. Hosting a small number of guests at a time allows owner Judy Herrick to furnish each one with a personal dose of western hospitality, which is how she wants it.

Breakfast, served as early or late as you like, is a hearty affair that'll keep you going on the river for most of the day. You can fish the Madison, one of the world's premier blue-ribbon streams, for trophy rainbow and brown trout, wading the waters or using a boat or raft available from the 9T9.

Overnights range from $70 to $125. For reservations or more information (including details on the available guide service), call the 9T9 Ranch at 682–7659, E-mail them at judy@9T9ranch.com or log on to their Web site at www. 9T9ranch.com.

As you travel north from Virginia City-Nevada City, a major attraction you definitely should not bypass, pull into the wide spot in the road known as Laurin (pronounced *Lor-ay*) and have a look at the resplendent **St. Mary of the Assumption Catholic Church.** The sturdy chapel, built of locally quarried cut stone, is listed on the National Register of Historic Places. In concert with its bucolic surroundings, the church lends the small town an air of peace, strength, and dignity.

Contrast the tranquillity at Laurin with what **Robber's Roost**, a few miles north, *might* have been like in an earlier day. Peter Daly built the important stage stop sometime in the 1860s, and according to some it was here that Henry Plummer's gang of road agents plotted their attacks on gold-bearing travelers. Others dispute this, claiming that the building wasn't constructed until 1867, three years after Plummer and his friends had met their maker.

Regardless of who did or did not spend time in it, the two-story, square-hewn log building is a picturesque and uncommon example of frontier architecture. An antiques and curio shop fills the interior of the former stage stop and tavern, providing an enjoyable browse.

Avid anglers will want to swing into the **R. L. Winston Rod Company** in Twin Bridges, where the Rolls-Royce of fly-fishing rods is fashioned. The company started in 1929 in San Francisco and quickly became known for its bamboo tournament-winning rods. It moved to Montana in 1976, by which time fiberglass was the material used in making most rods. Today, graphite (carbon fiber) is the substance of choice for Winston's state-of-the-art trout and saltwater rods, although they still produce bamboo rods for the traditionalist.

If you're thinking of shopping here, be sure your credit card's slate is fairly clean, for Winston's handcrafted rods begin at around $495 and go as high as $2,550 for the best bamboo models. Their new facility, located at 500 South Main, is open between 8:30 A.M. and 4:30 P.M. weekdays, with tours beginning at 2:00 P.M. Call 684–5674 for more information. For a preview of their wares, visit their Web site at www.winstonrods.com.

The town of **Pony**, almost a ghost town, is perched on the inclined flank of the Tobacco Root Mountains. So steep is the approach to Pony, and so tight the little nook it occupies, that one resident penned this little ditty about the Northern Pacific branch line leading to it:

> Pony, Pony the beautiful little town,
> where the train backed in 'cause it couldn't turn around.

The town is the namesake of Tecumseh "Pony" Smith, who filed the first placer claim here in 1868. Within a few years, the placer technique had yielded to more serious mining methods, and at least four steam- or water-driven stamp mills were pounding gold from ore in the hills surrounding Pony. Several impressive buildings remain, including the two-story brick Morris bank building and the splendid community church, revealing the fact that this was no mere overnight camp. You can also locate the decaying remnants of the Morris & Ellings Gold Stamp Mill.

Several late-Victorian houses are still used as residences, and a few new houses are popping up. Pony is simply too pretty to quit. The town is located up a paved road, 6 miles west of Harrison, which is 15 miles southeast of Interstate 90 from Cardwell.

If you think Pony is off the beaten path, travel the 7 miles south on gravel from there to **The Lodge at Potosi Hot Springs** and find out why it manages to remain one of Montana's best-kept secrets—even though it is one of the most sumptuous hot-springs resorts in the state. Soaking, gourmet dining, log-cabin accommodations, and all sorts of mountain recreation, including biking, horseback riding, and cross-country skiing, are available at the remote outpost. Call 685–3594 to find out more and to request explicit directions.

In Norris, 10 miles south of Harrison on Highway 287, check out the **Old Norris Schoolhouse Cafe**, specializing in south-of-the-border fare. Last used as a school in 1960, the restaurant features down-home—some might call it redneck—humor hanging on the walls. One of the more tame signs is a reference to many locals' opinion of the 1988 fire-management tactics used in nearby Yellowstone National Park: PLEASE

DON'T BE ALARMED BY THE SMOKE. EVERYTHING'S UNDER CONTROL. OUR COOK
WAS TRAINED BY THE PARK SERVICE.

Politics aside, you'll be served surprisingly good Mexican food, ribs, or
buffalo burgers as you relax at a slat-barrel table. The cafe is open noon
to 8:00 P.M. Wednesday and Thursday, and noon to 9:00 P.M. Friday and
Saturday. Call 685–3200 for more information.

After filling up on educational food, head ¼ mile up Highway 84 to the
Bear Trap Hot Springs, a good spot for a soothing soak (at $5.00 per
adult). The low-key resort, which also includes a campground and small
store, is open year-round, Tuesday through Sunday from 10:00 A.M. to
10:00 P.M. Call 685–3303 for more information. (Although the author
hasn't verified the claim, a Norris local told him that imbibing soaker-
campers definitely should sample a beer or mixed drink at the very fun
Norris Bar.)

Where Hope Shines On

*T*he proprietors of the **Free
Enterprise Health Mine,** *2 miles
west of Boulder, boast of their
"Unmedical Approach to Health." One
component of this approach: America's
only "ionizing Inhalatorium," where
those suffering from arthritis, asthma,
allergies, lupus, and a dozen other ailments inhale concentrated radon gases
purported to possess healing properties. Here Montana's first commercial
uranium mine opened for business in
1949 under the supervision of Wade V.
Lewis Jr., president of the Elkhorn
Mining Company. In the ensuing
years, thousands of pilgrims have traveled to Boulder to go underground in
old mines and breathe radon gas and
soak in pools. The ionizing radiation,
some say, is more effective than pre-
scription drugs, and testimonials of
miracle cures abound. (One theory is
that radon stimulates the pituitary*
*gland into producing greater quanti-
ties of health-enhancing hormones.)*

*Radon gas occurs naturally when
radium, in the process of breaking
down, oxidizes. It is, of course, the
same gas that thousands of residents
in the Rocky Mountains and other
regions of the country have spent
hundreds of dollars on, in attempts
to rid their basements of what is
generally considered a potentially
dangerous substance.*

*If you're hurting, though, or curious,
consider coming to have a look. Just
be sure to read the fine print before
descending! The Free Enterprise
Health Mine, "Where Hope Shines
On You," opens daily at 7:00 A.M.
The facility also maintains an RV
park. Call 225–3383 or visit the
Web site www.mt.net/hlthmine for
more information.*

The Domain of Copper Kings

Ahost of old mining camps lie rotting in the hills between Helena and Boulder, 30 miles south of the capital city. Foremost is impressive **Elkhorn**, mostly a ghost town, which contains striking examples of frontier architecture, including the marvelous old two-story, Greek Revival Fraternity Hall. The building once hosted boxing matches, dances, theatrical performances, and other social affairs. As you'll see, the streets of Elkhorn were laid out in a steep meadow sloping down from the flanks of Crow and Elkhorn Peaks. An intriguing side trip, weather permitting, leads to the old cemetery. Head from the north side of town along the road as it winds east around a mountainside. In approximately ¹/₂ mile, go right at the intersection and continue for several hundred yards. You'll see the cemetery, where graves from the late 1800s are still marked, on the hill to the right.

But first things first: To find Elkhorn, go 6 miles south of Boulder on Highway 69, and then travel 12 miles north on the gravel Elkhorn Road. On the way there, along the main highway you'll pass **Boulder Hot Springs** (225–4339), where the geothermal pools are an inviting 104 degrees and rooms in a turn-of-the-century hotel go for between $45 and $90. For more information on Elkhorn, call the Helena Area Resource Office at 449–8864, extension 154.

How does one begin to describe Butte? The city sits atop the Richest Hill on Earth . . . or atop part of it, anyway, for since excavations were begun in 1955 much of the hill has been carried away and smelted for copper. Now a gaping hole in the earth that's rapidly filling with toxic water, the 7,000-foot-long, 5,600-foot-wide, and 1,800-foot-deep **Berkeley Pit** is one of the city's primary tourist attractions and the butt of more than one Butte joke. To find the Berkeley Pit observation stand, simply head north from Interstate 90 on Continental Drive.

Butte residents are unwaveringly proud of their hometown, and given half a chance, many will expound on it *ad nauseum*. But when the newcomer first gazes on the source of this pride, he or she probably just won't get it, for to say that Butte is a little rough around the edges is a world-class understatement. The neophyte Butte visitor will probably wonder also at how row houses—this city that feels like an eastern-seaboard worker's town—ever came to be situated amid the gracious Montana landscape. One might wonder, finally, why anyone would even go to Butte on purpose.

But if you take the time to have a closer look and visit with some of those who call it home, you'll begin to glean an inkling of what it is that makes Butte special. It is a one-of-a-kind place, and its citizens are likewise unique; they even speak differently than anyone else in the state. Thankfully, not all are as wild as hometown boys and motorcycle madmen Evel and Robbie Knievel, but the

Montana's beavers and river otters give birth in April, the beavers safe in their lodges, and the otters secure in dens they've excavated into river and stream banks.

father-son duo seem an appropriate pair of ambassadors for this unorthodox place.

In the late 1800s, Butte became the world's leading copper producer, and by 1917 its population had mushroomed to over 100,000. The earliest skilled miners were of Cornish background, but word about the mineral wealth spread quickly, and soon workers and families from the world over headed to the new mining center. Those of Irish derivation became the largest group represented, hence Butte's renowned St. Patrick's Day celebration, which remains an all-out, spill-into-the-streets party. Others came from Italy, China, Finland, Croatia, Serbia, Lebanon, Mexico, Austria, Germany, and elsewhere.

The dangers of working underground and for sometimes ruthless mine owners led to Butte's becoming so solidly unionized that it earned a national reputation as the "Gibraltar of Unionism." At the 1906 organizational meeting of the Industrial Workers of the World in Chicago, the single largest delegation arrived from—where else?—Butte, Montana.

The best place to get a feel for how Butte became what it is, is at the *World Museum of Mining on Hell Roarin' Gulch.* By no means miss this attraction, but be warned: The place is big and captivating. You can easily while away a full day at the recreated town and adjacent mining museum, which occupy the twelve-acre site of the old Orphan Girl silver and zinc mine. This "town" of 1899 was a labor of love and completed only through the donation of thousands of hours of volunteers' time.

The cobblestone streets of Hell Roarin' Gulch are lined with dozens of buildings; they, in turn, are brimming with the relics of days gone by. You can visit the Chinese laundry and herbal-healing store, assayer's office, funeral and embalming parlor, lawyer's office, sauerkraut factory, millinery shop, general store and soda fountain, school, church. . . . Especially if you're a lover of antiques, you'll wonder at how the organizers ever got their hands on so much *great stuff.*

The two floors of the Orphan Girl's old hoist house, adjacent to Hell Roarin' Gulch, are dedicated to the World Museum of Mining. Included among the many displays is a collection of old photos of Butte, which offer a glimpse at the past and help the visitor understand just how big this town and its mining operations were (and just how bad the air pollution problem was).

To get to the World Museum of Mining on Hell Roarin' Gulch, go west on Granite Street until you can't go any farther. The attraction opens at 9:00 A.M. seven days a week from April 1 through October 31. It's closed November 1 through March 31. The entrance fee for those thirteen and older is $4.00, while kids twelve and younger (accompanied by an adult) are admitted for free. Call 723–7211 for more information.

The World Museum of Mining is one of many stops on the route of **Old Number 1**, a gas-powered replica of the electric trolley cars that once plied the hilly streets of Butte. One-and-one-half-hour outings depart from the Butte visitor center (located on p. 60) several times daily from June through September. Other stops along the way include the Berkeley Pit overlook, the **Mineral Museum** at Montana Tech, and the **Mai Wah**, a one-time noodle parlor containing displays on the Asian heritage of Butte.

As had been their custom in the Old Country, early Welsh and Cornish

Stop at the Red Light

*D*uring their hours above ground, some miners spent time in the two-story brothels that were common along the "Venus Alley" stretch of Mercury Street. Today all have been demolished except for the Dumas. The girls who worked at the Dumas and the clients who partook of their earthly pleasures there can be imagined (using very little imagination) by walking the halls and rooms of the **Dumas Brothel Museum**. The place was built in 1890 specifically as a brothel, a function it served for nearly one hundred years, making it Butte's longest-running house of ill repute.

Along with the rest of Butte, the Dumas experienced hard times in the early 1980s. It closed in 1982 because of community pressure, the result of a violent robbery there. Today it's an antiques and curios store with no admission charge. As you walk in and out of the similarly sized and shaped rooms—some with beds still in them—you'll see there's no disputing what they were designed for. This is no typical house floorplan.

The Dumas Brothel Museum, open from 10:00 A.M. to 5:00 P.M. daily, is located at 45 East Mercury Street. For more information call 723-6128.

miners in Butte often carried the bomb-proof pasty (pronounced *pass-tee*) in their lunch boxes and down into the mines. You needn't go underground to try one today, for the meat-and-potatoes pie has become a Butte institution, as grounded in tradition here as is corned beef and cabbage washed down with green beer on St. Patrick's Day. Several restaurants serve pasties, including *Joe's Pasty Shop*, at 1641 Grand Avenue.

A few, like Marcus Daly and William A. Clark, became fabulously wealthy from the mines at Butte and left behind a legacy of extravagant homes. Today you can visit—and sleep in, if you choose—Clark's home, now known as the *Copper King Mansion* bed-and-breakfast.

It took four years for nineteenth-century European craftsmen to build the home, which features white oak woodwork, hand-carved stairways, and mosaic floors. Its thirty-four rooms were completely restored in the 1960s and are open for tours daily, May 1 through September 30, from 9:00 A.M. to 5:00 P.M. It operates year-round as a bed-and-breakfast, with rooms going for $65 to $95 a night. The mansion is located at 219 West Granite. (Just east on Granite Street, rival copper king Daly built his Leonard Hotel, allegedly for the purpose of blocking Clark's expansive view.) Call 782–7580 for lodging reservations and tour information.

William A. Clark's son, Charles, also built an impressive home in Butte in about 1900. Located at 321 West Broadway, the lavish structure now houses the *Arts Chateau* and brings to mind a turreted king's castle amid a sea of serfs' dwellings. The Arts Chateau features a gallery and museum, with period furnishings on loan from The University of Montana. It's open Tuesday through Sunday in summer from 10:00 A.M. to 5:00 P.M., and in winter from 11:00 A.M. to 4:00 P.M. Call 723–7600 or visit www.artschateau.org for more information.

In the early 1980s, when the city's mining economy turned bad, Butte boosters began exploring ways to diversify. A few visionaries, perhaps reflecting on their childhood memories—neighborhood skating rinks are another Butte institution—proceeded to establish the *U.S. High Altitude Sports Center*. They were snickered at by many outsiders, and even by some insiders, who wondered, "Who would come to Butte in the winter to ice skate?"

Naysayers ignored, the facility was finished in 1987, and in November the outdoor oval served as the venue for the only World Cup speed-skating event held in America that year. By the time 1992 rolled around, of all the medal-winning speed skaters at the Albertville (France) Olympic Winter Games, only three had never trained and/or raced at the Butte facility. Bonnie Blair, America's greatest female speed skater and Butte's adopted daughter, attended Montana Tech in Butte and regularly trained at the center.

The oval, located at 1 Olympic Way just off Continental Drive on the south side of town, is open during the winter to public skating when not being used for competitions or training sessions. For information on using the facility and on upcoming competitions, call 494–7570 (winter only).

Probably the hardest-to-find attraction in the Butte area is the ***Granite Mountain Mine Memorial***, located off North Main up a bumpy dirt road near the neighborhood/village of Walkerville. The memorial marks the 1917 Speculator Mine fire, which took 168 miners' lives. It was the worst hard-rock mining disaster in American history. Not far from the memorial you can see remaining head frames from defunct mines standing hard against the horizon, looking like skeletons of timber and memorials of a sort.

Two-and-one-half-hour tours, beginning daily at the Plaza Mall Gift Shop at 3100 Harrison Avenue, climb high above town to visit one of Butte's easiest-to-spot but most difficult to access finds: ***Our Lady of the Rockies***. Our Lady, a 90-foot-high statue made of concrete and metal, can be seen from miles away at night, when it is brilliantly illuminated. Call 782–1221 for more details.

Before leaving what is arguably Montana's most fascinating city, visit the new ***Butte–Silver Bow Chamber of Commerce Visitor Center***, located at 1000 George Street, to find out what you have missed. It's located next to the KOA Kampground off Montana Street, north of Interstate 90 at Exit 126. To make a cyber visit to the facility, go to www.butteinfo.org. You can also call them at 723–3177.

Interstate 15 meets Interstate 90 a couple of miles west of Butte. A side trip of approximately 22 miles south on I–15 will lead first over the Continental Divide and then to the Moose Creek exit. Take this exit, then follow the dirt Moose Creek Road 3½ miles to the northeast, and you'll come to a trailhead for the spectacular, but little-visited ***Humbug Spires***.

The impressive spires, contained within an 11,335-acre wilderness area, are composed of a quartz monzonite called the Moose Creek Stock, which was intruded into the surrounding sedimentary rock many millions of years ago. From the trailhead you can take an easy out-and-back day hike along Moose Creek to view the spires or make a longer backpacking adventure of it. Rock nuts of all levels—

from beginning scramblers to those trained and equipped to handle 5.12-level climbs—can enjoy practicing their skills on the granite spires. For additional information call the Bureau of Land Management in Butte at 494–5059 and request the Humbug Spires recreation brochure.

Snags, or dead, standing trees provide homes to a wide array of Montana's cavity-nesting birds and mammals. They serve other critters, too, as hunting perches, food-cache stations, "diners" for insect-eating birds, and roosting and resting places for bats and birds of prey.

Anaconda was founded in 1883 when copper king Marcus Daly built the Washoe Smelter and Reduction Works. Today you can see the inactive ***Anaconda Smelter Stack***, at over 585 feet high one of the tallest brick structures in the world. You can also learn about the history of smelting and railroading in the Anaconda area at the ***Visitor Center Complex***. The center, located at 306 East Park Street, includes a replicated train depot and the historic City Hall center. Call 563–2400 for information.

Also in Anaconda is the ***Hearst Free Library***, built in 1889 as a gift to the Smelter City from Phoebe Apperson Hearst, mother of William Randolph Hearst. Mrs. Hearst built the library in memory of her husband, George, who was active in business with the Anaconda Company. Here, in one of the grand libraries of the West, artwork created by turn-of-the-century masters, also presents from Mrs. Hearst, still hangs on the walls. The library, located at Main and Fourth Streets, is open Tuesday through Thursday from 10:00 A.M. to 9:00 P.M., and Friday and Saturday from 10:00 A.M. to 5:00 P.M. Call 563–6932 for information.

A much newer addition to town, but one that is built with history prominently in mind: the Jack Nicklaus Signature ***Old Works Golf Course***, which opened to the golfing public in 1997. The first-rate eighteen-hole course, surprisingly affordable to play, meanders along Warm Springs Creek, incorporating old brick walls, smokestack flues, and additional features that were either left in place or added as expressions of the area's mining heritage. Bunkers, rather than holding the typical light-colored sand, are filled with fine black slag, a by-product of the smeltering process. To reserve a tee time, call 563–5989.

Spectacular ***Lost Creek State Park*** is up a back road, off a secondary route that branches from a low-use highway coming out of a one-horse town. So, typically only those who already know about it ever make it to this spot some Native American groups considered the "Gate to Heaven." Highlights include wildlife, especially the Rocky Mountain goats that are native to the area and a herd of bighorn sheep whose predecessors were transplanted to Lost Creek in 1967 from the Sun River area. Look high on the 1,200-foot-high canyon cliffs above Lost Creek to spot the critters and to view some impressive geology: Looking oddly out of place, grayish-pink granitic dikes cut diagonally across the cliffs of darker-colored limestone, deposited as layers of mud at the bottom of a shallow sea more than a billion years ago. The dikes were forced as molten material into fissures in the older rock when the Rocky Mountains began to uplift much more "recently"— some seventy-five million years ago.

The Basics of a Mule

The terms ass, donkey, and burro are interchangeable. The basic differences between a donkey and a horse are the former's longer ears, narrower hooves, straighter back, narrower body, and cow-like tail. A mule is the offspring resulting from the mating of a male donkey, or jack, and a female horse, or mare. Mules are sterile, as a result of the different chromosome count of the donkey and horse parents. A hinny is genetically like a mule, but it is a cross between a female donkey, or jennet, and male horse, or stallion. Donkeys are usually gray, whereas mules can run the gamut of standard horse colors.

From where the road ends inside the park, a short, wheelchair-accessible asphalt trail leads to another highlight, cascading Lost Creek Falls. Two campgrounds with a combined total of twenty-five campsites, each with a picnic table and fire grill, await on a first-come, first-served basis. Lost Creek State Park, open May 1 through November 30, is 1½ miles east of Anaconda on Highway 1, then 2 miles north on Highway 273, and 6 miles west on the park road. For information call 542-5500.

The town of Philipsburg's bold description of its surroundings, "possibly the most beautiful valley in the world," may or may not be true; the verdict is in the eye of the beholder. But even if it is an exaggeration, it won't be far off the mark in anyone's view, for the valley is unquestionably alluring.

A historic mining town designated as a National Historic District in 1983, Philipsburg contains dozens of intriguing structures and is literally surrounded by old mining camps: Twenty-odd ghost towns can be found within 40 miles of town, including Granite, once among the richest silver towns in the West and home to approximately 3,000 residents in 1900.

Southwest Montana's ghost town theme coalesces at the ***Ghost Town Hall of Fame***, located downtown in the old Courtney Hotel and Overland car dealership. The hall features a gallery containing a respectable collection of photos depicting dozens of the old Montana mining towns at their zeniths. The hall of fame is open daily from 10:00 A.M. to 4:30 P.M. during the summer, and noon to 4:30 P.M. after Labor Day (closed

Christmas through mid-April). Admission is $3.00. Call the Granite County Museum at 859–3020 for other information. (They also have a mining exhibit open by appointment.)

"Mountain canaries," as they were known to the miners, from throughout the Rocky Mountain states and western Canada gather in Drummond the second weekend in June for the annual *Montana Mule Days*. A parade with some 200 mules and donkeys marching through downtown Drummond caps the weekend, which also includes weight-pulling contests, team penning competitions, and various other events. More than 150 classes of mules and donkeys compete, ranging from miniatures to giants. Spectators are welcome and guaranteed a good time. For more information call the Drummond City Hall at 288–3231.

Cowboys, Cons, and the Capital

A quartet of unusual attractions is found in the 1100 block of Main Street in Deer Lodge, where you can take a guided tour through the *Old Montana Prison*, the first territorial prison established in the western United States. Also located within the old pen, which was built by convicts and used until 1979, is the *Montana Law Enforcement Museum*. The entertaining Old Prison Players hold summer performances inside—lending new meaning to being part of a "captive audience."

Adjacent to the prison is the *Towe Ford Museum*, a collection representing Edward Towe's lifetime passion for Ford automobiles. On display are more than one hundred vintage Fords, most of them in mint condition. Gracing the showroom are models dating from 1903 to the 1960s, including a Lincoln once owned by Henry Ford himself.

The two newest components of the museum complex are the *Frontier Montana Museum*, added in 1994, and *Lil' Joe,* a 270-ton electric locomotive residing in the parking lot outside. Lil' Joe was one of several similar locomotives built during the last stages of World War II by General Electric for Josef Stalin's Trans-Siberian Railroad. The Cold War quickly chilled during this period, however, and the engines never made it to the Soviet Union. Instead, the Milwaukee Road picked them up at bargain-basement prices, and Lil' Joe and his kin ran the rails between Harlowton, Montana, and Avery, Idaho, until the railroad discontinued its electric operations in 1974.

You can visit all the museums by purchasing one ticket that also will get you into the nearby *Yesterday's Playthings*, a doll and toy museum. Tickets are $7.95 for adults, $3.50 for those ten to fifteen years old, and $1.00 for seven to nine year olds; admission is free for children six and under. General hours are 8:00 A.M. to 8:00 P.M. daily in summer and noon to 4:00 P.M. Sunday through Tuesday and 10:00 A.M. to 4:00 P.M. Wednesday through Saturday the rest of the year. For more information call 846–3111.

There's a lot to see and do in Helena, the Montana state capital. Gold was discovered here in 1864 at Last Chance Gulch, and today the gulch (Main Street) is a closed-to-cars pedestrian mall between Sixth and Wong Streets.

Among the liveliest shops on Last Chance Gulch is **The Parrot Confectionery**, which doesn't need to spend much money advertising because, as the slogan goes, it "talks for itself." For nearly eighty years the Parrot has served Helena residents and visitors with heavenly handmade, individually dipped chocolates. Bill and Ianthe Post opened the shop in 1922 at 22 North Main, and then moved to the current headquarters in 1935. Though the store changed hands once—in 1957—the "new" and current owners, the Duensing family, have kept the original owners' intentions alive during their four-decade reign. Dave Duensing, who now runs the shop with brother Dusty, states matter of factly that the shop hasn't changed in seventy years.

And you'll believe it when you walk through the doors: From the soda fountain to the Wurlitzer jukebox to the green paint used on the old benches, the place screams Roarin' Twenties. It's not simply a cosmetic makeover: The recipes used for the chocolates and the Parrot's ever-popular ice-cream dishes and chili are the originals used by the Posts and are closely guarded secrets. Even when the prestigious likes of *Gourmet* magazine asked for the Parrot's chili recipe, the request was politely refused.

The Parrot, located at 42 North Main, runs through twenty tons of ingredients in an average year, so you'll hardly make a dent by sampling a few ounces of their products. Call 442–1470 for more information.

Located a few short blocks from Last Chance Gulch and dozens of other Helena attractions is the charming **Sanders Bed and Breakfast**. When the wife-and-husband team of Bobbi Uecker and Rock Ringling purchased the house in 1986 to convert it into an inn, they became only the third family to have owned it during its illustrious 111-year history.

As a concession to modern sensibilities and business needs, the proprietors have added a private bath, touch-tone phone, and data port to each room. Both the exterior porch and the high-ceilinged, oak-wainscoted parlor are ideal spots to relax, and the gourmet breakfast—featuring dishes like huckleberry pancakes and Grand Marnier French toast—offers the opportunity to chat with the owners and fellow guests. Additional touches include complimentary sherry and homemade cookies, and a newly added video library.

The home's original owners, the Sanders, were interesting, and the current ones are, too. Their flair for gracious hospitality and the personal touch is evident the minute you walk through the front door (and past Wilbur Sanders's mineral collection). Bobbi might share some tales of previous guests, who've included South Africa's Archbishop Desmond Tutu. Rock, of the famous Ringling Brothers Circus family, can relate stories about growing up on the family ranch in tiny Ringling, Montana, where elephants and other show animals were often hauled in for a little rest and relaxation. The seven-room inn is appointed with many of the original owners' furnishings.

An overnight at the Sanders, located at 328 North Ewing, goes for $90 to $110. For reservations and information call 442–3309, or E-mail thefolks@sandersbb.com, or visit the inn's Web site at www. sandersbb. com.

A block south of the Sanders, at 304 North Ewing, is the ***Original Governor's Mansion***, built in 1888 and resided in by Montana's leaders from 1913 to 1959. On the free guided tour of the gracious Victorian mansion, which is maintained by the Montana Historical Society, you'll see that it

Wilbur Sanders

*T*he house that today serves as the Sanders Bed and Breakfast was built in 1875 as a residence for Wilbur and Harriet Sanders, who arrived in Bannack in 1863 with the Sidney Edgerton wagon train. Edgerton, the first governor of the Montana Territory, was Wilbur Sanders's uncle. Wilbur soon began practicing law, and he was instrumental in organizing the Vigilantes Committee, the group responsible for hanging members of the Plummer gang and other road agents and for bringing some semblance of civilization to the wild Montana frontier . . . often using surreptitious and scarcely legal means themselves to do so.

These activities helped launch a political career for Sanders, which culminated in his becoming one of the state's first two U.S. senators when Montana gained statehood in 1889. He served in many other civil and official capacities and was founder of the Montana Historical Society, of which he was president for twenty-six years. Wife Harriet, also politically active, was a painter. Her work still hangs in the living room at the Sanders.

Sanders Bed and Breakfast, Helena

retains its original woodwork, wall coverings, and furniture. Tours are generally available from April 1 through December 31, on the hour from noon to 5:00 P.M. Tuesday through Saturday. Call 444–4789 for information.

The **Museum of the Montana Historical Society** should be on every Helena visitor's itinerary. Outstanding displays include an exhibition of the works of F. Jay Haynes, official photographer for the Northern Pacific Railroad and Yellowstone National Park during the final years of the nineteenth century and first part of the twentieth. The display includes not only Haynes's works and much of his equipment, but also railroad and park artifacts from his day.

The impeccable, 10,000-square-foot Montana Homeland exhibit holds more than 2,000 artifacts, arranged in dioramas that lead visitors through Montana's history: first, American Indians, who came into the region at least 12,000 years ago; then the earliest trappers and explorers and the first mineral exploiters; and finally, the stockmen, farmers, and others, through World War II. The display focuses on the lifestyles of the cast of characters who have called Montana home and on how they interacted with their natural surroundings.

As wonderful as the museum is in its entirety, the chief reason many people come is to take in the Mackay Gallery of Charles M. Russell Art. Russell, who left his St. Louis home at sixteen to pursue the life of a free cowboy on the open Montana plains, quickly became the state's best-known artist and one of its best-loved citizens.

The Mackay Gallery includes more than sixty Russell oils, watercolors, pen-and-inks, sculptures, and several of the comical illustrated letters for which he was famous. A gallery centerpiece, one of Russell's most beautiful works in the eyes of many, is the exceptional *When the Land Belonged to God*. The broad canvas depicts a herd of bison cresting a rise above a dry-country river bottom, timbered buttes and mountains in the distant background. The painting simply looks alive, with the early-morning sun banking off the beasts and steam rising from their nostrils and off their backs.

GOLD WEST COUNTRY

Montana Trivia

The white steel crosses gracing certain stretches of Montana's highways were placed by American Legion posts, as memorial markers for those who've died in traffic accidents and as reminders for others to drive safely.

The museum is located at 225 North Roberts, directly across the street from the state capitol building. (By the way, another famous Russell painting, the very large *Lewis and Clark Meeting the Flathead Indians at Ross' Hole*, hangs at the front of the House of Representatives floor in the capitol.) The museum, free to visit, is open daily Memorial Day through Labor Day and closed Sunday and holidays during the winter. Call 444–2694 for information on guided tours. You can also learn more at the museum's Web site, www.his.mt.gov.

Helena has many additional attractions to see. One favorite is the *Myrna Loy Center for the Performing Arts* (443–0287; www.helenapresents.com), named for Helena's famous hometown Hollywood girl. Entertainers of national repute perform in this converted county jail. Another is the resplendent *St. Helena Cathedral* (442–5825), a replica of the formidable Votive Church in Vienna, Austria. Pews and woodwork are all of hand-carved oak, and marble statues stand throughout the beautiful church.

A third is the *Archie Bray Foundation for the Ceramic Arts* (443–3502; www.archiebray.org). The grounds and gallery at this ceramic arts school of national repute are alive with the whimsical creations of both little-known and world-renowned ceramic artists (the latter includes Shoji Hamada, Peter Voulkos, and western-Montana mud-molding legend Rudy Autio). You can take a self-guided tour of the grounds, formerly the Western Clay Manufacturing Company brickyards, anytime during daylight hours, but the gallery is open only Monday through Saturday from 10:00 A.M. to 5:00 P.M., and Sunday 1:00 to 5:00 P.M.

And, finally, you can visit what are thought to be the oldest octagonal house west of the Mississippi and the "largest old barn" in the United States at the *Child Kleffner Ranch*. The three-level barn, built in 1888, encompasses 27,000 square feet of floor space. Still a working cattle ranch, the Child Kleffner Ranch was added to the National Register of Historic Places in 1977. To get there, take Highway 12 to East Helena and turn south onto Highway 518 toward Montana City, then turn right in approximately 1 mile. Call 227–6645 for information on tours.

To see more of Helena, including the historic *Reeder's Alley*, a neighborhood of restored brick miners' shanties, board the *Last Chance Tour Train* (442–1023). You can also learn more by visiting the city's chamber of commerce Web site at www.helenamt.com.

Lincoln, 55 miles northwest of Helena, is one of those places that could just as easily have ended up a ghost town like Bannack or Elkhorn, but didn't. In the 1860s folks came to Lincoln Gulch, named in honor of the day's president, looking for gold. The only evidence remaining today of the original town, which included several log homes and stores, is the old cemetery.

Modern-day Lincoln claims more than 1,000 residents (one fewer now, though, since Unabomber Ted Kaczynski was taken into custody after discovered to be living here). The town is home to **Hi Country Trading Post**, a surprisingly large and successful enterprise for such a tiny town. The headquarters of the employee-owned company, with its made-in-

A Price on Their Heads

*A*n 1887 bounty on ground squir- *rels and prairie dogs came close to bringing Montana's territorial trea- sury to its knees. Farmers, at their wits end, early that year implored the terri- torial legislature to add the hole-dig- ging little devils—called the "picturesquely pestiferous and festively fecund chipmunk" by the* New North- west *territorial newspaper—to the list of critters that could be killed for cash.*

On March 5, 1887, the Territorial Assembly bowed to that pressure, amending the existing law to offer a bounty of 10 cents for the hide of each ground squirrel killed and 5 cents for that of every prairie dog delivered to his maker. This was in addition to the higher bounties of between $1.00 and $3.00 already paid for the more tradi- tionally bounty-hunted bears, cougars, coyotes, and wolves. Appropriating $14,000 to cover everything, the assembly members figured they had erred on the side of more than enough. They were wrong: frontier creativity ran high, and folks found all sorts of inventive ways to kill hundreds of the rodents—including using a machine

that puffed smoke into holes, "from which the squirrel soon issues in a dazed condition and is smacked sense- less with a club."

According to a report issued by the ter- ritorial auditor, the amount paid in 1887 on bounties through August 21 totaled $48,012.50; of that, $41,060.05 had gone for the hides of prairie dogs and ground squirrels. Panicked, and recognizing that this couldn't go on much longer if the territory were to remain solvent, Territorial Governor Preston H. Leslie requested and received permission from President Grover Cleveland to convene a special session of the legislature aimed at revising the revision in the bounty law. Speaking to the gathered assembly, Gov. Leslie said, "It is seen that the pathway to the treasury from the killing of the animal at his home in the mountain is easily found, is full of temptation and very dangerous to the pockets of the people."

Agreeing with the governor, the legis- lature repealed all bounties on all creatures, great and small.

Montana gift and beef jerky sales shop, is located about 2 miles west of town on Highway 200. It opens Monday through Saturday from 8:00 A.M. to 6:00 P.M., and Sunday from 10:00 A.M. to 6:00 P.M. For more information call 362–4203 or visit the Web site www. hicountry.com.

The cowboying town of Augusta, situated 75 miles north of Helena on the broad plains that sweep down to the east from the Rocky Mountains, holds an annual rodeo called, unabashedly, *The Wildest One Day Show on Earth*. While visiting, motor up the roads leading west into the Sun River Canyon, home to one of America's largest herds of bighorn sheep, and Beaver Creek Canyon, where you'll encounter some of the most dramatic scenery in Montana. You can also drive or ride a mountain bike through the 20,000-acre *Sun River Wildlife Management Area*, just southeast of the canyon, where grizzly bears often visit, and hundreds of elk feed in the winter. For information call 562–3684 or 467–3234.

If you happen to be in the area on St. Patrick's Day (and you're not in Butte!), take in the *Wolf Creek Wild Game Feed*. This fundraiser for local emergency services features dishes such as breaded rattlesnake, bear meatloaf, elk chow mein, mountain lion strips, and beaver tail; more mundane meals like fried trout, grilled salmon steaks, and roast goose are available for the wary. The give-what-you-can-afford-per-plate feed gets underway at the Oasis Bar and Cafe at 3:00 P.M.; call 235–9992 for more information. Wolf Creek is located beside Interstate 15, 35 miles north of Helena.

Nestled against a backdrop of sandstone badlands and timbered arroyos, *The Bungalow* bed-and-breakfast resembles a miniature version of Yellowstone National Park's Old Faithful Inn—and with good reason: Both structures were designed by architect Robert C. Reamer. The place was built in 1911–1913 as a summer getaway for Helena entrepreneur Charles C. Power, its cedar logs hauled by rail from Sandpoint, Idaho, to Wolf Creek, then by wagon team from town to the isolated site. In 1946 the lodge and surrounding ranchlands were sold to Brian O'Connell, father of the current owner and hostess, Pat O'Connell Anderson, who has spent summers (and some winters) here most of her life. If you are lucky, Pat will haul out her files of fascinating old articles, photos, and letters, which include house-planning correspondences between Power and architect Reamer, who, it seems, was often snowbound in Yellowstone and late in getting his mail.

The Bungalow's four guest rooms go for between $85 to $90 nightly; three of them have shared baths; the other boasts a private bath with what surely is one of the world's longest and deepest clawfoot tubs. Two rooms still contain furnishings personally chosen for the home by the famous designer and department-store tycoon Marshall Field. Breakfast is a scrumptious affair that typically includes homemade breads, and evenings are usually spent melting into the deep chairs and sofas surrounding the massive fireplace in the sitting room. Anglers take note: The inn is only 7 miles from some of the Missouri River's most productive trout waters. You'll find the Bungalow, which in 1995 was added to the National Register of Historic Places, hidden in the hills 4 miles north of Wolf Creek by following Interstate 15, Highway 287, and a $1\frac{1}{4}$-mile-long, rutted ranch road. Call 235–4276 or E-mail alb4950@montana.com for reservations and precise directions.

**PLACES TO STAY IN
GOLD WEST COUNTRY**

BIG HOLE VALLEY
Nez Perce Motel, Wisdom;
(406) 689–3254

Jackson Hot Springs Lodge,
Jackson; (406) 834–3151

Grasshopper Inn, Polaris;
(406) 834–3456

Sundance Lodge,
Wise River; (406) 689–3611

Beaverhead National Forest
Recreational Cabins;
(406) 689–3243

DILLON
Best Western Paradise Inn,
650 North Montana;
(406) 683–4214

Comfort Inn,
450 North Interchange;
(800) 442–4667

Super 8,
550 North Montana;
(800) 800–8000

Creston Motel,
335 South Atlantic;
(406) 683–2341

ENNIS
El Western Resort
and Motel,
U.S. Highway 287 South;
(800) 831–2773

Sportsman's Lodge,
310 U.S. Highway
287 North; (406) 682–4242

Fan Mountain Inn,
204 North Main;
(406) 682–5200

9T9 Ranch,
99 Gravelly Range Road;
(406) 682–7659

BUTTE
Copper King Mansion Bed
& Breakfast,
219 West Granite;
(406) 782–7580

Scott Bed & Breakfast,
15 West Copper; (800)
844–2952

Ramada Inn Copper King
4655 Harrison Avenue;
(800) 332–8600

Comfort Inn,
2777 Harrison Avenue;
(800) 442–4667

Super 8,
2929 Harrison Avenue;
(800) 800–8000

DEER LODGE
Scharf Motor Inn,
819 Main; (406) 846–2810

Western Big Sky Inn,
210 North Main;
(406) 846–2590

Super 8,
1150 North Main;
(800) 800–8000

HELENA
The Barrister Bed
& Breakfast,
416 North Ewing;
(800) 823–1148

The Sanders Bed
& Breakfast,
328 North Ewing;
(406) 442–3309

Jorgenson's Holiday Motel,
1714 11th Avenue;
(800) 272–1770

Park Plaza Hotel,
22 North Last Chance
Gulch; (406) 443–2200

Days Inn,
2001 Prospect Avenue;
(800) 325–2525

**PLACES TO EAT IN
GOLD WEST COUNTRY**

BIG HOLE VALLEY
Big Hole Crossing
Restaurant, Wisdom;
(406) 689–3800

Rose's Cantina, Jackson,
(406) 834–3100

Jackson Hot Springs Lodge,
Jackson; (406) 834–3151

Elkhorn Hot Springs,
Polaris; (406) 834–3434

Wise River Club,
Wise River;
(406) 832–3258

DILLON
Longhorn Saloon & Grill,
8 North Montana;
(406) 683–6839

Subway, State Highway
41 North; (406) 683–6567

ENNIS
Yesterday's Restaurant &
Soda Fountain,
124 Main Street;
(406) 682–4246

Silver Dollar Saloon,
131 East Main Street;
(406) 682–7320

Continental Divide
(gourmet; closed in winter),
Main Street;
(406) 682–7600

BUTTE
Doreen's Family Restaurant,
138 West Park in Uptown
Butte; (406) 782–7625

Joe's Pasty Shop,
Harrison and Grand;
(406) 723–9071

Lydia's Supper Club,
4915 Harrison;
(406) 494–2000

Pekin Noodle Parlor,
117 South Main;
(406) 782–2217.

Pork Chop John's,
2400 Harrison and in
Uptown Butte at 8 West
Mercury; (406) 782–1783
(406) 782–0812

Uptown Cafe (gourmet),
47 East Broadway;
(406) 723–4735

DEER LODGE
Broken Arrow Steak House,
317 Main; (406) 846–3400

Scharf's Family Restaurant,
819 Main; (406) 846–2810

4-B's Family Restaurant,
North Interchange;
(406) 846–2620

Pizza Hut, 202 North Main;
(406) 846–2777

HELENA
Carriage House Bistro,
234½ East Lyndale;
(406) 449–6949

No Sweat Cafe
(breakfast and lunch),
427 North Last Chance
Gulch; (406) 442–6954

On Broadway (Italian),
106 Broadway;
(406) 443–1929

Park Avenue Bakery,
44 South Park Avenue;
(406) 449–8424

Stonehouse Restaurant
(fine dining),
120 Reeder's Alley;
(406) 449–2552

Windbag Saloon and Grill,
19 South Last Chance
Gulch; (406) 443–9669

Yellowstone Country

t is true that most of Yellowstone National Park lies in Wyoming, but that's certainly not to say that the Cowboy State has a monopoly on the Greater Yellowstone ecosystem's stunning scenery. In fact, many would argue—most of them Montanans, granted, and not Cowboy Staters—that even though Wyoming's Yellowstone claims the world-famous geysers and other thermal phenomena, the really stupendous country lies to the north of the park in the Big Sky State.

You'll begin touring Yellowstone Country in the headwaters region, where three rivers merge to become the Missouri, then press on to Bozeman. From the home of Montana State University, you'll go up the Gallatin River, passing the Big Sky Ski and Summer Resort enroute to West Yellowstone. From there, you'll pass into Wyoming and through the northwest corner of the world's first national park, then drop back into Montana along the Gardiner and Yellowstone Rivers. You'll then traverse the spectacular Paradise Valley to Livingston, a fun town filled with cowboys and fly-fishers, before continuing on to Big Timber and Red Lodge, where a side trip leads along the world-renowned Beartooth National Scenic Byway. Finally, on your way to Custer–Missouri River Country, you can venture onto outback roads to visit the remote Pryor Mountains National Wild Horse Range.

High Peaks and Hot Springs

The tranquil and history-rich **Headwaters State Park** lies 3 miles east of Three Forks on Highway 10, then 1½ miles north on Highway 286. Here you'll find pleasant campgrounds, displays interpreting the area's natural and human history, trails tracing the footsteps of Indians, and the ghost town remnants of Gallatin City. Angling is popular in the park, especially for the brown and cutthroat trout that inhabit the

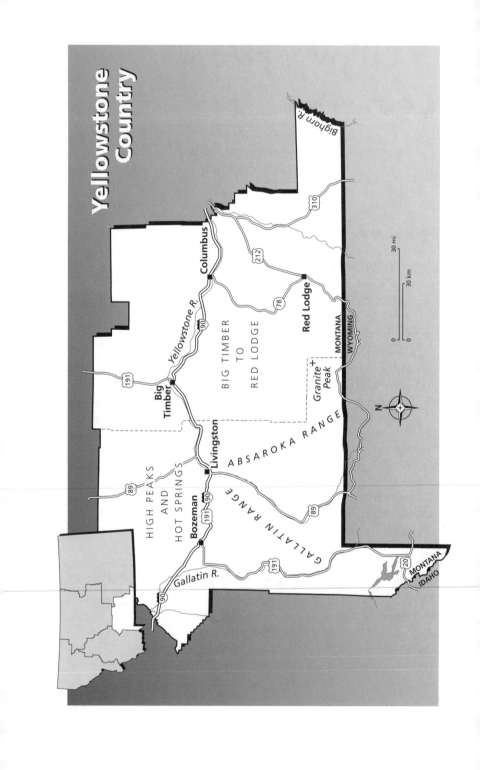

Yellowstone Country

Bighorn R.

310

212

78

Red Lodge

MONTANA
WYOMING

Granite
Peak

BIG TIMBER
TO
RED LODGE

Columbus

Yellowstone R.

90

191

Big
Timber

ABSAROKA RANGE

Livingston

HIGH PEAKS
AND
HOT SPRINGS

89

GALLATIN RANGE

191 90

Bozeman

89

191

Gallatin R.

90

20

MONTANA
IDAHO

N

30 mi

30 km

0

0

blue-ribbon waters of the Gallatin River. It's also a haven for bird-watchers: More than ninety species of birds can be seen throughout the seasons amid the park's rich mix of river-bottom and rocky-upland habitats. For more information on Headwaters State Park, call 994–4042.

The headwaters, where three major rivers flow together to form the Missouri, was long known by American Indians as one of the most game-abundant areas in the region. During the eighteenth century the Blackfeet, Gros Ventre, Shoshoni, and Flathead tribes shared the area, but by early in the nineteenth century the powerful and aggressive Blackfeet dominated. Lewis and Clark came through in 1805, naming the "three noble streams" the Madison, Gallatin, and Jefferson, after the U.S. secretary of state, secretary of the treasury, and president ("the author of our enterprize"). Not long after, trappers and traders in search of beaver pelts filtered in.

Two of the earliest into the beaver country were John Potts and world-class mountain man John Colter, both formerly of the Lewis and Clark expedition. Together they were dispatched in 1808 from Manuel Lisa's trading post at the confluence of the Big Horn and Yellowstone Rivers, armed with the mission of convincing the Indians to trade at Lisa's Fort Remon. But by this time the Blackfeet, who were hostile toward white Americans, controlled the scene, and the duo unfortunately encountered a party of several hundred Piegan warriors. Legend has it that Potts was killed immediately, but Colter was given a chance for survival: After convincing the Piegan chief that he was a poor runner (although known among fellow explorers as a very good one), Colter was stripped, given a head start, and permitted to run for his life, barefoot and bare naked.

The warriors chased Colter over a rough, rocky, and cactus-covered terrain, but he finally ditched them by hiding in brush along the Madison. He regained Fort Remon after an eleven-day odyssey, tattered, footsore, and hungry. The epic adventure enhanced Colter's reputation as one of the smartest and toughest of all the wild and wily mountain men.

BEST ATTRACTIONS

Headwaters State Park,
Three Forks;
(406) 994–4042

Willow Creek Cafe and Saloon,
Willow Creek;
(406) 285–3698

American Computer Museum,
Bozeman; (406) 587–7545

Rendezvous Ski Trails,
West Yellowstone;
(406) 646–7701

Gallatin Petrified Forest,
Corwin Springs;
(406) 848–7375

Chico Hot Springs,
Emigrant; (406) 333–4933

Buckin' Horse Bunkhouse,
outside Reedpoint; 932–6537

Tormgrimson Place,
Fishtail; (406) 328–6923

Grizzly Bar,
Roscoe; (406) 328–6789

Beartooth National Scenic Byway,
Red Lodge; (406) 446–2103

At the corner of Main and Cedar in Three Forks, visit the **Headwaters Heritage Museum**, one of Montana's best small-town shrines to the past. Among the ground-floor displays is a collection of pictures taken

John Colter Run

*T*he 7-mile **John Colter Run**, *an annual institution for more than twenty years, is hosted in early September by Bozeman's Big Sky Wind Drinkers running club. The race celebrates John Colter's epic trek. The first year I showed up for the race, in 1993, I must admit that I was relieved to find that today's contestants are permitted to retain their shorts and shoes. The early autumn morning was cool, but not cold; perfect for running. After the starting gun sounded, we were off, roughly 200 strong, trotting up the paved road leading from Headwaters State Park toward the railroad siding known as Trident. Soon, though, after about a mile of level pavement, we were directed across the railroad tracks and into the hills . . . and I* mean *hills. On the major ascents everyone, even the leaders, I think, were reduced to walking. On the other side, descending was basically a controlled fall/slide, as competitors concentrated hard to avoid close encounters with what are, perhaps, descendents of the prickly-pear cactus plants Colter had to contend with.*

After a half hour into the race, we were a mile-long string, with middle-of-the-pack runners diving down a steep ridge as the distant leaders inched up the next one. As the race director had prophetically informed us, "The 'iron horse' is something Colter didn't have to contend with, but it's part of the deal today." And sure enough, several

of the front-runners were brought to a screeching halt just a half mile from the finish line, while they waited for a train clanking south from Trident, permitting slower runners to catch up to them.

Relief is typically the emotion one feels on nearing the end of a running race, but here relief was clouded with dread, for one last hurdle remained: the Gallatin River. Depending on one's height, the river was belly- to neck-deep in the current—"the deepest I've ever seen it," according to more than one race veteran, owing to an unusually high snowpack the previous winter. Thankfully, the race organizers had secured a stout rope on opposite banks of the river and stationed hired hands dressed in wetsuits along the length of the rope to help shorter and/or spent competitors across.

H. M. Chittenden, in his seminal 1895 volume, The Yellowstone National Park, *wrote that when John Colter appeared back at Fort Remon after his eleven-day, 200-mile-plus odyssey, "The men at the fort did not recognize him at first and doubtless would not have believed his story if his terrible plight had not been proof of its truth." I can only imagine, because I know how badly I felt after only 7 miles and one hour.*

For information on the John Colter Run, call Universal Athletics in Bozeman at 587–4415.

MAJOR ATTRACTIONS WORTH SEEING

Museum of the Rockies,
Bozeman

*Big Sky Ski and
Summer Resort*

*Grizzly Discovery Center
and National Geographic
IMAX Theater,*
West Yellowstone

by local photographer Niels Olson, documenting Three Forks' history during the first half of the twentieth century. Another features several hundred hand-carved miniatures created in his spare time by a local railroad engineer, many of them microscopically inscribed with his name.

Filling another case are samples of the artifacts unearthed at the Three Waters Quarry, an archaeological excavation that has served as a hands-on classroom for hundreds of Montana State University students over the last two decades. The site is in the Horseshoe Hills, close to neighboring Willow Creek. On a nearby table a scrapbook overflows with articles on the Three Forks area's past happenings—including a report on the Great American Flatboat Expedition of 1976. The expedition, one of thousands of special events that took place in the United States during its bicentennial year, began on the upper reaches of the Missouri River near here and ended in New Orleans. One article reveals that the expedition leader won the heart of a Three Forks girl, and the two later married.

Among the goodies found upstairs in the museum are collections of barbed wire and old cowboy clothes and tack. The free museum is open from mid-May through mid-September, Monday through Saturday from 9:00 to 11:00 A.M. and 1:00 to 5:00 P.M., and on Sunday from 1:00 to 5:00 P.M.

For a look at some new clothes and tack, swing into the ***Three Forks Saddlery***, known as "The Working Cowboy's Store." You'll enjoy this shop—as fine a cowboy-outfitting store as there is north of the Pecos—whether or not you're a horse lover. (Perhaps you need a gift for a friend who's horsey or simply enjoy the smell of fresh-tanned leather.)

For forty years the store has outfitted area cowboys with custom chaps and saddles (you can watch 'em being made), including their popular Kelly Roper and Montana Packer models. They also offer a full line of western hats, boots, and clothing, and books and other merchandise relating to the cowboying life. The sign on the door at Three Forks Saddlery, located at 221 South Main, reads, COME IN AND SAY HELLO—YOU'RE ALWAYS WELCOME. Their phone number is 285–3459.

The ***Sacajawea Hotel***, named in honor of Lewis and Clark's female Shoshoni interpreter, is a grand hotel, listed on the National Register of Historic Places. Built in two stages, the original Madison House portion was erected in 1882 and then moved on log rollers from old Three Forks to its current site in 1910. The newer portion, built that same year, comprises the main lobby and guest rooms, while the older Madison House wing became the kitchen and dining room. Architect John Willson, responsible for many of the old homes in Bozeman, designed the Sacajawea, which was built to serve those traveling on the Milwaukee Road railway.

After recent renovations, each elegant room has a private bath. The outstanding restaurant, with prices ranging from moderate to expensive, is open daily for supper from 5:00 to 9:00 P.M. An overnight stay at the Sacajawea Inn, located at 5 North Main Street in Three Forks, runs from $60 to $105, double occupancy. The 30,000-square-foot inn is open year-round, although some of the thirty-three rooms are partitioned off during winter. For reservations and more information call 285–6515 or go to www.sacajaweahotel.com.

At the **Willow Creek Cafe and Saloon,** located 7 miles south of Three Forks in the tiny town of Willow Creek, they know how to make good coffee, and they know how to make food even better. Their sinful fresh-fruit pies and pastries are legendary in these parts; they purchase the pumpkins, huckleberries, and other ingredients from local growers and pickers. The dinner menu, with prices ranging from moderate to expensive, consists largely of sumptuous seafood, beef, and pasta

Best Annual Events

1. *Montana Powder 8's Championship, Bridger Bowl (Bozeman); early February; (406) 587-2111*

2. *Yellowstone Rendezvous Cross-Country Ski Race, West Yellowstone; early March; (406) 646-7701*

3. *Upper Yellowstone Fly-Fishing Expo, Livingston; early May; (406) 222-9369*

4. *National Parks Paper & Antique Show, Bozeman; early June; (406) 238-9796*

5. *Home of Champions Rodeo & Parade, Red Lodge; early July; (406) 446-1718*

6. *Mountain Man Rendezvous, Red Lodge; late July; (406) 446-1718*

7. *Festival of Nations, Red Lodge; early August; (406) 446-1718*

8. *Sweet Pea Festival, Bozeman; early August; (406) 586-4003*

9. *Montana Antique Aircraft Association Fly-In and Air Show, Three Forks; early August; (406) 285-4880*

10. *Barnes Steam & Power Show, Belgrade; late August; (406) 388-4433*

11. *John Colter Run, Three Forks; early September; (406) 587-4415*

12. *Bridger Mountain Raptor Festival, Bozeman; early October; (406) 586-1518*

dishes. The breakfasts are out of this world, and so are the lunches, which feature hearty, homemade soups.

The charming, antiques-appointed Willow Creek Cafe & Saloon sits at First and Main, in a historic building once a saloon-barbershop-dance hall complex. Not only is it the town's eatery, it's also the village "chattery." Sit a spell and you're bound to hear some interesting gossip or tall tales related by an old-timer. The restaurant is open for lunch and dinner Tuesday through Saturday and for all three of the day's meals on Sunday (closed on Monday). For dinner reservations call 285–3698.

Just south of the Willow Creek Cafe on Main Street is a nondescript old brick building adorned with a faded mural of a bucking bronco and rider, sporting a simple blue awning on the front. On the awning, in large white letters, are the words *Willow Creek Tool,* the only clue as to what fills the building's interior.

Inside you'll find a dizzying array of some of the best woodworking tools made. The business opened in 1983, and owner David Spencer had some major-league convincing to do when citified, suit-and-tie sales reps called on his fledgling outfit in laid-back Willow Creek. But he obviously was successful, for now he sells and travels as a distributor for some of the best names in tools.

Willow Creek Tool's regular hours are 8:00 A.M. to 5:00 P.M. Monday through Friday. For information on the associated Willow Creek Wood Productivity Training Center, call 285–3247.

Another surprise restaurant in the hinterland not far from Three Forks is the **Land of Magic Dinner Club**, which features a relaxed western ambience and great steak dinners. The place is found in Logan, 6 miles east of Three Forks on the frontage road paralleling Interstate 90. It's open 6:00 to 10:00 P.M. Monday through Friday, 5:00 to 10:00 P.M. on Saturday, and 4:00 to 9:00 P.M. on Sunday. For reservations call 284–3794.

But if you're still too full from the Willow Creek Cafe to partake of a spellbinding sirloin at Land of Magic, first motor out to visit **Madison Buffalo Jump State Park.** Here you can work on that appetite while learning about how some earlier residents procured their steak dinners.

Bone deposits, up to 60 inches deep in places, and projectile-point styles found at the site indicate that this buffalo jump, or pishkun, was active beginning at least 2,000 years ago. After being stampeded down rock-lined drive lanes by runners, herds of bison plunged over the steep cliff that rises beyond the observation deck now in place. Those only injured from the fall were quickly dispatched by hunters waiting below, and after the kill women would take over and butcher the animals. From this bounty, the Indians obtained much of their food for the winter, as well as the raw materials for clothing, tools, and shelter.

Look closely as you traverse these hills, and you'll spot stone circles, or tipi rings, and what investigators believe are eagle catch pits. After excavating a large enough hole, an Indian would hide in it beneath a cover of branches, with a rabbit or some other raptor's tasty tidbit atop the whole affair. If and when an eagle swooped down for the bait, the Indian would try to grab it by the feet and kill it. If things went according to plan, the brave became the proud owner of a new supply of valuable eagle's plumage.

As at any archaeological site, don't disturb the evidence: Even stone chippings should remain where seen on the ground. Madison Buffalo Jump State Park, open for day use only, is located 7 miles south of Logan on gravel. For more information call 994–4042.

Manhattan, Montana, received a good bit of national exposure because of its role in the "Real Beef for Real People" television ad campaign. But beef isn't the only thing raised and eaten in Manhattan; in fact, within Montana it's better known as the Seed Potato Capital. Fittingly, each

Native to the Area

We tend to think of whites as the newcomers to Montana's plains and mountains and American Indians as having lived here forever. Of course, they haven't been here forever—just 12,000 years or so. Most of the tribes whose names we associate with the state today, however—the Crow, Cheyenne, Flathead, and others—are relative newcomers themselves. The first tribe whose name we recognize, the Shoshone, moved in eight or nine hundred years ago, and by the 1500s they dominated the country east of the Continental Divide in the future state of Montana. It was they who worked the Madison Buffalo Jump during its most intensively used period.

The Shoshone began to migrate toward the southwest in the 1600s, and by the time Lewis and Clark passed through the area in 1805 and 1806, only a handful remained. Meanwhile, the Crow had moved in during the 1600s, and it was only in the late 1700s that the Blackfeet, Gros Ventre, Assiniboine, and Cheyenne established themselves in their respective portions of the state. By then horses also had arrived on the scene, obtained from tribes to the south who had, in turn, gotten theirs from early Europeans. The horse was the means to the Plains Indians' new-found mobility and to the development of an altogether different strategy for hunting bison. Pishkuns rapidly became a thing of the past.

August the town hosts the **Manhattan Potato Festival**. The most popular event in this spud-tacular festival is the mashed-potato fight in which entrants, dressed in plastic garbage bags, line up across from one another and throw huge scoops of the mushy white stuff at each other. Now, that's real fun!

Tinsley Homestead at the Museum of the Rockies, Bozeman

But if it's peace and quiet you're searching for, forgo the clamorous potatofest and opt instead to stay at one of several primitive **Gallatin National Forest rental cabins**. The forest, headquartered in Bozeman, claims twenty-four such cabins, most of them built in the 1920s and 1930s to house rangers and trail crews. They rent for $25 a night. They come equipped with cots or bunks, wood-burning stoves, cooking gear, and tables and chairs. Overnighters haul in their own sleeping bags, food, and, in most cases, water. Visitors also are asked to replenish the wood supply from the wood pile outside (axe or splitting maul provided).

Some cabins can be reached by car; others, however, are accessible only by trail, and many rent only during the winter. For information on the individual cabins, which are let out on a first-come, first-served basis, call the Bozeman Ranger District at 522–2520.

Bozeman never was a boomtown of the sort that commonly popped up throughout southwest Montana. Rather, it grew slowly but surely, primarily as a commercial center for the ever-expanding Gallatin Valley agricultural trade. Helping add to that stable economic base today are major attractions like the **Museum of the Rockies**, considered by many to be Montana's foremost treasury of things old, some of them very old. If you haven't had enough after spending hours at the outstanding museum, ask for directions to the facility's **Kirk Hill Nature Center**, which rests in the foothills nearby. Or, take a guided tour of Bozeman in a restored 1936 Yellowstone Park Bus. For more information call the Museum of the Rockies at 994–DINO.

The unusual **American Computer Museum**—a.k.a. "Compuseum"— is wrapped in a plain-brown building adjacent to the state liquor store

Montana Trivia

The National Parks and Conservation Association, in partnership with more than 200 Montana businesses, has launched a campaign entitled BISON BELONG. To learn about the program, which urges state and federal officials to find a way to prevent the killing of more of Yellowstone's bison, call (800) 628-7275.

at 234 East Babcock Street in downtown Bozeman. A wall display at the beginning of the guided tour reminds the visitor that you don't have to be a computer nerd to encounter computer chips on a daily basis. Rather, anyone who uses a video camera, microwave oven, compact-disc player, late-model car, automatic teller machine, digital watch, or any of a host of other gadgets depends on microchip computers.

The history of computing and computers—from the abacus (invented by the Babylonians in about 450 B.C.) to the slide rule to today's high-speed business microprocessors—is revealed in professionally prepared exhibits displayed in chronological order; the newest is entitled "From Thomas Jefferson to Personal Computers." Gadgets you've probably never seen, but which were common in times past, are displayed and explained. Kids, especially, will enjoy the museum's hands-on exhibits and its working robot.

An example of the little-known facts you can pick up here: Augusta Ada Byron, the only child of Lord Byron, can be considered the world's original "computer programmer," for she developed the first punch-card programs to be used with Charles Babbage's 1840s Analytical Engine. Another: It took $7^1/_2$ years to manually calculate the results from the 1880 U.S. census. Thanks to a punch-card system devised by Herman Hollerith, it took only one third the time, or $2^1/_2$ years, to tabulate the results from the 1890 census.

Also described is the 1942 development of the first electronic digital computer, forerunner to today's personal computers, at Iowa State University. Numerous early computer models are displayed, including a massive IBM similar to the one used in putting a man on the moon in 1969. The fascinating American Computer Museum is open daily from 10:00 A.M. to 4:00 P.M. during the summer and noon to 4:00 P.M. Tuesday, Wednesday, Friday, and Saturday the rest of the year. Admission is $3.00; call 587–7545 or visit the Web site www.compustory.com for information on the museum's expansion plans.

You say you've worked up a mean thirst and a hearty appetite from all the museum touring? Head to the **Spanish Peaks Brewery**, 120 North Nineteenth Avenue in Bozeman. Some of the best microbrews in the Northwest are hand-crafted here, including the popular Black Dog Ale. Lip-smacking Italian specialties, such as brick-oven pizza and seafood pasta, are also served inside the brewery. The enterprise opens its doors at 11:30 A.M. Monday through Saturday and at noon on Sunday. Children are permitted, and soft drinks are available. Call 585–2296 or visit the Web site www.spanish peaks.com for additional information.

People from throughout Montana assemble to greet old friends and meet new ones at Bozeman's annual *Sweet Pea Festival*. First held in the early 1900s as a celebration of the Gallatin Valley's beautiful and bountiful summers, the festival went on hiatus in 1916. Resurrected in 1978, the Sweet Pea Festival now focuses on the arts and features a full slate of outdoor art shows, parades, dance and music performances by big-time names, Shakespeare in the park, and bicycle and running races. The festivities happen during early August, with a flurry of activities concentrated around the month's first weekend. Call the Chamber of Commerce at (800) 228–4224 or go to their Web site at www.bozeman.avicom.net for details.

Before leaving the Bozeman area, consider a side trip up dazzling Bridger Canyon to partake of a good night's sleep at the *Silver Forest Inn*. Located 15 miles north of town near the Bridger Bowl alpine ski area, the inn was constructed of huge logs in the 1930s and originally served as a getaway for writers and artists. Several rooms, appointed with antiques and original western art, are available for rent, and the inn's inviting outdoor hot tub makes it tough to pass up a moonlight soak. Nightly rates range from $75 to $125; for reservations and further information, call 586–1882 or visit www.silverforestinn.com.

Just up the way from the Silver Forest Inn, at 16621 Bridger Canyon Road, is *Bohart Ranch*, a day-use cross-country ski area in winter. During the snowless months the center's trails double as paths for walking, hiking, running, and mountain biking, both for leisure- and competition-minded folks. Included among the special events held at Bohart throughout the year are summer biathlons, which combine cross-country running and target shooting. Bohart also boasts a summer Frisbee Golf course. Call 586–9070 for information or log on to www.bohartranchxcski.com.

From Bohart you can wind northeasterly on the gravel-in-places State Highway 86, then head south along U.S. Highway 89 to Clyde Park. Hidden outside of town well in view of the Crazy Mountains is *Dead-Rock*, part working ranch, part guest ranch, and part Old West town.

Guests hole up in one of two lodges or four cabins; in the great outdoors beyond, they can take in horseback riding, mountain biking, and trout fishing in the ranch's forty-acre lake. The enterprise, which also features gourmet dining, is open year-round (come winter, snowmobiling and cross-country skiing are popular). Call 686–4428 or E-mail crazymount@aol.com to request more information or to make reservations.

If the air is chilly when you bid adieu to Bozeman, it's bound to become even nippier as you near West Yellowstone. To find something cozy to ward off that chill, stop by the *Montana Woolen Shop*, which features products from Amana, Woolrich, Hudson Bay, and other companies at uncommonly low prices. The interior of the small store is a free-for-all, with woolen goods hanging over every available stationary object and from every square inch of wall space. Multicolored blankets, robes, Navajo rugs, sweaters (2,987 at last count!), and fabrics are among the merchandise.

The Montana Woolen Shop is located 3 miles west of downtown at 3100 West Main Street (also known as Highway 191). It's open Monday through Friday from 9:00 A.M. to 7:00 P.M., Saturday from 10:00 A.M. to 6:00 P.M., and Sunday from 11:00 A.M. to 5:00 P.M. Call 587–8903 for more information.

Another interesting stop is the *Inventors Hall of Fame*, found $2\frac{1}{4}$ miles west of the woolen shop on Highway 191. Actually just a wall of fame found inside the headquarters of King Tool, the display consists of a variety of photos, newspaper articles, and plaques celebrating the creative spirit of a select group of Montanans.

Casey Emerson, proprietor of King Tool and a successful inventor in his own right, scaled back his vision of creating a national inventors hall of fame when he discovered that one already existed. He established this attraction, said to be the only state inventors hall of fame, hoping to inspire more Montanans to develop ideas they've had for inventions. The criteria one must meet in order to earn a spot on the wall are simply stated if not simply accomplished: He or she must have lived in Montana when the idea for the invention came about, and the final product must have resulted in at least $1 million in sales.

A couple of the honorees include Curt Phillips of Rudyard, who developed an air-blower attachment for combines that helps to minimize crop loss, and Bozeman resident Keith Barner, inventor of several specialized widgets for archers and bow hunters.

Let It Snow

*A*ny skier worth his or her boots, bindings, and boards knows that Montana boasts a trio of destination ski resorts: the Big Mountain, Big Sky, and Red Lodge Mountain. Less known is that the state features a dozen other ski resorts. These tend to be "locals" hills, although some of them, such as Bridger Bowl north of Bozeman and Montana Snowbowl outside Missoula, claim statistics that are anything but small town. Here's a summary of where you can go downhill schussing or shredding under the big sky, and what to expect when you get there:

Bear Paw Ski Bowl,
Havre; 265–8404 *Vertical Drop: 900'* *Average Snowfall: 140*

Big Mountain,
Whitefish; 862–1900 *Vertical Drop: 2,300'* *Average Snowfall: 300*

Big Sky,
Big Sky; (800) 548–4486 *Vertical Drop: 4,180'* *Average Snowfall: 400*

Blacktail Mountain,
Lakeside; 844–0999 *Vertical Drop: 1,440'* *Average Snowfall: 250*

Bridger Bowl,
Bozeman; (800) 223–9609 *Vertical Drop: 2,000'* *Average Snowfall: 350*

Discovery Basin,
Anaconda; 563–2184 *Vertical Drop: 1,300'* *Average Snowfall: 200*

Great Divide,
Marysville; 449–3746 *Vertical Drop: 1,330'* *Average Snowfall: 150*

Lost Trail,
Conner; 821–3211 *Vertical Drop: 1,200'* *Average Snowfall: 300*

Marshall Mountain,
Missoula; 258–6000 *Vertical Drop: 1,500'* *Average Snowfall: 150*

Maverick Mountain,
Polaris; 834–3454 *Vertical Drop: 2,120'* *Average Snowfall: 180*

Montana Snowbowl,
Missoula; 549–9777 *Vertical Drop: 2,600'* *Average Snowfall: 300*

Red Lodge Mountain,
Red Lodge; 446–2610 *Vertical Drop: 2,400'* *Average Snowfall: 250*

Showdown Ski Area,
Neihart, 236–5522 *Vertical Drop: 1,400'* *Average Snowfall: 240*

Teton Pass,
Choteau; 466–2209 *Vertical Drop: 1,100'* *Average Snowfall: 300*

Turner Mountain,
Libby; 293–4317 *Vertical Drop: 2,110'* *Average Snowfall: 200*

To learn more about any of these areas, Internet users can tap into http://travel.mt.gov and click the Winter Recreation button. The Winter Recreation Web site features snow reports (updated daily), information on groomed cross-country trails, details on snowmobile rentals and trails, and a lot more.

The official address of King Tool is 5350 Love Lane. Because of the lovely nature of the name, however, the street's sign is a popular target for road-sign thieves. Because you'll likely not find a sign reading Love Lane, know this: Turn north onto the first road west of the big sign reading Winchester Angus, then continue for ¼ mile. Another surprise inside King Tool is a gymnasium/basketball court; to inquire as to why it's there, or to request more information on the Inventors Hall of Fame, call 586–1541.

Continue west on Highway 191 to Four Corners, where you do *not* want to miss sampling one of the amazing sandwiches at **New York Pizza & Deli** (582–1986). From there, turn south following Highway 191 and the Gallatin River. In 6 miles turn into the **Gallatin Gateway Inn**, an opulent Spanish Colonial Revival-style structure sporting a stucco exterior and a hard-to-miss red-tile roof. The Milwaukee Road railway built the inn, one of the first hotels designed to serve a burgeoning number of tourists traveling to Yellowstone National Park, in 1927 at the southern end of their branch line from Three Forks. They believed that Salesville (soon to become Gallatin Gateway) would be the ideal spot to entertain visitors who would be traveling by bus the rest of the way to the park.

The inn features twenty-five rooms, which seems too few in relation to its expansive dining and lounging areas. The reason: The builders assumed that after tourists savored the inn's amenities, the majority would return to Pullman cars to sleep. But their timing was not good, for within a decade most were traveling to Yellowstone by car, and the venture failed. The Milwaukee Road sold the inn in the early 1950s, and not long after, it fell into disrepair.

Following an extensive renovation in the late 1980s, however, the Gallatin Gateway Inn has reclaimed its initial grandeur and is again welcoming the Yellowstone-bound. Rooms, available in a choice of single or double occupancy or two-room suites, are decorated in the subdued hues of the Western landscape. The immense dining room features a menu that changes with the seasons and attracts a strong local and regional clientele.

The high ceiling, original Polynesian mahogany woodwork, hand-carved beams, and tall windows create a distinctive atmosphere that has made the lounge and ballroom area a popular spot for weddings and other social events. The inn also now has an outdoor pool and hot tub, a fly-casting pond, and mountain bikes available for exploring area back roads. Rooms at the Gallatin Gateway Inn range from $70 to $175 per night. For information and reservations call 763–4672. You can also learn more at the inn's Web site, www.gallatingatewayinn.com.

Continue south on U.S. Highway 191 up the Gallatin River, past the entrance to the Big Sky Ski and Summer Resort, then through the northwest corner of Yellowstone National Park. At the junction with U.S. Highway 287, continue south and in 8 miles you'll reach West Yellowstone.

Like Gallatin Gateway, West Yellowstone once was a terminus for a railroad spur line, but this one came from Ashton, Idaho, to the south. The rustic Oregon Short Line (now the Union Pacific) Depot, built of native materials, was designed to blend into the landscape and echo the style utilized for the National Park Service buildings in Yellowstone National Park.

Today the old depot houses the *Museum of the Yellowstone,* and its displays on Native Americans, the U.S. Cavalry, mountain men, wildlife, the wildfires of 1988, and other subjects relating to the natural and human history of the Yellowstone region. Perhaps the most fascinating finds are in the Famous Indian Portrait Gallery, with its vintage photographs of the great chiefs of the Cheyenne, Nez Perce, Blackfeet, and other tribes. The Museum of the Yellowstone, located at 124 Yellowstone Avenue near the entrance to the park, is open May through October from 8:00 A.M. to 10:00 P.M. daily. For information call 646–7814.

If your visit to West Yellowstone comes during the town's long and snowbound winter, try kicking and gliding along the *Rendezvous Ski Trails*, where seasoned cross-country skiers can enjoy hours of fun, and Nordic neophytes couldn't pick a better place to learn the basics.

The trail system, first carved out of Gallatin National Forest lands in the 1970s by the Neal Swanson family, has gained a reputation over the years as one of the premier ski-trail systems in the entire Rocky Mountain region. The trails are maintained and immaculately groomed by the community for the visitor. For information on the Rendezvous Ski Trails and area ski-rental possibilities, call the West Yellowstone Chamber of Commerce at 646–7701.

For lodging while in "West," as the locals call it, consider the nearby *Hibernation Station*, 212 Gray Wolf Avenue. Luxurious, hand-built log cabin accommodations—featuring classic Old West artwork and furnishings—are available year-round, with nightly rates ranging between

$79 and $269. Rooms range from single queen units to large family cabins with kitchens included. Hibernation Station also maintains a hot-tub room, and some rooms boast private hot tubs as well. Obtain additional information or make reservations by calling (800) 580–3557. The enterprise also maintains a Web site: www.hibernationstation.com.

After exploring the wonders of Yellowstone, most of which lies within the borders of Wyoming, head north from Mammoth Hot Springs back into Montana. If you're struck by the beauty of the upper Yellowstone River region, you're not the first. Consider the words Crow Chief Arapooish once used to describe to a white fur trader why this country, the historic home of his people since the 1600s, was so special to them:

> The Crow country is a good country. The Great Spirit has put it in exactly the right place; when you are in it you fare well; whenever you go out of it, whichever way you travel, you fare worse. . . . Everything good is to be found there. There is no country like the Crow country.

The easiest way to find the next attraction in this uncommonly good country is to backtrack from the town of Gardiner. At the second bridge spanning the river south of town, 2½ miles inside the North Entrance of the park, you'll see a parking area. Pull in, hike the short trail leading down to the **Boiling River**, and enjoy a hot dip near the forty-fifth parallel, halfway between the equator and the North Pole.

Most of the park's thermal features are dangerous and therefore off-limits to swimming, but at Boiling River soaking has long been an accepted and relatively safe and common practice. Unfortunately, during the 1970s, rowdy parties also became common, culminating in two tragic drownings in 1982. This prompted the National Park Service to alter the rules at the hot springs, and today family-oriented soakers have largely supplanted the once-common party animals. The hours at the rustic river-cobble pools are 5:00 A.M. to 9:00 P.M. in summer; 5:00 A.M. to 6:00 P.M. in winter. During spring high water, the pools are closed altogether.

If you'd prefer to soak in lavish surroundings with all the amenities at hand, keep driving north on Highway 89 and into the alluring Paradise Valley. Before reaching your destination, however, there are a couple of highlights you shouldn't miss.

From Gardiner, it's a short side trip to **Jardine**, one of Montana's classic almost-ghost towns. Gold was first discovered in Bear Gulch in 1866, but no large-scale extracting operations were established until the turn of the century, when Harry Bush organized the Revenue Mining Company. The easier-to-get gold played out and Jardine nearly died, but it was resurrected in the 1920s as an arsenic-mining center. That substance's value as a pesticide lost favor in the 1940s, however, with the development of DDT, and again the town fell on hard times.

Today at Jardine, located 5 miles up Bear Gulch on the Jardine Road, you'll see the old residences of miners and the well-preserved remains of the Revenue forty-stamp gold mill. You'll also find that Jardine has yet again returned to life: In 1987 the Jardine Joint Venture began mining gold in the area. (All no trespassing signs in this area should be obeyed unquestionably because of the potentially dangerous minerals that were mined and exposed to the air.)

In Corwin Springs pull in for some good home cooking at the **Cinnabar Store** cafe and general store, owned and operated by the Church Universal and Triumphant. While church members and some of their activities are controversial topics in Park County, there's no debate over the quality of the moderately priced buffet and deli dishes served here—everyone who tries them likes them. Many of the fruits, vegetables, and meats used are grown on the adjacent, church-owned Royal Teton Ranch. The Cinnabar Store is open daily from 7:00 A.M. to 10:00 P.M. For information, call 848–7891.

The phrase *hardwood forest* takes on an uncommonly literal meaning at the **Gallatin Petrified Forest,** a 26,000-acre special management area set aside by the Forest Service in 1973. The petrified trees are the result of vol-

Hot Springs Celebrities

*D*on't be surprised if, while taking in the doins' at Chico Hot Springs, you spot someone who looks familiar, for the Paradise Valley has attracted more than its share of Hollywood celebrities. Among those who are or have been regulars at Chico: Peter Fonda, Dennis Quaid, Meg Ryan, and Jeff Bridges, who met his wife when she was working as a cocktail waitress there. Visitors of an earlier day included Steve McQueen, while even earlier on the scene were notables such as Teddy Roosevelt and the artist Charlie Russell.

Some swear that even today you can encounter certain turn-of-the century Chico regulars. The ghosts of Bill and Percie Knowles, who owned the resort in 1900, reportedly still frequent the halls of the main lodge, and Percie-sightings in a third-floor room have been reported by guests and employees alike. A psychic staying in the lodge in the late 1980s made repeated visits to the front desk to report that the hotel was inhabited by ghosts before the staff finally convinced her that, yes, they knew that, their names are Bill and Percie, and they're already accepted as residents!

canic activity in the region some fifty million years ago, when a mixture of ash and water covered standing forests. Through the centuries, silica-containing water percolated through and turned the trees to rock, while preserving their structure. The trees of rock then were lifted high above the valley when the mountains rose some thirty-five million years ago.

From the Tom Miner Campground, a trail new in 1991 leads for about $1/2$ mile up to a line of cliffs, where the remains of petrified trees can be found. A more strenuous hike of 3-miles-plus leads into the heart of the preserve, where there's much more to be seen, including tree trunks still standing. In that area it's permissible to pick up small pieces of petrified wood, provided you first obtain a collection permit from the Forest Service office in Gardiner or Bozeman.

To find Montana's hardest hardwood forest, travel 12 miles north from Corwin Springs on Highway 89 and then 12 miles on the gravel road leading southwest to the Tom Miner Campground. For more informa-

Fly-Fishing Central

*T*he Federation of Fly Fishers is a national organization headquartered in Livingston's old Lincoln School, at 215 East Lewis Street. In addition to its administrative offices, the FFF maintains a museum/education center at the facility.

Previously located in West Yellowstone, the FFF moved its offices to Livingston in the summer of 1994, largely due to the lobbying efforts of John Bailey, owner of Dan Bailey's Fly Shop. In the mid-1980s Bailey and other town leaders had unsuccessfully attempted to attract the FFF to Livingston's old Burlington Northern Depot (which today houses the Depot Center). When in 1993 the old three-story Lincoln School came up for sale, Bailey jumped in to action and formed the Lincoln School Foundation to raise funds to purchase the building and again try to lure the FFF to town.

This time the FFF took the bait offered by the city. And Livingston certainly is a fitting home for an organization representing more than 200,000 avid fly fishers: It boasts no fewer than a half-dozen fly shops, claims an unknown but very large number of outfitters and guides, embraces the legendary Yellowstone River, and is in close proximity to the Paradise Valley's numerous private spring creeks, which reputedly offer some of the best trout fishing found anywhere on earth. Livingston even landed the role of Missoula in A River Runs Through It, the Robert Redford film based on Norman Maclean's memorable novella concerning the interrelatedness of family, fishing, and religion.

The FFF's yearly calendar comprises a slate of clinics, classes, and other activities. For details call 585–7592.

tion, directions, and a map detailing the longer hike, call the Gardiner Ranger District at 848–7375.

Now, 12 miles farther north along Highway 89, at the town of Emigrant, turn east to cross the Yellowstone River and proceed to **Chico Hot Springs Lodge.** Rooms, chalets, and log cabins are available for rent, and the Continental cuisine served in the Chico Inn is expensive but good—so good that the establishment is rated by many as the best restaurant in Montana. Chico also boasts of its "gourmet junk food," obtainable poolside by those soaking in the lusciously warm waters. Chico's western-style saloon features live dance music on weekends. For information and for dinner and lodging reservations, call 333–4933 or (800) HOT–WADA! or go to the Web site www.chicohotsprings.com. The resort is open year-round.

In the historic railroading and tourist-servicing town of Livingston, stop at the **Depot Center,** located in the imposing old Northern Pacific railroad station at 200 West Park Street. The depot was designed by the Minnesota firm of Reed and Stem, the railroad-architecture specialists responsible for Grand Central Station in New York City. Built in 1901–1902 to the tune of $75,000, the building remains one of the most impressive ever constructed in Montana.

The depot was abandoned by the railroad in the 1980s, and members of the newly created Livingston Depot Foundation took it upon themselves to raise the funds necessary to restore the building to its original splendor. They clearly were successful, and today visitors find distinctive exhibits on railroading, Indian artifacts, western history and art, and more on permanent display at the Depot Center. Traveling exhibitions also are commonly shown; recent ones have included an impressive traveling art show from Russia and the "Beautiful, Daring Western Girls: Women of the Wild West Shows," on loan from the Buffalo Bill Historical Center in Cody, Wyoming. (Livingston was a fitting place for this show, for past residents have included the likes of Calamity Jane.)

The museum is open daily until 5:00 P.M., mid-May through early October, and is closed the rest of the year. Various community events are also held at the Depot Center throughout the year. For a schedule and other information, call 222–2300.

At the **Chatham Fine Art** gallery you'll find displayed originals by the owner, the well-known Montana writer, fisherman, painter, and intellectual good ol' boy, Russell Chatham. He's also a gourmand: Next door is **Chatham's Livingston Bar & Grille,** where the artist's dreamy, brooding landscapes are displayed and French country cuisine is served. Chatham's oils have captivated hundreds of worldly art collectors and scores of not-so-worldly ones, too. Also on display at Chatham Fine Art are the paintings, photographs, and handiwork of a select group of additional artists from the region. The gallery (222–1566) is open in summer Monday through Saturday from 10:00 A.M. to 5:00 P.M., and the rest of the year Tuesday through Saturday from 10:00 A.M. to 5:00 P.M. The restaurant (222–7909) is open daily year-round (5:30 to 10:00 P.M. in summer and 5:00 to 9:30 P.M. in winter). The Chatham complex is located in the 100 block of North Main. For additional information, and to view a sample of his works, visit Chatham's Web site at www.russellchatham.com.

In the classified section of the Saturday, January 6, 1917, Livingston newspaper a notice appeared for rentals available with "nicely furnished

Home on the Range

After making reservations to stay a Saturday night in late September at Livingston's historic **Murray Hotel***, I informed Nancy that I'd been told we might be holing up in the Sam Peckinpah Room. Peckinpah, the late movie director known for his bloody westerns and other violent flicks, stayed often at the Murray; in fact, he considered the hotel one of his homes.*

Naturally, I had in mind a room with a masculine decor, featuring plenty of dark-stained woodwork, leather furniture, and paintings of things like mallards and moose. As soon as we walked into our suite, though, Nancy began laughing loudly. It was as frilly a place as we'd ever seen, brimming with lace and trimmed with a color scheme that I'm certain Peckinpah would not have selected. I still don't know if that's the Sam Pekinpah Room—but if it is, I'd say it must have him rolling around in his grave at a pretty good clip.

In the mezzanine above the lobby we discovered a permanent display fea-turing the paintings of Parks Reece, whose work reminded me of a cross between Gary Larson's ("The Far Side") and that of Missoula's popular Monte Dolack. Hilarious stuff, and great to look at, too.

After arriving late that afternoon, it had been difficult even making it to the registration desk, and because of street barricades, we'd been forced to park two blocks away. The reason: Unbeknownst to us it was the day and evening of Livingston's annual Oktoberfest, and the celebrating was centered right in the lobby of the Murray and on the surrounding streets. Microbrew and bratwurst vendors were doing brisk businesses in the cold evening air. Cowboys and noncowboys alike were keeping warm by dipping and twirling in the crowded, vibrant streets, to the sounds of a hard-core country band. It definitely was a "Livingston Saturday Night" that would have done Jimmy Buffet proud.

bedrooms, heat and bath" at 122 South Yellowstone. Today at that address you'll find that the rooming house has become the *Greystone Bed and Breakfast*.

Given the history of the residence, it seems ironic that proprietors Gary and Lin Lee were forced to go through an arduous process of filing petitions, appearing at City Board of Adjustment hearings, responding to letters to the editor, and more in order to accomplish their goal of opening a bed-and-breakfast—a basically innocuous type of enterprise—in this residential neighborhood.

The visitor to wind-blown Livingston should savor the fact that the Lees were successful in their endeavor, for their turn-of-the-century, four-bedroom inn serves as an ideal home away from home when enjoying the local sights. At the Greystone, rooms rent for $90 per night, May 1 through September 30, and $70 in the off season. The price includes a sumptuous breakfast. There's also a cabin renting for $165, which has a kitchen and can accommodate four comfortably. Call 222-8319 for reservations.

Up Mission Canyon, approximately 12 miles southeast of Livingston at the base of the glorious Absaroka Range, awaits an altogether different sort of lodging. The *Sixty Three Ranch*, a Montana dude ranch of proud tradition, began operations in 1863 (hence its name), and since 1929 it's been in the hands of the same family, the Christensens. Still a working cattle spread in addition to its guest-serving function, in 1982 the Sixty Three became the first dude ranch in Montana to be listed as a National Historic Site.

Trail rides, hiking, photography workshops, pack trips into the Absarokas, bird-watching, and fishing on Mission Creek, which rambles through the ranch for a lengthy 3½ miles, are popular outdoor pursuits at the Sixty Three. Activities in or closer to the lodge include volleyball, horseshoes, billiards, square dancing, and "sweat-lodging." A week at the Sixty Three goes for $1,100 per adult and $960 per child eleven years and under. It includes a private cabin, three meals daily for seven days, and the use of a saddle horse and all ranch facilities. For reservations call 222–0570.

Big Timber to Red Lodge

Downtown Big Timber is interesting for its abundance of historic masonry buildings constructed toward the end of the Victorian Age. The *Grand Bed and Breakfast*, built in 1890 and once a center of social activity for Big Timber, served turn-of-the-century travelers who arrived in town on the railroad. The inn was recently renovated and now features seven rooms, most with shared bath, which rent for $59 to $145 per night. The rate includes a hearty breakfast. The old hotel includes a first-rate supper club, as well. You can call 932–4459 for reservations or visit www.thegrand-hotel.com to learn more.

The name may stink, but the food is great at the **Road Kill Cafe.** "From your grill to ours" is the slogan at the tongue-in-cheek eatery, where patrons are reminded, "This is not Burger King and you cannot have it your way."

Delicious hoagie sandwiches, hot chicken wings, and bear scat (deep-fried cheese balls) top the menu. Rest assured that as you dine, local cowboys and the occasional celebrity—the Boulder Valley is another hot spot for the stars, and Tom Brokaw, Brooke Shields, Michael Keaton,

Careful Where You Drive

*T*he puns run as wild as the wool-bearing beasts in Reedpoint at the annual **Big Montana Sheep Drive,** where in years past celebrities including Meryl Sheep and Ram-bo have been spotted. The event began as a spoofy spin-off of the well-publicized Montana Centennial Cattle Drive of 1989, but that first summer's sheep drive was successful beyond anyone's wildest dreams: It raised nearly $12,000—twice what organizers had optimistically expected and enough to add a wing to the town's library. "And I don't think we fleeced anybody," said one official.

Originally envisioned as a one-time happening, the unexpected success of the premier event prompted a "rebleat performance" in 1990. That summer the Associated Press reported: "They're ba-a-a-c-k.... While coyotes salivate in the hills, hundreds of sturdy Montana-bred woolies will charge down the six blocks of Main Street in an event some say is matched only by the running of the bulls in Pamplona, Spain."

The sheep drive now draws a crowd in excess of 8,000 to witness the wooly wonder of countless sheep darting through the street of tiny Reedpoint, population one hundred (give or take a few). The theme of a recent drive, in honor of upcoming November elections, was "Ewe've got to be kidding." Several Montana political candidates were there, providing the voters in attendance with an opportunity to decide in person—in the words of another event organizer— "who's trying to pull the wool over their eyes."

Also on the roster at the annual event are a sheepherder poetry reading, a sheep-shearing contest, a street dance and barbecue, and competitions for the ugliest sheep, prettiest ewe, and smelliest sheepherder. The Big Montana Sheep Drive is held in Reedpoint on the Sunday before Labor Day. Call 326-2288 for additional details.

and others have places nearby—will keep the adjacent McLeod Bar lively and the jukebox loud.

The Road Kill is located near the tiny town of McLeod, 16 miles south of Big Timber on Highway 298. Even if you're not hungry for road kill, the drive up the Boulder River, a nationally famous trout stream, is well worth the time spent. As you head upstream, fingers of timber begin reaching down from the slopes above as the mountains claim more and more cropland. Watch for deer on the road—the valley is swarming with them—or you may fashion a new creation for the cafe! The Road Kill Cafe can be reached by calling 932–6174.

Twelve miles south of McLeod on Highway 298 is *Natural Bridge State Monument*, whose name is now a misnomer, for the great arch that once spanned the Boulder River collapsed in 1988. But the 100-foot-high waterfall still flows strong, and the spot is as serene and seductive as ever. Trails radiate out from the parking area, leading to viewing sites above the falls.

If you leave I–90 at exit 384 a few miles west of Reedpoint and head south on gravel up the canyon of Bridger Creek, in 3½ miles you'll arrive at the *Buckin' Horse Bunkhouse*. You'd be hard pressed to find a prettier and more isolated piece of overnighting property anywhere. Horseback riding and fishing are popular activities for those bedding down in the attractive log cabin, which can sleep four and includes a washroom and basic kitchen facilities. There's also a room with a shared bath available in the adjacent main ranch house (it was featured in the June 1997 issue of *Log Home Living*). Call 932–6537 to make reservations or request further information, or check out their Web site at www.buckinhorse.com.

In Columbus, drop into the *New Atlas Bar*, an ancient masonry structure housing a collection of more mounted animal heads than Teddy Roosevelt could have shaken his big stick at. The interior of the old place is smoky, yellowed, and grimy, and in need of a good bath, but stop in and have a cool drink anyway. Among the dead critters on display are an albino deer, a two-headed calf, and a pair of battling bobcats, frozen in action.

For an altogether relaxing experience, arrange to stay at the *Tormgrimson Place*, located on the Bench Ranch a few miles south of Fishtail. (Fishtail is 20 miles southwest of Columbus on Highways 78 and 419.) From the outside, the guest house still looks like what it was: an old log cabin built around 1903. Only its sound roof, new white chinking, and unbroken windows distinguish it from a hundred other homesteaders' cabins in the region.

But on the inside of this old cabin, you'll discover a touch of the modern West and what might be termed *lavish-rustic* accommodations. Jack and Susan Heyneman, owners of the Bench Ranch, have surely performed a little miracle in creating this sanctuary.

You'll have the run of most of the Bench Ranch's 3,000 acres when staying over. The Heynemans, who operate the ranch under a conservation easement with the Montana Land Reliance, abide by the practices of Holistic Resource Management. In order to preserve the resources and protect the ecosystem for all living things, they use no chemical fertilizers or herbicides in raising their sheep and acclaimed red Angus cattle. (You can read more about the Bench Ranch in the Crow Country section of Wallace and Page Stegner's book, *American Places*.)

A stone's throw from the cabin is the sparkling West Rosebud River, perfect for tube-floating or fly-fishing (catch-and-release only on the ranch). And rising abruptly to the south are the crags of the Beartooth Range, the highest mountains in all of mountain-filled Montana.

The Tormgrimson place features two bedrooms with big, log-frame feather beds, a completely equipped kitchen, a living room with a wood fireplace, and plenty of western art on the walls and books on the shelves. And, as the Heynemans boast, no TV. For one full day the house rents for $200 ($225 for three people or more). You can also rent the place for an entire week—after which you almost certainly will not want to leave. Call 328–6923 for reservations and detailed directions to the place.

Two bar-restaurant combinations within only a few miles of the Tormgrimson Place could readily throw your taste buds into a tug-of-war. It's a toss-up as to which is the better; about the only way for you to decide is to stay at the Tormgrimson place for two days minimum and sample supper at both.

The **Trout Hole Restaurant** is one of three businesses found at the Montana Hanna's complex in Dean, 8 miles southwest of Fishtail on Highway 419. (The other two are the Stillwater Saloon and the Fish Montana Fly Shop.) The soup and steaks are great at the Trout Hole, and the rack of barbecued pork ribs is beyond belief. Vintage snowshoes, skis, and fly-fishing gear adorn the walls, making the place feel downright Montana homey. Call 328–6780 for information and reservations.

Option number two: the **Grizzly Bar** in Roscoe, whose regulars for years have included local sheep and cattle ranchers and others from far afield and all walks of life. The interior is classic West, with cattle brands burned into the woodwork, while outside the East Rosebud

Grizzly Bar, Roscoe

River rushes by under a cover of huge cottonwoods, and a life-size grizzly bear roars down from the roof at those entering. The establishment is open daily, serving meals between 11:00 A.M. and 9:00 P.M.; call 328–6789 for reservations.

From Roscoe wend your way toward Red Lodge along the gravel roads paralleling Highway 78 to experience some real Montana backcountry. The roads are poorly marked—they're mostly for the benefit of local ranchers who already know where they are—so you may become temporarily lost here or there. If so, just ask a local for directions.

The annual *Festival of Nations* has been staged in the mountain town of Red Lodge for nearly fifty years. Conducted in early August, the festival is dedicated to promoting peace and goodwill among the citizens of all countries of the world. Ethnic crafts, foods, and music are featured throughout, and each of the nine days is designed around a different nation. Nearly 15,000 visitors participate in the sing-alongs, street dances, and dozens of other activities. You can find out more about the Festival of Nations by calling the Red Lodge Chamber of Commerce at 446–1718 or logging on to their Web site at www.wtp.net/redlodge.

Red Lodge is a popular destination year-round, with downhill and Nordic skiing popular during winter and dozens of diversions readily at hand in the summer. Like most tourist-serving towns, Red Lodge has spawned its share of restaurants, T-shirt shops, gift stores, and other businesses, some more unusual and interesting than others. Among the more interesting is *Kibler and Kirch*, found at 22 North Broadway in the Home Place Building, where you'll want to stop in to lust over the wide selection of lavish furnishings. Most of the merchandise sports a uniquely Montana flair: log and iron furniture, original sculptures, wil-

Long in the Beartooth

Early in the twentieth century a group of Red Lodge-vicinity citizens, headed by a medical doctor named Dr. J. C. F. Siegfriedt, dreamed of building a new road to Yellowstone, an attraction that would bring in an influx of sorely needed tourism dollars. The vision of the physician and his fellows came true in 1931, thanks largely to their lobbying, when President Hoover signed into law the Leavitt Bill, which included the "Park Approach Act." Crews from the Civilian Conservation Corps and a number of private contractors commenced construction, finishing their astounding, $2.5-million task in June 1936. The full length of the Beartooth Highway they constructed extends 68 miles, from Red Lodge to the Northeast Entrance of Yellowstone.

low baskets, classy picture frames featuring classic cowboy scenes, and a whole lot more. The women who own the shop also offer a full range of home and business decorating services.

This store somehow appeals even to those of us who aren't natural-born shoppers. For more information on Kibler and Kirch, open daily, call 446–2802 or E-mail the good folks at kibler@wtp.net.

Another shop worth visiting is **Magpie Toymakers**, located at 115 North Broadway. The front of the store is dedicated to 101 types of toys on display, handmade and otherwise, many of them wonderfully whimsical. The back half is shop space, where visitors watch toymakers creating their articles of amusement. You can call Magpie Toymakers at 446–3044.

Finally, before heading up the big hill, appease your sweet tooth by swinging into the **Montana Candy Emporium**, housed in the old 1925 Iris Theater. The large assortment of candy inside is reason enough to wander into the old building, but once there you may be drawn away from the candy containers to the wall filled with historic photos and posters. The wall honors Red Lodge—area rodeo stars, including the celebrated Greenough and Linderman families, both of which have claimed national champions among their clans.

If the rodeo display intrigues you, you'll find more about the Greenough family and Red Lodge rodeoing at the **Carbon County Historical Museum**, located at the south end of town and open daily from Memorial Day through Labor Day. Also on display is the intact homestead cabin of legendary mountain man John Johnston, better known as "Liver Eatin' Johnson," who served for a spell as the first constable of Red Lodge.

Don't leave Yellowstone Country before negotiating the **Beartooth National Scenic Byway**, arguably the most beautiful and exciting roadway in America. In a typical year, the road cresting lofty, 10,947-foot Beartooth Pass is open to cars from Memorial Day through mid-October (and to snowmobiles the remainder of the year), although brief snowstorms can cause temporary closures even in the middle of summer.

YELLOWSTONE COUNTRY

If you tackle the byway in early summer, in places you'll be driving through a virtual tunnel of snow, with high snowbanks lining both sides of the road. Kids will get a kick out of battling it out with snowballs in the middle of summer. One day each July, on an undisclosed date that changes with the year, the Red Lodge Chamber of Commerce opens their Top of the World Bar, offering nonalcoholic drinks and world-class photo opportunities to those who stop by.

Columbus, the seat of Stillwater County, was originally known as Sheep Dip.

In 1989 the Nashville-based Gibson Guitar Company opened a manufacturing plant in Bozeman, where today they build their world-famous acoustic guitars, mandolins, and banjoes.

Once you reach the high, treeless alpine realm of the Hellroaring Plateau, trails beckon. The broad and surprisingly gentle landscape is dotted with small lakes, many of them brimming with golden, brook, and cutthroat trout. Dozens of varieties of tiny, colorful wildflowers blanket the ground during the short growing season; you might also notice polygons formed in the ground's surface, the product of constant freezing and thawing.

From Red Lodge, the 68-mile Beartooth Highway switchbacks its way up, up, up. It dips into Wyoming before veering north to return to Montana and then connects with the isolated outpost of Cooke City, Montana, and the Northeast Entrance into Yellowstone National Park. For more information on the roadway, call 446–2103.

The remote ***Pryor Mountains National Wild Horse Range*** occupies the extreme southeast corner of Carbon County and an adjacent chunk of Wyoming. The Secretary of the Interior in 1968 designated this 30,000-acre area as the first federal wild horse range.

Some believe the resident horses are direct descendants of the mustangs brought to North America by the Spanish conquistadors in the 1500s, and that the isolation provided by the area's deep canyons and remote mountains have kept them genetically pure. Others, typically those less fond of wild horses, are quick to argue that the horses descend from domesticated stock that escaped or was released back into the wilds, and that they're no more closely related to the Spanish mustangs than are the horses seen in every other farmer's pasture. Lending credence to the former theory is the fact that some of the Pryor Mountain horses lack the sixth lumbar vertebra, as the wild mustangs did.

Regardless of their genetic heritage, horses run wild along the eastern and southern fringes of the Custer National Forest and on adjacent Bureau of Land Management lands. In the past, the isolated Pryor Mountains also have been home during parts of the year to the Crow

Indians and to a rich legacy of Native Americans preceding them. It's estimated that more than a thousand cultural sites are hidden in these hills, so watch closely for evidence of prehistoric human beings.

The range is reachable by dirt roads, some impassable when wet, leading southeast from the town of Warren. If you prefer to get there entirely on pavement, first go to Lovell, Wyoming, and then negotiate the 25-mile Bad Pass Road between that town and Barry's Landing, Montana. Bighorn sheep can often be seen close to the Bad Pass Road in the fall, near the Devil Canyon Overlook. Another good strategy for seeing bighorn sheep and wild horses: Hike into the juniper-studded canyon behind the Hough Creek Ranger Station, where a natural spring attracts the animals.

This is exceedingly remote country, so obtain good travel directions and stock up on water and provisions before striking out. Call 248–9885 or 666–2412 for maps and additional information.

**PLACES TO STAY
IN YELLOWSTONE COUNTRY**

THREE FORKS
Sacajawea Hotel,
5 North Main;
(406) 285–6515

Broken Spur Motel,
124 West Elm;
(406) 285–3237

Fort Three Forks Motel,
10776 U.S. Highway 287;
(406) 285–3233

Bud Lilly's Angler's Retreat,
16 West Birch;
(406) 285–6690

BOZEMAN
Fairfield Inn by Marriott,
828 Wheat Drive;
(406) 587–2222

Holiday Inn, 5 Baxter Lane;
(800) 366–5101

Voss Inn,
319 South Willson;
(406) 587–0982

Silver Forest Inn, 15325
Bridger Canyon Road;
(406) 586–1882

Lehrkind Mansion
Bed & Breakfast,
corner of East Aspen and
North Wallace;
(406) 585–6932

Gallatin Gateway Inn,
12 miles southwest of
Bozeman; (406) 763–4672

Gallatin National Forest
Recreational Cabins,
various locations;
(406) 522–2520

WEST YELLOWSTONE
Stage Coach Inn,
209 Madison Avenue;
(800) 842–2882

Three Bear Lodge,
217 Yellowstone Avenue;
(406) 646–7353

West Yellowstone
Conference Hotel,
315 Yellowstone Avenue;
(406) 646–7365

Comfort Inn,
638 Madison Avenue;
(406) 646–4212

Firehole Ranch,
situated northwest of town
on the southwest side of
Hebgen Lake;
(406) 646–7294

LIVINGSTON
Paradise Inn,
U.S. Highway 89 at I–90;
(800) 437–6291

The Murray Hotel,
201 West Park;
(406) 222–1350

Comfort Inn,
114 Love Lane;
(406) 222–4400

Super 8,
105 Centennial Drive;
(800) 800–8000

Greystone Inn Bed & Breakfast, 122 S. Yellowstone Street; (406) 222–8319

The River Inn on the Yellowstone, 4950 Highway 89 South; (406) 222–2429

RED LODGE
The Pollard Hotel, 2 North Broadway; (406) 446–0001

Yodeler Motel, 601 South Broadway; (406) 446–1435

Super 8, 1223 South Broadway; (800) 800–8000

Pitcher Guest Houses, various locations; (406) 446–2859

Rock Creek Resort, 4 miles south on U.S. Highway 12; (406) 446–1111

PLACES TO EAT IN YELLOWSTONE COUNTRY

THREE FORKS
Sacajawea Inn, 5 North Main; (406) 285–6515

Headwaters Restaurant, 105 South Main; (406) 285–4511

Willow Creek Cafe and Saloon, located 7 miles south of Three Forks in Willow Creek; (406) 285–3698

Land of Magic Dinner Club, 6 miles east of Three Forks in Logan; (406) 284–3794

BOZEMAN
Azteca (Mexican), 134 East Main; (406) 586–5181

The Baxter (Italian and other), 105 West Main; (406) 586–1314

Fred's Mesquite Grill, northwest corner of Church and Main; (406) 585–8558

MacKenzie River Pizza Company, 232 East Main; (406) 587–0055

Pickle Barrel, East Main downtown and in the university area at 809 West College; (406) 587–2411.

WEST YELLOWSTONE
Stage Coach Inn, 209 Madison Avenue; (406) 646–7381

The Gusher (pizza, etc.), corner of Madison & Dunraven; (406) 646–9050

Jocee's Baking Company, located on Canyon Street; (406) 646–9737

Oregon Short Line Restaurant, located in the West Yellowstone Conference Hotel at 315 Yellowstone Avenue; (406) 646–7365

Three Bear Restaurant, 205 Yellowstone Avenue; (406) 646–7811

LIVINGSTON
Chatham's Livingston Bar & Grille, 130 North Main; (406) 222–7909

Winchester Cafe & Grill, 201 West Park (in the Murray Hotel); (406) 222–2708

The Wok, 117 West Park; (406) 222–9009

The Pickle Barrel, 113 West Park; (406) 222–5469

The Pizza Garden, 101 North Main; (406) 222–7400

RED LODGE
Bridge Creek Backcountry Kitchen & Wine Bar, 106 West 12th; (406) 446–9900

Gunsmoke Bar-B-Que, 403 North Broadway; (406) 446–1897

Round Barn Restaurant & Dinner Theater, 2 miles north of town on U.S. Highway 212; (406) 446–1197

Old Piney Dell Restaurant, at the Rock Creek Resort; (406) 446–1111

Custer—Missouri River Country

Custer Country and Missouri River Country encompass two of the state's designated travel regions. Combined, the two "countries" cover the eastern third of Montana, a region teeming with wide-open vistas and creatures such as mule deer and pronghorn antelope, but lacking in humans. The twenty-one counties included are inhabited by just over 200,000 people—a figure that is particularly impressive once you consider that more than half of them live in Yellowstone County, Montana's most populous county (home to Billings, the state's largest city). So, as you can imagine, the twenty counties excluding Yellowstone offer some uncrowded possibilities, indeed.

This route begins in that major city of Billings, with side trips leading east to Pompeys Pillar, north to Roundup, and south to the Crow Indian Reservation and Bighorn Canyon National Recreation Area. From Hardin you'll travel to the outback of extreme southeast Montana. Miles City, Baker, and Glendive, towns you may or may not have heard of, are the major "metropolitan areas" in this part of the state. From there you'll drive to the Big Open, the most remote and least visited region of this immense state. From Jordan, after leading you on a loop around the northeast corner of Montana—through towns that include Circle, Sidney, Culbertson, and Plentywood—the route covers the country north of monstrous Fort Peck Lake, where settlements with names like Glasgow and Saco grace the broad prairie expanses.

Crow Country

It is easy to draw generalizations about Montana's larger towns: Missoula, for instance, is a timber town, while Butte's economy is based on mineral extraction, and Bozeman is an agricultural center. Billings, nestled against the rimrocks carved by the Yellowstone River,

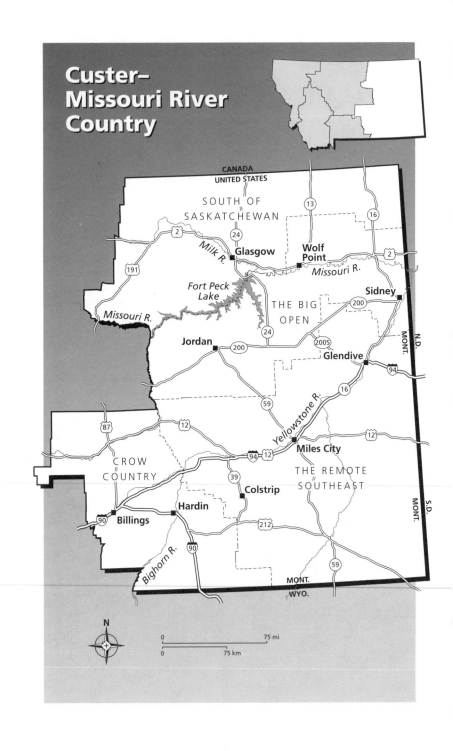

Custer–Missouri River Country

CANADA
UNITED STATES

SOUTH OF SASKATCHEWAN

13

16

2

24

Milk R.

Glasgow

Wolf Point

Missouri R.

191

Fort Peck Lake

THE BIG OPEN

Sidney

200

Missouri R.

Jordan

200

200S

Glendive

94

24

16

N.D.
MONT.

59

Yellowstone R.

87

12

12

Miles City

12

94 12

CROW COUNTRY

39

THE REMOTE SOUTHEAST

Colstrip

S.D.
MONT.

Hardin

90 Billings

212

Bighorn R.

90

59

MONT.
WYO.

N

0   75 mi
0   75 km

has perhaps the most diverse economy of any city in Montana, with an emphasis on cattle, farming, and minerals—specifically, oil.

You might begin touring the Magic City by driving up to the rimrocks via Twenty-seventh Street, then turning east onto Highway 3 and, in 1 mile, right onto the Black Otter Trail. As you bang along this chuckholed road, you'll catch breath-stealing glimpses of the river basin below. At just over 2 miles is a turnaround; as you circle a knob in another ¾ mile, stop at *Yellowstone Kelly's Grave*, which is set off by a split-rail cedar fence.

A sign at Kelly's gravesite reads:

A LONG BREACH-LOADING SPRINGFIELD RIFLE COVERED FROM MUZZLE TO STOCK WITH THE SKIN OF A HUGE BULLSNAKE WAS CARRIED BY MAJOR LUTHER SAGE 'YELLOWSTONE' KELLY, SHAKESPEARE-QUOTING INDIAN FIGHTER AND SCOUT. KELLY, A NEW YORKER BORN APRIL 19, 1849, AND CIVIL WAR VETERAN, GUIDED GOVERNMENT EXPEDITIONS IN THE 1870S AND '80S IN THE YELLOWSTONE RIVER VALLEY. HE LATER SERVED WITH THE MILITARY IN ALASKA AND THE PHILIPPINES AND THEN RETIRED TO CALIFORNIA BEFORE HIS DEATH DECEMBER 17, 1928. HE ASKED TO BE BURIED ON THIS POINT OVERLOOKING THE AREA HE HAD SCOUTED. . . . YELLOWSTONE KELLY WAS THE LITTLE BIG MAN WITH A BIG HEART.

You can appreciate why Kelly so loved this spot, for the view is splendid (the smoke-belching refinery immediately below notwithstanding): the city, the Yellowstone River Valley, the Pryor Mountains, and, beyond, the distant Beartooths, Bighorns, and other ranges. Early morning is the best time to visit the tranquil spot, before the city below has awakened.

The *Moss Mansion*, at 914 Division Street, is a piece of opulent evidence left behind by one who profited handsomely from the natural wealth of this country. The veritable castle of stone-block construction, with its red-tiled roof, remains nearly unchanged from the day in 1903 when the Preston B. Moss family moved into their new domicile. It cost $105,000 to build the mansion—this at a time when the price for an average house was about $3,000.

BEST ATTRACTIONS

Chief Plenty Coup Memorial Park,
Pryor; 252–1289

Rosebud Battlefield State Monument,
between Busby and Decker; 232–0900

Range Riders Museum and Memorial Hall,
Miles City; 232–4483

Medicine Rocks State Park,
Ekalaka; 232–0900

Makoshika State Park,
Glendive; 365–6256

Evelyn Cameron Gallery,
Terry; 635–4040 or 635–5442

Fort Union Trading Post,
Fairview;
(701) 572–9083
(visitor center is in North Dakota)

Medicine Lake National Wildlife Refuge,
Medicine Lake; 789–2305

Grandruds' Lefse Shack,
Opheim; 762–3250

Sleeping Buffalo Resort,
Saco; 527–3370

Moss Mansion, Billings

Moss, who moved to Billings in 1892, became president and owner of the First National Bank and delved into numerous other enterprises, including the hotel, utilities, and publishing businesses. Many of his family's original furnishings decorate the ornate rooms of the three-story house, which was designed by famous turn-of-the-century architect Henry Janeway Hardenbergh. Finely woven Persian rugs, stained glass, and woodwork of polished mahogany, oak, and red birch were all used extensively, lending rich tones and a vibrancy to the library, lounge, and other rooms.

For decades the mansion was cloaked in secrecy, as Miss Melville Moss continued living there alone after the rest of her family had passed away. A hedge eventually covered the lower level, so that only second- and third-story windows were visible to those passing by, and rarely was anyone seen being admitted into the house by its lone resident. Miss Moss died at the age of eighty-eight in 1984, and soon thereafter Billings residents finally had the opportunity to view what lay inside the mansion long camouflaged by brush and ivy vines. Its elegance stunned visitors, and a community-wide determination quickly mounted to save the grand home.

No secret today, the Moss Mansion has even been discovered by Hollywood. Several scenes of *Son of the Morning Star*, a television miniseries about George Armstrong Custer, were shot in its interior.

The nonprofit Billings Preservation Society administers the mansion and raises funds for its maintenance. Guided tours are offered on the hour from 10:00 A.M. to 4:00 P.M. daily in summer, with reduced hours in winter (1:00 to 3:00 P.M.); admission is $6.00 for adults and $3.00 for children twelve and under. For information on the many seasonal events held at the Moss Mansion, call 256–5100.

Duffers will find a most unusual course at the *Circle Inn Golf Links*, located behind the Circle Inn restaurant. The entire nine-hole course is less than 800 yards long, or about one-quarter as long as a typical course, and the average hole is only 89 yards. A round takes less than an hour,

MAJOR ATTRACTIONS WORTH SEEING

ZooMontana,
Billings

Little Bighorn Battlefield
National Monument,
Hardin

and even novices will have a good time without holding up the players behind.

A round of golf, cocktails, and dinner at the Circle Inn, featuring some of the best beef cuts to be found in this beef eater's town, is a popular way for Billings residents to while away a summer evening, when lights permit play to continue until 1:00 A.M. The golf links and restaurant are located at 1029 Main; green fees are $5.00 for nine or eighteen holes ($6.00 after 6:00 P.M.), and you can rent the two or three clubs needed. For dinner reservations and more information, call 248–4201.

Another terrific restaurant, with fare that's a little more exotic: **Mikado,** located right downtown at 109 North Broadway (252–8278).

Billings citizens are justifiably proud of their **Riverfront Park**, a greenbelt featuring a system of trails and recreation sites surrounding two small lakes. One of them, Lake Josephine, was named after the sternwheeler *Josephine,* which reached Billings in June 1875—the farthest upstream a steamboat ever made it on the Yellowstone River. Cycling, canoeing, picnicking, bird-watching, and fishing are all popular activities in the summer, while ice-skating on the lakes and cross-country skiing on the 2-mile Lake Loop and 3-mile Forest Loop trails gain favor in the colder months. The park, open from 5:00 A.M. to 10:00 P.M. daily, is located along Mulowney Avenue, just south of King Avenue (exit 446) on Interstate 90.

Before leaving the Billings area, take a trip along the scenic, 5-mile back road leading to **Pictograph Cave State Historic Site**, where some of Montana's most significant archaeological finds were unearthed. Take the Lockwood interchange on Interstate 90 (exit 452) and turn right at the stoplight and then immediately right again at the sign pointing toward the pictographs. In $2\frac{1}{4}$ miles the road turns to gravel and descends into a dramatic, sandstone-rim canyon, punctuated with stands of ponderosa pine. After $2\frac{3}{4}$ miles of gravel is the parking area, from which a narrow asphalt trail winds steeply up into the caves.

Pictograph Cave was named a national historic landmark in 1964, and in 1969 the Montana Department of Fish, Wildlife and Parks assumed responsibility for its protection. It's now open to visitors, at an admission fee of $3.00 per car, year-round from 8:00 A.M. to 8:00 P.M. For more information call 245–0227.

From 5 miles north of Billings on Highway 87, turn east onto old Highway 10 and take a side trip through the verdant portion of the

Yellowstone River Valley known as the Huntley Project, a shortened version of the Huntley Irrigation Project. The Bureau of Reclamation opened the headgates for the irrigation project in 1907, making it one of the first of its kind after Congress passed the Reclamation Act of 1902. The project comprises four towns—Huntley, Ballantine, Worden, and Pompeys Pillar.

Prehistoric Montana

*T*here's not a lot of evidence remaining at Pictograph Cave of the early Americans who once resided there, but by using one's imagination it's not hard to picture a place swarming with prehistoric human activity.

Amid the harsh environment of the prehistoric plains, the surrounding area was an unusually attractive spot to reside. Water was abundant, and the caves are situated such that they're protected from cold northerly winds and are hit full-force by the sun's warming rays during the short days of winter. Moreover, the point where Bitter Creek, the stream just below the parking lot, empties into the Yellowstone River was a natural river ford. For millennia animals traveled the route, and for centuries people followed.

Dozens of edible foods were available in the pine- and bramble-filled ravines surrounding the caves: fruits like chokecherry, wild grape, gooseberry, currants, and buffaloberry; and roots, bulbs, and herbs, such as arrow-leaf balsam root, wild onion, asparagus, wild turnip, and yucca.

The three rock overhangs lining the Eagle Sandstone cliffs are known as Ghost Cave, Pictograph Cave, and the smaller and shallower Middle Cave. The floors of Ghost and Pictograph were excavated by a Works Progress Administration crew in 1937; 30,000 artifacts were recovered at several distinct levels of occupation. Projectile points, stone knives, and animal bones were dug from as deep as 40 feet below the ground surface in Pictograph, the largest of the three caves. Among the most significant finds unearthed were the rock paintings, also of various ages, on the wall of Pictograph. (Although badly faded, some of these can still be made out.)

In 1940, William T. Mulloy, a doctoral candidate at the University of Chicago, took over the project. Most of the excavations were already completed, so Mulloy's primary task was to inspect and interpret what had been found. He concluded that the Empty Gulch area had been occupied during four distinct periods, ranging from around 2600 B.C. to historic times. The chronology Mulloy devised to relate specific artifacts to particular time periods became the standard still used to date artifacts found throughout the Great Plains. Mulloy went on to a long and distinguished career at the University of Wyoming and became well known in the archaeological world for additional works on the plains and on isolated Easter Island in the Pacific Ocean.

CUSTER–MISSOURI RIVER COUNTRY

"A thousand smiles and a million memories" await those who visit the **Huntley Project Museum of Irrigated Agriculture**, at the site of the former town of Osborn in Homesteader Park, 3 miles east of Huntley. The museum, featuring artifacts used in the early days of farming and irrigation, details the way in which this dry country was converted into the lush, crop-filled valley seen today. Perhaps the best time to visit is on the third weekend in July, when the Huntley Project Lions Club hosts the celebration known as Homesteader Days at Homesteader Park.

Garryowen, a name attached to a small town near the Little Bighorn Battlefield National Monument, is taken from a popular Irish tune that served as the official song of George Custer's 7th Cavalry.

The town of Pompeys Pillar, at the eastern end of the Huntley Project, was named after **Pompeys Pillar National Historic Landmark**, the nearby, prominent sandstone butte. On his trip back east through the Yellowstone Valley in 1806, Captain William Clark carved his name on the face of the butte, where it can still be seen today. This is significant because it's the only known physical evidence remaining in Montana from the Lewis and Clark expedition.

Long before Captain Clark visited on July 25, 1806, the butte was known as a good camping spot by American Indians, and Clark found that numerous petroglyphs had been carved into its face by his predecessors. Quite taken with the view after climbing to the summit, Clark wrote that he could see the snow-capped Rockies to the southwest and the Bull Mountains to the northwest, while huge numbers of buffalo, elk, and wolves were on the prairie before him.

Clark called the feature "Pompy's Tower" in honor of Baptiste Charbonneau, Sacajawea's young son, whom Clark had nicknamed Pompy, or "little chief" in Shoshonean. The name was changed to Pompeys Pillar when the journals of Lewis and Clark were published in 1814.

The pillar figured heavily for the next several decades as a landmark for trappers and explorers and as a campsite for both Indians and U.S. troops. When the Northern Pacific Railroad was completed in 1882, Pompeys Pillar became a popular stop, and the railroad placed a protective grate over Clark's signature. The landmark was privately held from 1906 until 1991, when it and the surrounding 366 acres were purchased, for just under $900,000, by the Bureau of Land Management. The site is being progressively developed and is open to the public Memorial Day through Labor Day from 8:00 A.M. to 8:00 P.M. daily and through the rest of September from 9:00 A.M. to 5:00 P.M. daily. For information call 875–2233 or 896–5000.

Before heading south to the Crow and Cheyenne reservations, consider a loop trip north to the broad sweep of rolling farm and ranch country surrounding the Musselshell River. Begin the 120-mile route by going northwest on Highway 3 through Acton and Broadview, then cross the Musselshell and turn east onto Highway 12 at Lavina. In another 20 miles you'll arrive at Roundup, which served as the kick-off point for the Great Centennial Cattle Drive of 1989. Thousands of head of cattle were moved to Billings by some 3,500 drive participants, who ranged from saddle-sure cowboys to saddle-sore novices.

A few miles northwest of Roundup is *Lake Mason National Wildlife Refuge,* a 16,000-acre stretch of prairie marsh and adjacent uplands that provide ample opportunity to see an assortment of critters. Migrating waterfowl, like Canada geese and white pelicans, are common during the spring and fall, and nesting shorebirds, such as avocets and sandpipers, can be seen during the summer. Watch also for pronghorn antelope, coyotes, and red fox.

The verdant scent of the marsh and its buzz of activity, especially during the evening and early morning, make the place seem uncommonly alive in contrast with the surrounding dry and quiet prairie. To reach the refuge, take Golf Course Road west from town, turn right in about 6 miles, and arrive at Lake Mason in another 3 miles.

From Roundup, Highway 87 leads south over the Bull Mountains and back to Montana's largest city. From the Interstate 90 Lockwood Interchange (exit 452), go south for ½ mile and turn right onto Old Pryor Road. The road soon rolls into a stunning landscape of timbered buttes, sandstone cliffs, and bottomlands brimming with hayfields and huge cottonwoods—in all, some of southeast Montana's prettiest country. From the ridge tops along the route, you'll earn long-range vistas of this land, historic home to the nomadic Plains Indians and to endless herds of buffalo.

After 10 miles, turn right, following Old Pryor Road. On reaching the Crow Indian village of Pryor in another 23 miles, turn right at the stop sign, go ¾ mile, and turn into *Chief Plenty Coups Memorial Park.* This park celebrates *Aleck-chea-ahoosh*—which translates to "Many Achievements" or "Plenty Coups"—the last great war chief of the Crow. It's an uncommonly peaceful place: The Castle Buttes of the Pryor Mountains rise to the south, and Pryor Creek gurgles below a stand of box elders near the base of a protective sandstone rim on the north. Black-capped chickadees, revealed through Plenty Coups' dreams as his own good medicine, flutter about.

The park museum houses Plenty Coups's personal items and displays examining the Crow culture, and nearby is the chief's stout, square-hewn log house. The original central section of the house was built around 1885, the eastern portion in 1906, and the west wing was added at an unknown date; its fireplace was constructed of bricks salvaged from Fort Custer, which was situated near present-day Hardin. It is said that Plenty Coups drank daily from the Medicine Springs, still flowing beneath the huge cottonwoods next to his house, the waters of which he considered a source of strength and power.

Chief Plenty Coups Memorial Park is open from 8:00 A.M. to 8:00 P.M. daily (with the museum open 10:00 A.M. to 5:00 P.M.) May through September, and between October and April by appointment. Admission is 50 cents per person; for more information call 252–1289 or visit the Web site www.nezperce.com/pcmain.html.

Follow the paved road leading east from Pryor for some 35 miles to Saint Xavier, then turn south onto Highway 313, and shortly you'll arrive at the *Bighorn Canyon National Recreation Area*. Most of the

Plenty Coups

*P*lenty Coups was born near present-day Billings in 1848 and died in 1932. Inviting, grassy picnic sites surround his grave, where Strikes the Iron and Kills Together, two of Plenty Coups's wives, also are buried. (In Crow fashion, after the death of Kills Together, Plenty Coups took her sister, Strikes the Iron, as his next wife.) An American flag flutters atop a tall pole, reminding us that here lies not only a great Indian chief, but also an American hero.

When chosen to represent all Indians of the Americas in a ceremony at the Tomb of the Unknown Soldier in 1921, Plenty Coups's brief but stirring speech was said to have brought tears to the eyes of more than one old hard-edged cavalry man: "For the Indians of America I call upon the Great Spirit . . . that the dead should not

have died in vain, the war might end and peace be purchased by the blood of red men and white." It was on this trip east that Plenty Coups visited George Washington's Mount Vernon, instilling in him the idea of donating his home as a historic site for the enjoyment of the American people.

Plenty Coups was a proud Indian who had come to terms with the whites, realizing that to continue fighting them would do more harm than good for the Crows. A proponent of goodwill among all people, when deeding his property to the nation in 1928, Plenty Coups asserted that it must be a park for all people to use together. "It is given as a token of my friendship for all people, both red and white," he said, further stipulating that the park was not to be a memorial to him alone, but to the entire Crow Nation.

63,000-acre recreational haven, straddling the Montana-Wyoming border, is easily reachable only by boat, on the waters of 71-mile-long Bighorn Lake. The northernmost 47 miles of the reservoir lap against the walls of the dazzling, multihued Bighorn Canyon, considered by many as this region's small-scale version of the Grand Canyon.

Up Rosebud Creek

*A*nother battle, much better known and documented than the Crow-Piegan skirmish mentioned later, took place about 30 miles away as the raven flies, at the Little Bighorn Battlefield National Monument. At this major attraction the National Park Service maintains outstanding interpretive displays and facilities. Yet another battle—somewhere between these two in importance and public awareness—exploded several miles southeast of the Little Bighorn. It was the Battle of the Rosebud, where General George Crook and forces were attacked on June 17, 1876, by the same Sioux and Cheyenne warriors who annihilated Custer and his troops eight days later along the Little Bighorn.

Crook's army consisted of 1,000 cavalry and infantry troops, along with roughly 450 Crow and Shoshone warriors and aides. Among the warriors: a twenty-eight-year-old Crow Indian named Plenty Coups. Crook, an old-hat Indian fighter, was moving his men north from Fort Fetterman, Wyoming, as one line of a huge military operation designed to close in on "hostiles" along the Bighorn, Tongue, and Powder Rivers. However, before nearing the other two parties, which were coming in from central Montana and Bismarck, Dakota Territory, Crook was trapped and repeatedly attacked on Rosebud Creek by Crazy Horse and his warriors.

Although Crook later maintained that he won the battle, just about anyone who was there would have said otherwise. The Cheyenne-Sioux victory at Rosebud Creek readied the Indians, mentally and physically, for the battle a week later, in which George Armstrong Custer and his detachment out of Bismarck were decimated. Not incidentally, when Custer attacked the Indian encampment on the Little Bighorn, he fully believed Crook's soldiers and warriors were still heading in his direction, and that they would be there to provide backup if needed. In reality, though, they'd been turned back at the Battle of the Rosebud and had retreated into Wyoming.

Today at **Rosebud Battlefield State Monument,** you'll find a well-preserved buffalo jump, displays on pioneer cattle-ranching efforts in the area, and a self-guiding tour interpreting the battle's back-and-forth action. To get there, from I–90 go east on U.S. Highway 212 for approximately 25 miles. Just inside the Northern Cheyenne Indian Reservation, but before reaching Busby, turn south onto Route 314. You'll come to the battlefield site in about 20 miles. Don't look for a water supply or restrooms, but do keep your eyes peeled for rattlesnakes. For additional information you can call Montana Fish, Wildlife & Parks in Miles City at 232–0900.

Afterbay Reservoir, the 2-mile stretch of water between Yellowtail Dam and the much smaller Afterbay Dam, has garnered a reputation as an extraordinary spot for winter bird-watching. Meanwhile, the waters downstream from Afterbay Dam are a nationally known, blue-ribbon trout fishery.

At the Yellowtail Visitor Center, operated by the National Park Service for the Bureau of Reclamation, you'll find displays on Crow tribal history and the Yellowtail Dam, which was constructed in the late 1960s, as well as exhibits explaining how the project helps to serve the irrigation, hydro-electric, recreation, and flood control needs of the region. You'll also learn about the rich natural history and prehistory of the region, and perhaps you'll pick up a tip on where to hike to find an ancient buffalo jump or vision-quest site. Inquire here also about arranging a ranger-led tour to the site of Fort C. E. Smith (now on private land), established in 1866 to protect gold prospectors traveling the Bozeman Trail from attack by Sioux Indians. The visitor center is open daily from 9:00 A.M. to 5:30 P.M., Memorial Day through Labor Day, and on an abbreviated schedule the rest of the year. Call 666–2412 for additional information.

As you drive through this area, gaze up at the cliffs above the Grapevine Creek Drainage. According to Crow Indian history and also to the journal of trapper Zenas Leonard, these hills hosted an unusually ferocious and bloody battle in 1834 between two Indian tribes. A band of Piegan (Blackfeet) warriors who had strayed far from their homeland, which ranged between present-day Browning, Montana, and Calgary, Alberta, surely knew they were treading on dangerous ground in this Crow territory. And they were. A group of Crows attacked and annihilated the band of Piegan, but not before at least thirty Crows were killed.

Crow Fair, held the third weekend in August at Crow Agency (the "Teepee Capital of the World"), boasts one of the biggest rodeos in Montana, a horse-fest including bareback show riding by Crows—known as the best riders among the Plains Indians—and horse racing with parimutuel betting. Crow Fair is one of the preeminent powwows for all of North America's Indians, and members of tribes from throughout the United States and Canada come for the dance competitions, parades, and other events. Neophyte participants are coached by announcers at the various events regarding what actions are expected or are taboo. Crow Fair is held at the tribal campgrounds along the Little Bighorn River. You can't miss it—just look for the sea of tipis flooding the bottomlands.

Before heading east, consider taking a side trip 13 miles north to Hardin to visit the ***Big Horn County Historical Museum and Visitor***

Center. First opened in 1979, the museum complex incorporates eleven buildings on twenty-four acres of grounds. Within view is the site of old Fort Custer, presently a wheat field but once one of the most modern of the frontier forts. A number of abodes and places of business, worship, and schooling have been moved from various outlying locations to the museum grounds. They're filled with old-time goodies, such as farm machinery and railroad memorabilia, designed to lend the visitor a sense of what life on the frontier must have been like for white settlers.

The free museum, located just off Interstate 90 at exit 497, is open during the summer from 8:00 A.M. to 8:00 P.M. seven days a week in summer, and the rest of the year Monday through Friday from 9:00 A.M. to 5:00 P.M. Call 665–1671 or E-mail the museum at historical@mcn.net for further information.

Best Annual Events

1. *Cowtown Beef Breeders Show,*
   Miles City; early February;
   (406) 232-2890

2. *Montana Women's Run,*
   Billings; early May; (406) 656-6973

3. *Peter Paddlefish Day and*
   Kite Festival, Sidney; early May;
   (406) 482-1916

4. *Miles City Bucking Horse Sale,*
   Miles City; mid-May;
   (406) 232-2890

5. *Custer's Last Stand Reenactment*
   and Little Big Horn Days,
   Hardin; late June; (406) 665-1672

6. *Fort Union Rendezvous,*
   Sidney; late June; (406) 482-1916

7. *Longest Dam Run,*
   Glasgow; late June; (406) 228-2222

8. *Governor's Cup Walleye Tourna-*
   ment, Glasgow; early July;
   (406) 228-2222

9. *Wild Horse Stampede,*
   Wolf Point; early July;
   (406) 653-2012

10. *Big Sky State Games,*
    Billings; mid-July; (406) 254-7426

11. *Northeast Montana Fair,*
    Glasgow; late July; (406) 228-8221

12. *Hispanic Fiesta,*
    Billings; early August;
    (406) 245-4111

13. *Montana Fair,*
    Billings; early August;
    (406) 256-2400

14. *Eastern Montana Fair,*
    Miles City; late August;
    (406) 232-9554

15. *Mosquitofest,*
    Saco; late August;
    (no phone number)

16. *Crow Fair,* Crow Agency;
    late August; (406) 665-1672

17. *Northeast Montana Threshing*
    Bee, Culbertson; late September;
    (406) 787-5265

18. *Christmas at Pioneer Town,*
    Scobey; early December;
    (406) 487-2061

The Remote Southeast

*H*ighway 212 heads east into the 444,000-acre Northern Cheyenne Indian Reservation, home to around 3,500 Cheyenne Indians. For a decade, beginning in 1874, the Northern Cheyenne were a homeless people. First uprooted from the Black Hills and southeastern Montana when gold fever hit the region, they were shuffled off to the valleys of the Tongue and Powder Rivers; then they were sent to live in Indian Territory (present-day Oklahoma) with the Southern Cheyenne. In 1878, in a heroic journey eloquently documented in Mari Sandoz's poignant book, *Cheyenne Autumn*, Northern Cheyenne chiefs Little Wolf and Dull Knife struck out to lead their people back to the north country they loved. En route, they were trapped by soldiers and incarcerated at Fort Robinson, Nebraska, then moved to the Sioux reservation at Pine Ridge, South Dakota, where they spent several years. Finally, in 1884, they returned home to the newly designated Northern Cheyenne Indian Reservation.

From Lame Deer, 42 miles east of Crow Agency, travel 21 miles east on Highway 212 to the town of Ashland, where the reservation abuts Custer National Forest lands. The *St. Labre Mission and Cheyenne Indian Museum* offer visitors the chance to gain a better appreciation for the enduring spirit of the Morning Star People. Free tours of the mission, the museum, and the St. Labre Indian School, founded in 1884—all located at the edge of town—are available from 8:00 A.M. to 5:30 P.M. daily, Memorial Day through Labor Day. For more information call 784–4500.

Colstrip, 22 miles north of Lame Deer on Highway 39, is "the town that coal built." The Northern Pacific Railway established Colstrip in 1923 to house the workers the company had employed to mine the local coal to fuel its locomotives. By 1959, however, diesel had replaced coal as the preferred fuel for powering trains, and Colstrip was sold to the Montana Power Company. During the construction of two gargantuan power plants in the 1980s, the town's population mushroomed to more than 8,000 but has since leveled off to 3,500. Well-planned and unexpectedly attractive, Colstrip is obviously a company town, although most of the businesses and residences are privately owned.

In the county seat of Forsyth—tucked into a pretty, protected setting below pine-studded bluffs—stop by to see the *Rosebud County Courthouse*, a grand neoclassical building capped with an ornate copper dome and listed in the National Register of Historic Places. The top floor of the building explodes in a colorful display of murals and stained glass. Next door you'll find the *Rosebud County Pioneer Museum*, worth visiting while in the neighborhood. The museum is open May through September 15, 9:00 A.M. to 7:00 P.M., Monday through Saturday, and on Sunday from 1:00 to 7:00 P.M.

Before heading eastward along Interstate 90, consider making the 40-mile side trip northwest on Highway 12 to the far-from-anywhere settlement of Ingomar. The town once was a major wool-shipping railhead along the now-defunct Milwaukee Road, boasting nearly fifty businesses. Some 2,500 homestead claims were filed in the area between 1911 and 1917. But today the spot in the road is all but a ghost town. Of what remains, the surprising *Jersey Lily Cafe* is known throughout Montana for a plate of beans considered by some the best in the West. The restaurant (358–2278) is open daily from 7:00 A.M. until 10:00 P.M.

In Miles City, shoot straight for the *Range Riders Museum and Memorial Hall*, a monument dedicated to the great American cowboy and cowgirl. Miles City, the oldest white settlement in this part of Montana, became its primary cowtown after the Northern Pacific Railway pushed through in 1881. Herds were driven hundreds of miles from the central and eastern ranges of Montana and beyond to the railhead here. (The popular TV miniseries *Lonesome Dove* was based on a fictional cattle drive that takes place between Texas and Miles City.) Lending the downtown color today are classic western taverns, with names like Range Rider Bar, Montana Bar, and Log Cabin Saloon, all aglow in bright neon.

Cattle and horses meant cowboys, of course, and the area produced some of the country's best bronc riders. Realizing the significance of what already in 1938 was a colorful history, a group of Miles City stock growers and fellow townspeople formed the organization now known as the Range Riders. Their first facility was constructed of logs cut in western Montana and shipped to town, gratis, by the Northern Pacific Railroad.

It was built near where the Tongue River empties into the Yellowstone—fittingly, the very site where some sixty years earlier General Nelson A. Miles had constructed Cantonment 1, a temporary quarters for soldiers waiting for the completion of nearby Fort Keogh. Miles had been dispatched, in the wake of Custer's defeat at the Little Bighorn, to establish this fort—named after Captain Myles Keogh, who was killed at the Little Bighorn—along the Yellowstone River to serve as a headquarters for the Indian campaign.

Range Riders Museum, Miles City

The Range Riders' original log building now serves as the hub of a complex of buildings gracing the museum grounds. There's a lot to be seen. Memorial Hall features plaques honoring some 500 pioneering range riders, plaques that include a brief biography of each honoree's life. Found inside the vaultlike Gun Building is a priceless, 500-piece collection of firearms donated in 1987 by the Bert Clark family. The guns span at least 300 years of history and include an early wick-ignition, matchlock Arabian rifle; guns that won the West; and World War I and World War II weapons.

Additional buildings house the Wilson Photo Collection of Old Timers, the Fort Keogh Officers' Quarters, and the Homestead House. The museum, found at the west end of Main Street just over the Tongue River Bridge, is open between April 1 and October 31 from 8:00 A.M. to 8:00 P.M. daily. For more details call 232–4483.

An event not unrelated to Miles City's vivid cowboying past is the Jaycees' *World Famous Bucking Horse Sale*, held every third weekend in May. The town pulls out all the stops for this one, and the partying continues without break from Friday through Sunday. Festivities include a wild-horse drive, street dances, cowboy poetry readings, bar-becues, the always-popular rodeo, and much more. "Buck-outs" are contested, with the wildest, buckingest horses drawing top dollar from rodeo-stock contractors from throughout North America. Wedged between buck-outs are somewhat more tame but no less exciting thor-oughbred horse races, with parimutuel betting offered.

The Bucking Horse Sale is a popular and nationally known event. Since beginning in 1950, it's attracted a lot of well-known personalities—including Ted Kennedy, who, when campaigning for brother John in 1960, lasted about five seconds on a wild bronc. For information on the popular Bucking Horse Sale, call the Miles City Chamber of Commerce at 232–2890 or E-mail them at mcchamber@midrivers.com. Make your reservations early!

Ekalaka, named for the Sioux Indian bride of early settler David Harrison Russell, is not on the road to anywhere. It's one of those places to which you must intend to go in order ever to get there. Either that or you must become incredibly lost.

Where Have All the Horses Gone?

*I*n the 1930s, a Midwest-based outfit called Chappel Brothers Company employed dozens of Montana cowboys, who were assigned to riding the ranges surrounding Miles City. These cowboys should have been called horseboys, however, because it was equines and not bovines that they spent their days herding and tending to.

Across hundreds of acres of open range, much of it composed of former homesteads abandoned by failed farmers, the cowboys grazed thousands of horses. The best of the bunch were sold to the U.S. Army as cavalry mounts, but most of the horses wound up at a cannery in Rockford, Illinois, where they were butchered. The finer cuts were sold to European markets for human consumption, while the trimmings went into Ken-L Ration dog food. At one point CBC was the second-biggest user of tin cans in the U.S., runner-up only to the Campbell Soup Company. "I think they fed practically the whole dog population of Philadelphia with those trimmings," said Phil Rich, an Ohio business executive who attended a 1994 gathering of former CBC riders, bosses, and descendants of those who worked for the company during the era. The group congregated at the Range Riders Museum in Miles City during the 44th annual Bucking Horse Sale festivities.

Responding to a recent publication that had included an article saying that CBC stood for Christian Brothers Company, master of ceremonies John L. Moore, a rancher whose father worked for the company, said, "The North Side [range north of Miles City, that is] was not a monastery, Sid Vollin [one of the CBC trail bosses] was not a monk, and the last time I checked, the Christian Brothers were making wine, not horse flesh."

A growing network of roads in the Midwest had led to a decline in the number of horses in that region, which is what persuaded CBC to expand its range into Montana. Although CBC got out of the horse business after selling Ken-L Ration to Quaker Oats in 1943, the company still holds the mineral rights on many ranches in eastern Montana.

CUSTER—MISSOURI RIVER COUNTRY

Montana Trivia

Some of the town names in eastern Montana hint at their isolation: for instance, Lonesome, located south of Malta, and Faranuf, south of Glasgow.

To get to Ekalaka entirely on paved roads, drive the 77 desolate miles of piney hills and rolling grasslands separating Miles City and Baker, then turn south onto Highway 7 and continue for 35 miles. (At the *O'Fallon Historical Museum* in Baker, you might be able to coax directions out of an old-timer for side trips to prehistoric human sites or ruts carved by wagon trains passing through the area.)

Why bother going to Ekalaka? Well, it's one of most marvelously empty corners of Montana; other than that, perhaps the best excuse is the *Carter County Museum*, located on Main Street. The museum houses a large collection of fossils and artifacts found throughout the area, including a complete skeleton of an Anatosaurus, or duck-billed dinosaur—the Montana State Fossil—dug in 1937 just a few miles from town. Also on display are a Triceratops skull and a mammoth skeleton. The museum building itself is a fossil of sorts, with its construction of native stone and petrified wood. For information on the Carter County Museum, call 775–6886.

On your way to Ekalaka perhaps you noticed protruding from the rolling prairie and pine-covered hills the pockmarked pillars of *Medicine Rocks State Park*. On the way back north, stop and have a look, as Teddy Roosevelt did in 1883. Of his camping trip here, Roosevelt later wrote, "Altogether it was as fantastically beautiful a place as I have ever seen; it seemed impossible that the hand of man should not have something to do with the formation."

Native Americans, conversely, held that the unearthly landscape must have been created by the Great Spirits. Historically, the area has been of spiritual significance to the Cheyenne and Sioux, who held spirit-renewal ceremonies at these rocks containing "big medicine." Many stone circles and other prehistoric artifacts have been found at Medicine Rocks, indicating that it was also an important spot for the nomadic groups preceding the Sioux and Cheyenne.

You, too, may find the remote and unusual park, 10 miles north of Ekalaka on Highway 7, a magical place. Camping is available; for more information, call 232–0900.

From Ekalaka, return to Baker and continue north on Highway 7 for 45 miles to Interstate 94. Go west onto Interstate 94 for 25 miles to Glendive where, at the southeast edge of town, you'll find yet another starkly spectacular parcel of lands administered by Montana Fish, Wildlife and Parks: *Makoshika State Park*. *Makoshika* means "bad

Makoshika State Park

country" or "badlands" in Sioux, a name you'll appreciate after traversing the fantastically eroded, pine- and juniper-studded wildlands. The park is brimming with hogbacks, fluted ridges, pinnacles, hoodoos, and other oddly shaped sandstone buttes capped and protected by harder rock.

Camping, picnicking, and exploring the scenic roadways and nature trails are among the most popular activities at Makoshika. Although Montana's largest state park, it covers only about one-sixth of the 56,000-acre Makoshika badlands area. Most of the park's geological strata belong to the 65-million-year-old Hell Creek Formation, which formed from decaying vegetation in a verdant coastal swamp where ancestors of today's sequoia, magnolia, oak, and palm trees thrived. This was the Age of Reptiles, and the Hell Creek Formation is renowned among paleontologists for its abundance of dinosaur fossils. No fewer than ten species are found in the formation, including the notable Triceratops and Tyrannosaurus rex.

In recent years folks have been coming from throughout the country to help dig dinosaurs at Makoshika, paying handsomely for the privilege of working hard under the hot eastern Montana sun, under the auspices of the Milwaukee (Wisconsin) Public Museum and the Museum of the Rockies in Bozeman. Findings from their work have lent support to the theory that dinosaurs perished in a cataclysmic event, such as a meteor crashing into Earth. For more information call 994–2251. You can also learn more about this area by visiting the Museum of the Rockies' Web site at www.montana.edu/wwwmor.

It's illegal for private parties to remove fossilized animals or plants, but you are asked to report to park headquarters any that you come across. The park is open all year and charges an entrance fee of $4.00 per car; for information call 365–6256.

When gawking at dinosaurs or sampling caviar *a la Montana*, consider holing up at the **Hostetler House**. Hosts Craig and Dea Hostetler guarantee you'll arrive at their two-room inn as a guest but leave as a friend. The country decor features handmade quilts on the beds and family-heirloom furnishings. Rounding out the comfortable surroundings are a relaxing hot tub, sun porch, gazebo, and full breakfast, featuring homemade breads and muffins. The historic home, built in 1912, is located at 113 North Douglas, and rates are around $50 per night. Call (800) 965–8456 or 377–4505 for reservations.

In Terry, 35 miles southwest of Glendive on Interstate 94, you can enjoy

The Paddlefish

*T*he only places the odd paddle-fish—a living fossil, of sorts—is known to exist are in the lower Yellowstone River and in China's Yangtze River. Also known as the spoon-billed catfish, the paddlefish possesses shark-like fins and a long snout that looks like a paddle. They can grow to be 3 feet long, weigh 140 pounds, and live to be 30 years old. This ancient and unlikely bottom-feeder, or some reasonable ancestral facsimile, has swum the waters of the region for millions of years. Thought to be extinct in the United States since 1912, one of the monsters was pulled from the river near Glendive in 1962, and since then their numbers have been increasing.

Therefore, the May and June **Paddle-fish Spawning Run** is cause for great celebration in Glendive. In 1989 the Montana legislature revised a state law prohibiting the use of game fish parts for commercial use, expressly so that the Glendive Chamber of Commerce could collect paddlefish roe, process it, and sell it as caviar! The ruling forbids the chamber to pay for the eggs; rather, they must be donated. So,

they're collected from among the 3,000 or so fishermen who gather May 16 through June 30 for the spawning run at the diversion dam at Intake, 16 miles northeast of town. In turn, the fishermen benefit by having their fish cleaned free of charge by chamber-hired employees. (Formerly, the eggs would simply have been tossed aside after a fisherman snagged one of the beasts and tugged it to shore.)

The eggs are washed, salted, cooled, and then packaged for sale. The snagged paddlefish seems to be the only party who doesn't profit from the arrangement, for money raised through caviar sales is split evenly between the chamber and the state, which uses its portion to improve eastern Montana fisheries. The chamber uses its share to enhance local recreational opportunities. And, in what might be thought of as one prehistoric beast coming to the aid of another, some of the funds have helped to finance the community's Triceratops project. Curious? Call the Chamber of Commerce at 365–5601 to find out more.

a twenty-first-century rarity: a moving-picture show in the comfort of your car. For forty years the **Prairie Drive-In Theatre** has been showing current attractions, and as the only such theater in the region it draws moviegoers from Glendive, Miles City, Baker, and other towns.

Still photos, in the form of the captivating **Evelyn Cameron Gallery** are what visitors come to view at the Prairie County Museum, housed in the attractive, marble-floored 1915 State Bank of Terry building.

Big Open Debate

*T*he Big Open encompasses a vast spread of wild, wide-open spaces. Here refuges teem with bird and animal life, and signs of prehistoric human beings are abundant—and so is evidence of failed homesteads.

Even for those homesteaders who managed to hang on in the Big Open, life typically has been tough. By 1930, after twenty years of settlement by homesteaders, only twenty-five of Garfield County's more than one thousand farms had piped-in water. Electricity came to Jordan in 1951, and telephone service five years later. The long-awaited railroad never did make it there.

This hard living in a lonely land has spawned a fiercely independent spirit. You may recall that in the mid-1990s Jordan was the site of the infamous "Freemen" standoff. Several years prior to that event, a group of romantics and visionaries, under the auspices of Missoula's Institute of the Rockies, proposed that residents of the 15,000-square-mile Big Open (which includes all of Garfield County and portions of several others) should consider a new way to make ends meet. Because raising cattle and wheat are such marginal endeavors in this harsh country, they maintained, bison and other native species should be returned in great numbers, while domestic stock and grain are phased out. Landowners would keep their lands and simply change jobs: Basically, they would become outfitters, guiding tourists on hunting, photography, and wildlife-viewing expeditions into the Great Plains' answer to Africa's Serengeti.

For many the idea is compelling, but it wasn't exactly met with a resounding "Let's do it!" by the folks living there. Bizarre, outrageous, insulting, and monstrous are adjectives one Montana newspaper quoted residents as using when voicing their opinions of the plan.

Their sentiment is perhaps best summed up in a counterproposal offered by a group of Big Open citizens: Why not build a huge dam on the Clark Fork River downstream from Missoula, causing the immense basin occupied by prehistoric Lake Missoula to fill again? The new megalake would create hundreds of recreation-oriented jobs and also rid Montana of its worst pollution and congestion problem—Missoula (while also ridding the free-minded Big Open residents of meddling western Montanans).

The Big Open, Garfield County

Evelyn Cameron, an Englishwoman, came to the Terry area in 1889 to ranch with her naturalist husband, Ewen. (He's known, among other things, for having killed the Boone and Crockett record grizzly bear for Montana, in 1890, at the Missouri Breaks.) Lady Cameron took up photography in 1894, and for more than thirty years lugged her large 5 x 7 Graflex camera and associated paraphernalia around the prairie, incessantly photographing the eastern Montana landscape and its homesteads, wildlife, and legion of characters. Under the watchful eye of her neighbor and friend, Janet Williams, more than 1,400 of Cameron's glass-plate and nitrate negatives survived the years following her death. In 1990 they were donated to the Montana Historical Society by the Williams family.

Excerpts from the celebrated biography of Lady Cameron, *Photographing Montana (1894-1928): The Life and Works of Evelyn Cameron*, by Donna Lucey, appear alongside the strikingly sharp photographs of cowboys, wolves, sheepherders, badlands, wagon trains, and other turn-of-the-century eastern Montana subjects. The Prairie County Museum is located at 204 South Logan; for more information call 635–4040 or 635–5442.

The Big Open

From Miles City, pull onto long and lonesome Highway 59 going northwest and proceed to that part of Montana known as The Big Dry or The Big Open. For many, the greatest attraction here is the very lack of attractions, of the modern, human-made variety.

Jordan, the most isolated county seat in the lower forty-eight states, is Garfield County's center of enterprise. Several Tyrannosaurus rex

Montana Trivia

skeletons have been taken from the Hell Creek Formation in the surrounding hills, including specimens that for decades were displayed at the American Museum of Natural History in New York City and the Carnegie Museum in Pittsburgh. At the **Garfield County Museum** you can learn about the area's numerous excavations and view some of the fossils found nearby. To learn more about the museum, call the town's Senior Center at 557–2501.

Hell Creek State Park and Marina is situated on the Hell Creek Arm of formidable Fort Peck Lake. As you traverse the 26-mile road leading north from Jordan, you'll suspect that you're headed to the middle of nowhere (or maybe you already thought you were there when in Jordan!). Wild turkey, pronghorn antelope, golden eagles, and mule deer are commonly seen along the route.

At your destination, however, you'll discover a buzzing oasis of activity. There's a campground, grocery and concession stores, boat rentals (Fort Peck Lake is known for its world-class walleye fishing), and more. For information on the park, which opens for the season in mid-April, call 557–2345.

If you prefer sleeping in a cabin with a roof overhead, head for nearby **Hell Creek Guest Ranch.** The remote badlands spread was homesteaded in 1913 by Elmer Trumbo, father of current owner John Trumbo, and several of his original buildings remain. Hell Creek offers ranch-style home cooking, rustic yet modern accommodations, and family-oriented hiking, photography, and fossil-digging tours. In the fall, ranch hands guide hunters in pursuit of wild turkey, elk, antelope, and trophy mule deer. Hell Creek Guest Ranch is located 21 miles north of Jordan; for reservations and further information, call 557–2224.

It'll probably never gain the notoriety of the Baseball Hall of Fame in Cooperstown, New York, but nevertheless at the McCone County Museum in Circle you'll find the **Montana Sheepherders Hall of Fame.** Outside the entryway stands a life-size concrete statue of a sheepherder holding a lamb, and inside are listed the names of more than 300 local sheep growers, many displayed with their brands. (Circle was named for a cattle brand, by the way.) Also within the museum are farming implements, Indian artifacts, and the wildlife collection of the Orville Quick family. The animal mounts, accumulated over the span of forty years, include more than 200 birds in dioramas resembling their natural habitats.

The McCone County Museum, located at 801 First Avenue South in Circle, is open weekdays year-round, from 8:00 A.M. to 5:00 P.M. (but it sometimes closes for the lunch hour). Call 485–2414 for more information.

A great deal of work has gone into creating the **MonDak Heritage Center** in Sidney, a well above average museum and art center. The pride of the museum is its two galleries, where monthly revolving shows from throughout the country are displayed. Exhibits beyond the galleries include a complete homesteader-days "town" and a model of the nearby historic Fort Union Trading Post. The MonDak Heritage Center, located at 120 Third Avenue Southeast, is open in summer from 10:00 A.M. to 5:00 P.M. Tuesday through Friday and 1:00 to 5:00 P.M. Saturday and Sunday; in winter from 10:00 A.M. to 4:00 P.M. Wednesday through Friday

Prairie Beauty

I spent most of the summer of 1979 living in a motel room in Sidney. From there I ventured to the surrounding prairies of Montana and North Dakota to survey proposed oil-well sites for evidence of prehistoric artifacts. For a fellow accustomed to living in the Rocky Mountains, the days were relentlessly hot in that country, and the nights weren't all that cool, either. I remember listening to the radio early in the mornings, when the mercury often had already climbed to around seventy degrees, and hearing reports of temperatures in the forties back in Missoula. It made me want to go home.

But I did see some amazing things as I walked through those unpeopled badlands fashioned by the erosive action of wind and water. Much of the country bordered on the Little Missouri, the river responsible for carving the maze of terrain known as Theodore Roosevelt National Park,

which I often worked in close proximity to. As the summer wore on I learned that the prairie possesses a brand of beauty unlike any I'd previously known. Occasionally, when I was assigned to survey a particularly remote site, a Shell Oil Company helicopter would deliver me there, then retrieve me a few hours later. I felt like it was just me and the mule deer, alone on the Great Plains . . . along with the occasional rattlesnake.

Two things from that summer particularly stand out: a full skeleton of a prehistoric bison that I found, eroding out of the cut banks of Bennie Peer Creek; and the drive across the extraordinary Fairview Bridge. The bridge, located 3 miles east of Fairview, has railroad tracks running the length of its driving surface. The only lift bridge on the Yellowstone River, it once carried car and train traffic across the river . . . but not at the same time, one supposes.

and 1:00 to 4:00 P.M. Saturday and Sunday. Admission is $2.50 for adults and $1.00 for students. Call 482–3500 for more information.

What remains of the full-scale version of *Fort Union Trading Post* is found 23 miles northeast of Sidney, astride the Montana–North Dakota border. Traders and settlers became interested in the area when William Clark, of the Lewis and Clark expedition, wrote in his journal that whoever came to control the confluence of the Missouri and Yellowstone Rivers would probably command the fur trade of the entire Northwest.

The Canadians beat the Americans to the punch when, in the late 1820s, Kenneth McKenzie built his namesake fort. The American Fur Company's John Jacob Astor was close behind, however, and in 1829 he built Fort Union at the confluence of the great rivers. For two decades thereafter Fort Union was the center of the upper Missouri fur trade. Assiniboine Indians from the north, Crow from the south, Blackfeet from the Missouri headwaters, and other tribes from elsewhere brought beaver pelts and buffalo hides to trade. At its zenith, the fort employed some one hundred workers, many of them with Indian wives and families. Men from throughout the world found their way here: Inhabitants included Americans (black, white, and Native), Russians, Spaniards, Italians, Germans, Englishmen, Frenchmen, and others.

By the mid-1830s, the demand for beaver was tapering off in Europe and on the East Coast, as silk replaced fur as the favored material for men's hats. Simultaneously, however, the market for tanned buffalo robes burgeoned, and trade at Fort Union was brisk until late in the 1830s, when a smallpox epidemic arrived via the steamboat *St. Peter* and decimated some of the Indian tribes. Trade slowed for a while and then again picked up, until another smallpox scourge hit in 1857. By the time the Civil War heated up, trade at Fort Union was sluggish, and the post was badly in need of repair. Most of the buildings were dismantled in the 1860s by federal soldiers, and the logs were moved a mile downstream to be used in constructing Fort Buford.

Recent National Park Service archaeological excavations turned up scores of valuable artifacts and shed new light on Fort Union's past. Their efforts have resulted in the reconstruction of portions of the fort's stone bastions, the Indian trade house, and the Bourgeois House, the imposing former quarters of the post commander. The lofty exterior of the house now looks much as it did in 1850, and the interior serves as a visitor center and reference library.

Fort Union Trading Post National Historic Site is located at 15550 Highway 1804 (not coincidentally, the year the Lewis and Clark expedition wintered in North Dakota). To get there, go north from Sidney on Highway 200 for 14 miles; after crossing the North Dakota border just past Fairview, turn north onto Highway 1804 and continue for 8 miles. The site is open Memorial Day through Labor Day from 8:00 A.M. to 8:00 P.M. (Central time, since the visitor center is on the North Dakota side of the complex). During the remainder of the year it's open from 9:00 A.M. to 5:30 P.M. For more information call (701) 572–9083.

From Sidney, travel 37 miles northwest on Highway 16 to Culbertson, then 33 miles west on Highway 2 to Poplar, headquarters for the Fort Peck Assiniboine and Sioux Indian tribes. The American dream thrives at *A & S Tribal Industries*, where industrial products for government and private use are manufactured. Products include camouflage netting, hydraulic presses, computer-controlled punch presses, medical chests, and many others.

A & S Tribal Industries opened in 1975 and now employs approximately 400 persons, 80 percent of them tribe members. The management invites visitors to drop by any time during working hours (Monday through Friday from 6:00 A.M. to 4:00 P.M.) and enjoys giving guided tours to groups or individuals. Call 768–5151 to find out more. (Note: The facility closes for a period of two weeks around the Fourth of July.)

In Wolf Point, 21 miles west of Poplar, cowboys and cowgirls whoop it up at the granddaddy of Montana rodeos, the *Wild Horse Stampede*, first held at the turn of the century. In the wild horse race, an unusual addition to the more typical rodeo events, teams of three cowboys compete to be the first to saddle and ride a wild horse across the finish line. Held on the second full weekend in July, the three days of rodeoing and revelry also include a carnival, parades, and Indian cultural displays. For more information you can call the Wolf Point Chamber of Commerce at 653–2012.

South of Saskatchewan

ocated a mile south of the town of Medicine Lake (which is 25 miles north of Culbertson) on Highway 16 is a diamond in the rough: the *Medicine Lake National Wildlife Refuge*. The refuge, established in 1935 under the management of the U.S. Fish and Wildlife Service, contains a proliferation of potholes and swamps left behind when the last great glacier retreated. In all, 40 percent of its 31,000 acres are covered by lakes, ponds, and marshes, with the remainder in prairie and meadow. The largest body of water, 8,700-acre Medicine Lake, now enjoys added protection as the centerpiece of the 11,000-acre Medicine Lake Wilderness. The wilderness also holds the adjacent dunes of the Sand Hills.

Like other national wildlife refuges, Medicine Lake is financed largely through the sale of migratory bird stamps, or "duck stamps," which waterfowl hunters must purchase annually. A staggering variety of birds—as many as 75,000 at a time—call the place home: Canada geese, double-crested cormorants, grebes, ruddy ducks, yellow-headed blackbirds, American bitterns, and sharp-tailed grouse, to name only a few. The refuge is important both as a stopover for migrating birds and as a breeding ground for dozens of species.

The headquarters, with mounted birds and prehistoric artifacts on display, is open from 7:00 A.M. to 3:30 P.M. Monday through Friday, and during other daylight hours visitors are welcome to stop at employees' residences to make inquiries. At the office you can obtain a key to the 100-foot viewing tower; be sure also to pick up a route brochure for the 14-mile car tour. Destinations include the new Bridgerman Point observation deck, where the largest colonies of white pelicans in the U.S. can be viewed. The brochure pinpoints where you can expect to see many other bird species, as well.

Glaciers aren't all that left evidence after passing. Surrounding Medicine Lake, and included in the scenic drive, are the *Tipi Hills*, listed on the National Register of Historic Places because of the dozens of tipi rings found there (tipi rings are circles of stones that once encircled the edges of tipi skins). Clearly, the area was abundant hunting ground in prehistoric times and served as a "wildlife refuge" long before the U.S. government designated it so. For more information on Medicine Lake National Wildlife Refuge, call the visitor center at 789–2305.

Sitting Bull, the prominent Sioux chief, surrendered to U.S. troops in July of 1881 near present-day Plentywood, located 22 miles north of Medicine Lake on Highway 16. A monument to him now stands just outside the *Sheridan County Museum*, located along Highway 16 at the entrance to the county fairgrounds. Near the museum in the Civic Center you'll find one of the longest murals in Montana, a 74-foot canvas by Bob Southland depicting the county's history, from the days of the prehistoric Americans to the present.

Not long after Sitting Bull and his people were subdued, gangs of outlaws—including Butch Cassidy's infamous Wild Bunch—traveled through this area on the Outlaw Trail, occasionally hiding out in the rough breaks of the Big Muddy River Valley. You can find out more about the region's Indians, outlaws, and homesteaders at the museum, open daily May through September.

Nowadays hostile Indians and bad guys are mostly history, but the area surrounding Plentywood has become a "hideout" of sorts for exotic animal species. No fewer than a dozen ranches in Sheridan County raise unusual animals, such as the Sicilian spotted donkey, Russian Romanov sheep, Nubian ibex, Muntjac deer, and pygmy goat, most of them operating under the umbrella of the Mon-Dak Game Breeders Association, headquartered in Plentywood. Among the critters you can see at the **Rolling Hills Llamas and Exotics**, 8 miles north of Westby, are Australian cashmere goats, Vietnamese potbellied pigs, and the remarkable Tennessee fainting goat. When startled, these animals stiffen and tip over onto their backs in a dead faint, typically reviving in about fifteen seconds.

Visitors are welcome at Rolling Hills Llamas and Exotics. The place is easy to find, for it claims the distinction of being the northeastern-most

The Missouri Coteau

*T*he town of Westby, situated 26 miles east of Plentywood, occupies a wetlands-filled corner of Montana that is within the Missouri Coteau. This glacier-created landscape of rolling hills and prairie potholes stretches from northern South Dakota into Saskatchewan. The Missouri Coteau (coteau is French for hill) provides vital nesting grounds for a large number of species of passerines, or perching songbirds. Their annual migrations have turned isolated Westby, nestled against the North Dakota border, into somewhat of a mecca for bird-watchers from throughout the country. The Missouri Coteau also contains some of the richest prairies of native mixed grasses remaining on the Great Plains, making the region an early summer haven for fans of wildflowers, too.

For information on the Missouri Coteau, and to inquire about the times of spring and summer for optimum bird- and wildflower-viewing, you can call the **Hilltop House Bed & Breakfast** in Westby, at 385–2508 or 385–2533.

ranch in Montana. The headquarters is located 1 mile from the North Dakota state line and 3 miles south of the international border. For more information call 385–2597.

In Daniels County, dozens of decaying cabins attest to the fact that many hundreds more people than live here now once tried their hands at it. Of the hundreds of would-be dryland farmers who moved to Daniels County during the homesteading boom of 1910–1920, it's estimated that only about 15 percent stuck it out. In 1963 the town pulled out all the stops to celebrate that minority at the Homesteaders' Golden Jubilee.

The festival spawned the notion of building a monument of permanence to the past. The idea matured and grew into the twenty-acre **Pioneer Town and Museum**, found today at the west edge of Scobey, a small plains town situated at the junction of Highways 5 and 13, 41 miles west of Plentywood. More than forty buildings, most of them reconstructed and spilling over with artifacts, line the streets— a blacksmith shop, one-room school, general store, completely furnished homestead shack, and many others. An extensive collection of early-day farm equipment is featured, and some fifty restored, antique automobiles fill two adjacent buildings. In the museum visitor center are additional displays, such as antique lamp and gun collections.

At the Rex Theatre on the museum grounds, various shows are given throughout the summer, including the annual performance by the Dirty Shame Dance Hall Girls and Dixieland Band, held during Pioneer Days on the last weekend in June. Tours of the museum complex are conducted daily between 12:30 and 4:30 P.M. from Memorial Day through Labor Day. Winter hours are 1:00 to 4:00 P.M. on Friday. Admission is $5.00 for adults and $2.50 for kids. Call 487–5965 for information.

In the late seventies, at a Lutheran Church lutefisk dinner, Glasgow gift-shop owner Marge Forum sampled some of the hand-rolled *lefse* produced by Myrt Grandrud and her friend, Arlene Larson. Their lefse, a Scandinavian tortilla-like Christmas treat made of potatoes and cream, was so good that Marge convinced the two ladies to make more to sell at her shop. It went over even bigger than Marge had anticipated, and soon the ladies couldn't make enough to keep up with the demand.

So Myrt's husband, Evan, began helping to roll out mashed potatoes in the evenings after returning from work at the Opheim radar station. Although the ladies at first maintained that hand-driven rolling pins were the only acceptable means by which to roll out the dough, Evan finally convinced them otherwise by tinkering away in his shop and devising an ingenious, automated rolling pin. The rest, as they say, is history.

Today **Grandruds' Lefse Shack** operates out of a double garage at the Grandruds' home, a mile south of Opheim, a tiny burg found 46 miles west of Scobey on Highway 248. Potatoes—most of them Evan's home-grown Norland reds—are cooked, twenty-five pounds at a time, mixed, chilled in ice cream buckets, and packed into round cylinders. Evan's machines then kick into action and roll out the rounds, and the lefse is cooked on griddles.

The shop turns out twenty tons of lefse in a season. Approximately 800 pounds of potatoes are cooked in a typical shift, and in an average week they go through 6 gallons of cream, 40 pounds of butter and 300 pounds of margarine. The operation is as large as the Grandruds want it, fearing that additional growth would mean losing control of quality and working more than they like. The lefse is sold primarily in stores in Montana and North Dakota and through the mail-order operation handled by Myrt. They advertise very little, depending instead on word of watering mouth to get the message out.

The key to running a successful operation in tiny Opheim? Timing, according to Evan. "We started at about the time all of the old-time Scandinavian grandmas were either gone or had arthritis in their hands. Twenty years ago people made their own lefse, but a lot of the wives are working now and don't have the time."

Visit during the lefse-making season (fall and early winter) and you'll be impressed by the friendliness of the staff of twelve to fifteen and the laid-back, yet industrious, atmosphere. You'll also be treated to hot-off-the-griddle lefse with your choice of white or brown sugar. Call 762-3250 or E-mail the business at lefseshk@nemontel.net to find out more.

"From Dinosaur Bones to Moon Walk" is the theme at the **Valley County Pioneer Museum** in Glasgow, 50 miles south of Opheim on Highway 24. The eclectic collection includes area fossils, the late Chief Wetsit's original tipi (made from twenty-three elk hides), an outdoor machinery exhibition, wood carvings by the late master carver Frank Lafournaise (including what "Ripley's Believe It or Not" once recognized as the world's tiniest workable violin), a miniature model of the 1930s Fort Peck Dam project, and a display on the history of aviation in Valley County.

Montana Trivia

The museum showpiece, to which an entire large room is dedicated, is the **Stan Kalinski Collection**. For years on display at Stan's Bar on Front Street, the collection includes some 300 mounted animals, such as an albino deer; an extinct Audubon sheep; many reptiles, birds, and mammals from the far corners of the earth; and a bison that was butchered for the feast honoring Franklin Roosevelt when he visited Glasgow in the 1930s. Stan's ornate Buffalo Bill Cody bar—bullet hole and all—resides here, too.

The Valley County Pioneer Museum is open from Memorial Day through Labor Day, 9:00 A.M. to 9:00 P.M. Monday through Saturday, and 1:00 to 9:00 P.M. Sunday, free of charge. Located on Highway 2 West in Glasgow, it's tough to miss—it is the only building in the vicinity with an Air Force jet protruding from the front. For more information call 228–8692.

People drive from afar to the tiny town of Nashua, 12 miles southeast of Glasgow on Highway 2, to enjoy **Bergie's** homemade ice cream. The place is a northeast Montana tradition, having been in business as a Miller Drug Store for decades prior to 1985, when Larry and Jeannie Bergstrom bought it, even though they already had jobs, in order to prevent it from closing for good. Over the antique marble counter, ice cream aficionados can order one of seven flavors, several of which change with the seasons (chokecherry and rhubarb are popular in summer). Sodas, sundaes, and milk shakes are staples at Bergie's, too. For more information call 746–3441.

When informed in 1932 by U.S. Corps of Engineers officials of their intention to build a dam across the Missouri River a few miles south of his town, Glasgow mayor Leo B. Coleman is reported to have exclaimed, "My god, man! It would cost a million dollars to build a dam across there!"

But President Roosevelt gave the go-ahead in 1933, and over the span of six years the **Fort Peck Dam** was erected. Even today it is the largest earth-filled dam in the United States—with embankments reaching 4 miles across the Missouri River—and ranks sixth among dams in the world in the volume of water impounded.

The stated purposes for the dam were to aid in flood control and to make the Missouri River more navigable, but even more important at the time was the creation of jobs. Montana was reeling from the

Depression and from several straight years of drought. The Fort Peck public works project was a godsend: Construction at its peak provided jobs for nearly 11,000 individuals. Eighteen boomtowns, with a combined population of nearly 40,000, buzzed where months before only a few hundred had quietly resided. It was the Wild West all over again, a sight that moved Pulitzer Prize winner Ernie Pyle to write, "You have to see the town of Wheeler to believe it . . . it is today the wildest wild-west town in North America. Except for the autos, it is a genuine throwback to the '80s, to Tombstone and Dodge City." (Wheeler was a small, makeshift town that no longer exists.)

The Fort Peck Dam backs up the waters of the Missouri into its main valley and dozens of side drain-ages to create Fort Peck Lake, which at full pool is 134 miles long and claims an astounding 1,520 miles of shoreline. The lake is entirely surrounded by the public lands of the equally formidable *Charles M. Russell National Wildlife Refuge*. At 1,100,000 acres, C. M. Russell is the largest contiguous wildlife refuge in the lower forty-eight states and the most untrammeled stretch of the northern Great Plains remaining. It encompasses the native prairie, badlands, timbered coulees, and bottomlands so often depicted in the works of the cowboy-turned-painter for whom the refuge was named.

Incidentally, little did Mayor Coleman know that eventually the project would cost nearly $150 million and the lives of six men killed in a slide (they are still buried in the dam today). Guided tours of the Fort Peck Dam and surroundings can be arranged between Memorial Day and Labor Day by calling the Corps of Engineers at 526–3431. An ambitious new visitor center, boasting an IMAX theater, dinosaur museum, and interpretive center, are under development at the dam.

The *Fort Peck Theatre*, listed on the National Register of Historic Places, is a beautiful wooden structure built in the style of a large Swiss chalet. It, too, was constructed in the thirties, designed for showing movies to the dam workers and their families. The 1,100-seat structure now houses the Fort Peck Summer Theatre, presenting professional shows from mid-June through Labor Day on Friday, Saturday, and Sunday evenings at 8:00 P.M. Reservations are not needed, and the box office opens at 7:30 P.M. For more details call the Glasgow Chamber of Commerce at 228–2222 or 228–9219.

Natural hot springs aren't common in the eastern reaches of Montana, so why is there one near Saco, 60 miles northwest of Fort Peck on Highways 24 and 2? Well, it's not exactly natural, but at least at

The Fort Peck Theatre, Glasgow

Sleeping Buffalo Resort the water is naturally heated. In 1922 a wild-catter exploring for oil hit a fantastic flow of gushing hot mineral water at about 3,200 feet below the ground surface. Allegedly, he proceeded to go broke trying to cap the flow!

Luckily, he wasn't successful. During Franklin D. Roosevelt's presidency, the Soil Conservation Service joined with the Phillips County American Legion to develop a complex around the springs, and the Works Project Administration built several rock buildings at the "Saco Health Plunge." In 1958 a new well was drilled after a flow stoppage occurred; unfortunately, the following summer the Madison Canyon Earthquake struck near Yellowstone, causing the ground here to shift and break the casing. So, another new well was drilled.

The history continues, but what is really important is what you'll find today at Sleeping Buffalo Resort (renamed in honor of the large bison-resembling boulder moved to the locale a few years ago). Three pools of different temperatures, one as toasty as 106 degrees, await soakers the year around. Some 600,000 gallons of fresh water flow through the pools every day. Because the water contains unusually high concentrations of minerals, it's purported to possess therapeutic values for those suffering from arthritis and similar ailments.

Probably not even the buffalo slept on the summer day in 1992 at the resort when Butte native Robbie Knievel flew on his motorcycle over a 125-foot line of twenty covered wagons—arm in a cast, no less, owing to a broken bone suffered from a fall in another recent stunt.

Sleeping Buffalo Resort, open year-round, features rustic cabins, a cafe, steakhouse, waterslide, campground, bar, and nearby golf course. It's located 10 miles west of Saco on Highway 2, near the Nelson Reservoir. Call 527–3370 or log on to www.ereaux.com for more information.

Finally, a couple of museums you might want to take in before continuing into Russell Country: the *Huntley School*, situated in the town park in Saco, where television newsman Chet Huntley began his education; and the *Phillips County Historical Museum*, (654–1037), open May 15 through September 15 at its new facility on Highway 2 East in Malta (just watch for the dinosaur silhouette). Just east of Malta you'll pass the turn into *Bowdoin National Wildlife Refuge*, a marshland environment where you can spot pelicans, white-faced ibises, and a noisy cast of other winged things.

PLACES TO STAY IN CUSTER–MISSOURI RIVER COUNTRY

BILLINGS

Sheraton Billings Hotel, 27 North 27th; (406) 252–7400

Best Western Ponderosa Inn, downtown at 2511 1st Avenue North; (800) 628–9081

Comfort Inn of Billings, 2030 Overland Avenue; (800) 221–2222

Billings Super 8, 5400 Southgate Drive; (800) 800–8000

The Josephine Bed & Breakfast, 514 North 29th; (406) 248–5898

HARDIN

American Inn, 1324 North Crawford Avenue; (800) 582–8094

Hardin Super 8, 201 14th Street; (800) 800–8000

Western Motel, 830 West 3rd Street; (406) 665–2296

MILES CITY

Best Western War Bonnet Inn, 1015 South Haynes; (406) 232–4560

Days Inn, 1006 South Haynes; (406) 232–3550

Historic Olive Hotel, 501 Main; (406) 232–2450

Motel 6, 1314 South Haynes; (406) 232–7040

BAKER

Sagebrush Inn, 518 U.S. Highway 12 West; (406) 778–3341

Lakefront Bed & Breakfast, 402 Lake Street; (406) 778–2727

Montana Motel, 716 East Montana Avenue; (406) 778–3315

GLENDIVE

Budget Western Jordan Inn, 223 North Merrill; (406) 365–5655

Days Inn, 2000 North Merrill; (800) 325–2525

Super 8 Motel, 1904 North Merrill; (800) 800–8000

Hostetler House Bed & Breakfast, 113 North Douglas Avenue; 377–4505

JORDAN

Hell Creek Guest Ranch, 21 miles north of town; (406) 557–2224

Fellman's Motel, State Highway 200; (406) 557–2209

Garfield Hotel & Motel, State Highway 200; (406) 557–6215

SIDNEY
Lone Tree Motor Inn,
900 South Central;
(406) 482–4520

Richland Motor Inn,
1200 South Central;
(406) 482–6400

Angus Ranch House Motel,
2300 South Central;
(406) 482–3826

PLENTYWOOD
Sherwood Inn,
515 1st Avenue West;
(406) 765–2810

Plains Motel,
626 1st Avenue West;
(406) 765–1240

GLASGOW
Cottonwood Inn,
U.S. Highway 2 East;
(406) 228–8213

Koski's Motel,
U.S. Highway 2 East;
(406) 228–8282

Star Lodge Motel,
903 6th Avenue North;
(406) 228–2494

Historic Fort Peck Hotel,
18 miles southeast of town;
(800) 560–4931

MALTA
Edgewater Inn, Jct.
Highway 242 and
U.S. Highway 2;
(406) 654–1302

Great Northern Motel,
2 South 1st Avenue;
(406) 654–2100

Riverside Motel,
8 North Central;
(406) 654–2310

Sleeping Buffalo Resort, 18
miles northeast of town;
(406) 527–3370

**PLACES TO EAT
IN CUSTER–MISSOURI
RIVER COUNTRY**

BILLINGS
Cactus Creek,
2928 King Avenue West;
(406) 656–9090

Walker's Grill,
301 North 27th Street;
(406) 245–9291

Cafe Jones, 2712
2nd Avenue North;
(406) 259–7676

Juliano's,
2912 7th Avenue North;
(406) 248–6400

The Granary,
1500 Poly Drive;
(406) 259–3488

MILES CITY
Historic Olive Hotel,
501 Main; (406) 232–2450

600 Cafe, 600 Main;
(406) 232–3860

Hole in the Wall,
602 Main; (406) 232–9887

Club 519, 519 Main;
(406) 232–5133

BAKER
Sakelaris's Kitchen, Lake
City Shopping Center;
(406) 778–2202

GLENDIVE
Bacios Ristorante,
302 West Towne;
(406) 365–9664

Jordan Coffee Shop,
223 North Merrill;
(406) 365–5655

CC's Family Cafe,
1902 North Merrill;
(406) 365–8926

JORDAN
Hell Creek Bar, Main Street;
(406) 557–2302

SIDNEY
Triangle Nite Club, south of
town on Highway 23;
(406) 482–9936

The South 40,
207 2nd Avenue Northwest;
(406) 482–4999

Depot Pizza & Fine Food,
2300 South Central;
(406) 482–4650

Lalonde Hotel,
217 South Central;
(406) 482–1043

PLENTYWOOD
Randy's Restaurant,
323 1st Avenue West;
(406) 765–1661

Laura Belle's,
101 North Main;
(406) 765–1080

Blue Moon Supper Club,
east of town on Highway 5;
(406) 765–2491

GLASGOW
Johnnie Cafe, 433 1st
Avenue South;
(406) 228–4222

Sam's Supper Club,
307 1st Avenue North;
(406) 228–4614

Eugene's Pizza,
193 Klein; (406) 228–8552

MALTA
Great Northern Hotel,
2 South First Street East;
(406) 654–2100

Westside Restaurant, west
of town on U.S. Highway 2;
(406) 654–1555

Russell Country

R ussell Country encompasses the high plains, tall buttes, and muddy waters of north-central Montana, a landscape depicted often in the evocative works of Charlie Russell, America's cowboy artist. The region also holds a lot of flat farming country, lying north of the Missouri River, as well as a broad sweep of the Rocky Mountain Front, where massive mountains give way to the endless Great Plains.

From southwest of Malta, wind along the Missouri Breaks Back Country Byway to Lewistown, an attractive, mid-sized community that serves as the geographical hub of Montana. From there head northwest to Fort Benton, a town that, arguably, played a more important role than any other in the taming of Montana. From Havre, situated northeast of Fort Benton, U.S. Highway 2 heads west along the Hi-Line to Shelby; from there it is on to the Rocky Mountain Front settlement of Choteau. U.S. Highway 89 will then lead you to Great Falls, where history buffs can fill up on the lore of Lewis and Clark. Next heading southeast on U.S. Highway 87, you'll turn south onto U.S. Highway 191 before regaining Lewistown. Continue on to Harlowton. Finally, a trip heading west along U.S. Highway 12 leads to White Sulphur Springs by way of interesting spots in the road known as Twodot and Martinsdale.

Charlie Russell's Canvas

N ature clocked eons of overtime in fashioning the jumble of geology known as the Missouri Breaks, described by Lewis and Clark as "the deserts of America." Seventy miles southwest of Malta on Highway 191, at James Kipp Park (just south of the Fred Robinson Bridge), you'll find the kick-off point for the *Missouri Breaks Back Country Byway*.

The river and adjacent floodplains, timbered coulees, and prairie comprise a diverse range of habitats, and perhaps nowhere in the contiguous United States can such a medley of wildlife be met (outside of Yellowstone National Park, anyway, and you'll definitely see fewer tourists here

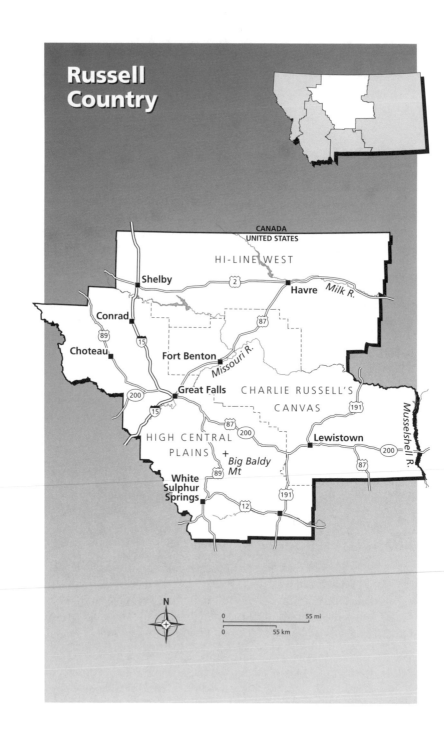

Russell Country

CANADA
UNITED STATES

HI-LINE WEST

Shelby

2

Havre

Milk R.

Conrad

87

89

15

Choteau

Fort Benton

Missouri R.

200

Great Falls

CHARLIE RUSSELL'S
CANVAS

191

Musselshell R.

HIGH CENTRAL
PLAINS

87

200

Lewistown

200

+ Big Baldy
Mt

89

87

White
Sulphur
Springs

191

12

N

0   55 mi

0   55 km

than there). More than 60 species of mammals, 200 varieties of birds, and 20 types of reptiles and amphibians have been identified in the Breaks. Along the eastern portions of the Lower Two Calf Road, for instance, you've a good chance of spotting prairie elk in the river bottoms. Bighorn sheep also are regularly seen atop the ridges and in the coulees of this area—not the Audubon bighorn described by Lewis and Clark (which has since become extinct), but the introduced and apparently thriving Rocky Mountain bighorn.

From James Kipp Park head west on the Knox Ridge Road. After 27 miles turn north onto the Lower Two Calf Road, which loops back east, eventually rejoining the Knox Ridge Road 4 miles west of the beginning point. Along the 34-mile Lower Two Calf Road are several spur roads leading to overlooks and river-bottom sites.

The entire loop, sans side trips, is about 65 miles long. All of the Knox Ridge Road, except for its easternmost 4-mile portion, is surfaced for all-weather travel, while long stretches of Lower Two Calf Road are unsurfaced. The gumbo clay of the Missouri Breaks is notorious for becoming absolutely impassable when wet, so keep a close eye on the weather or you may spend more time in the Breaks than planned.

If the weather is dry and has been for some time, with little chance of rain in the forecast, you'll probably do fine in a passenger car, although a high-clearance vehicle is recommended. Because of the isolated nature of the country, go equipped with plenty of provisions and water. For more information on how to prepare and for detailed maps and brochures, call the Bureau of Land Management in Lewistown at 538–7461.

Lewistown, sitting at the center of Montana, is a popular spot for Yogo sapphire rock hounding and for world-class fishing and big-game and bird hunting. To get there from James Kipp Park, follow Highway 191 south for 20 miles, and then continue south along Highway 19 for 21 miles. Turn west onto Highway 87 near Grassrange and proceed across the southern flank of the Judith Mountains, earning a good view of attractive Lewistown just before dropping into it.

BEST ATTRACTIONS

Missouri River Back Country Byway, Lewistown; (406) 538–7461

Charlie Russell Chew Choo, Lewistown; (800) 735–7886

Square Butte, Square Butte; (406) 538–7461

Montana Agricultural Center and Museum of the Northern Great Plains, Fort Benton; (406) 622–5316

Havre Beneath the Streets, Havre; (406) 265–8888

Bear's Paw Battlefield, Chinook; (406) 357–3130

Pine Butte Swamp Preserve, Choteau; (406) 466–5526

Heaven on Earth Ranch, Ulm; (406) 866–3316 or 452–7365

Charles M. Bair Family Museum Ranch, Martinsdale; (406) 727–8787

Bonanza Creek Country Guest Ranch, Lennep; (800) 476–6045

Montana Trivia

Considering that it's smack in the middle of central Montana's arid plains, Lewistown in summer is a surprisingly verdant spot. The town's storm-attracting location along the base of the Judith Mountains is responsible. In an average year Lewistown receives half again as much rainfall as Missoula, for instance, which sits on the "wet," western side of the Continental Divide.

The Judith Basin is nothing if not cowboy country; it was here that Charlie Russell came as a kid to learn the ways of the range. Cowboy poetry, a unique art form, expounds on the life of the open-range rider, and the emotions it triggers range from joy to heartbreak. If you've never had the opportunity to hear it read by those who write it, consider making the annual Montana **Cowboy Poetry Gathering**, convening in Lewistown in late August at the Park Inn convention center. Rhymin' wranglers from throughout Montana and beyond get together to share their poetry and music and to participate in workshops, jam-session readings, and social activities. Past performers have included the well-known (in cowboy poetry circles) Wally McRae, Hank Real Bird, and Sandy Seaton. Sessions are conducted for cowboy poetry neophytes and old-timers alike. Call 538–5436 or visit the chamber's Web site at www.lewistownchamber.com for more information.

One of the world's largest freshwater springs feeds **Big Spring State Hatchery** and also provides Lewistown's delicious supply of 99.9 percent pure drinking water. Flowing at over 3 million gallons per hour at Big Spring, the water originates in the nearby Big Snowy Mountains. Several strains of rainbow and other types of trout are raised at the facility, and lots of them: Big Spring supplies approximately half of all trout stocked in Montana lakes each year. An idyllic picnic grounds, maintained by the Department of Fish, Wildlife and Parks and the local Lions Club, sits adjacent to the placid pools fed by the spring.

In 1968 a nineteen-pound brown trout was taken from Spring Creek, downstream from the hatchery. For an idea of just how big a fish that was, glimpse into the open-air pond filled with giant trout, many of them in the twelve-to-sixteen-pound range. By putting a nickel into the nearby "candy machine," you can obtain a handful of stinky treats to feed the fish. Toss some food into the tank and then stand back, or prepare to get wet as a consequence of the splashing feeding frenzy you've incited.

RUSSELL COUNTRY

MAJOR ATTRACTIONS WORTH SEEING

C. M. Russell Museum Complex, Great Falls

Lewis & Clark Interpretive Center, Great Falls

Big Spring State Hatchery is located 6½ miles south of Lewistown on Spring Creek Road. (En route to the primary unit you'll first go by the hatchery's lower component.) Group tours are available on request; call 538–5588 for more information.

The *Charlie Russell Chew Choo* dinner train departs from the Kingston depot outside Lewistown on Friday and Saturday evenings throughout the summer and early fall. Boasting the "best prime rib east of the Rockies," the three-hour excursion also promises bountiful wildlife viewing, thrilling trestles and tunnels . . . and the very real possibility of being chased down and robbed by the Denton Gang. The cost for the outing, which follows the old Milwaukee Road line (now operated by Central Montana Rail), is $75 per person. Call (800) 735–7886 for reservations and information on special hotel/train packages.

Several gold-mining camps lie rotting in the ranges surrounding Lewistown, the most accessible being *Maiden Ghost Town*. Although gold prospectors had been interested in the Judith Basin country for years, fear of hostile Indians precluded their exploring too far afield. It wasn't until the early 1880s, by which time the Indian wars had ended, that claims began appearing and makeshift towns popping up in the Judith and North Moccasin Mountains.

In 1885 Maiden claimed around 700 residents and 150 buildings. The Spotted Horse, the most important mine in the area, paid out more than $2 million in gold over the years. Among the things still to be seen is the foundation of the Spotted Horse's gold-stamp mill, found just east of Maiden on Warm Springs Road. To get to Maiden, go north from Lewistown on Highway 191 for 9 miles to its junction with Highway 81, and then turn east onto Warm Springs Canyon Road and continue for 9 miles.

At the junction of Highway 81 and Highway 191, turn west onto Highway 81. This low-trafficked road dips and twists through the heart of the Judith Basin country, possibly the prettiest blend of mountains and plains you'll ever lay eyes on. (*Judith* is a big name in these parts: Judith River, Judith Basin, Judith Mountains. The river was first to receive the name—Captain William Clark named it in honor of his bride-to-be.) The wind is free to blow without obstruction here, so beware of opening both front car doors at the same time, or you may lose anything not tied down!

Five miles west of the junction of Highway 191 and Highway 81 note the sign on the north side of the road reading *Gigantic Warm Spring*, a descriptive name if ever there was one. Follow the gravel road for a mile to the Dave Vanek Ranch, pay the $3.00 fee, and head on down to the pool, which holds warm water diverted from nearby Warm Springs Creek. The springs formerly provided the water for the mining town of Kendall, using a system of ditches and viaducts. A pleasant picnic ground sits beside the waters, which are open to the public between 10:00 A.M. and dark. Call 538-9825 for more information.

Inspect some of Charlie Russell's paintings, and you'll notice that one of his favorite backdrops was a prominent, timber-covered square butte rising from the arid plains. The imposing feature—known, not surprisingly, as *Square Butte*—is home to a whopping variety of four-legged and two-winged creatures and was used prehistorically as a vision-quest site by American Indians. The Bureau of Land Management has designated Square Butte an "outstanding natural area" and protects it for its extraordinary geological, historical, and scenic attributes.

Square Butte is a volcanic pillar—technically a *laccolith*, or huge, solidified bubble of molten rock—that stands at 5,684 feet, roughly 2,000 feet above the surrounding prairie. Raptors such as golden eagles, prairie falcons, and great horned owls nest in the butte's protected alcoves, while pronghorn antelope, deer, and occasionally elk are seen

"What the Hay?"

*T*he Utica Road (Routes 238 and 239) connects the small towns of Hobson and Windham, en route meandering around the upper Judith River Valley and passing through tiny Utica. To the sides of the road, on a specified day early each September, some three dozen local ranchers create strange and wonderful things out of hay, as they vie to bring home the prize money in the "What the Hay?" competition. The contest, sponsored by the Utica Rod and Gun Club, transforms the normally sleepy byway into a road brimming with rigs, as folks travel

from miles around to see what sorts of whimsical and hilarious sculptures have been piled up this year.

Although the works of hay art are often conceived weeks, even months in advance, the ranchers-turned-artists wait until the last minute to build the creations, in order to keep their plans secret. The sculptures usually remain standing for a few days after the official day of competition, until the wind blows them over or the local bovine population discovers them and begins snacking away.

144

Best Annual Events

around the base. A herd of shaggy, white mountain goats resides on top and along the vertical cliffs below. The goats were moved here in the 1970s to replace a herd transplanted three decades earlier. The earlier herd abandoned the butte in the 1960s, apparently concluding that the nearby Highwood Mountains looked like a preferable place to call home.

From the town of Square Butte, 64 miles northwest of Lewistown, turn onto the gravel road leading west and go 1 mile. At a ranch entrance you'll find a sign describing the butte and a registration box with instructions; be sure to follow them carefully, for public access to the butte is permitted only through the kindness of the ranch owner. After checking in, follow the road (impassable when wet) to where it ends. From that point, it's a tough and steep, but rewarding, hike of about a mile to the top of Square Butte.

On top you'll notice charred evidence of the lightning fire that raged through in 1956. The view of Charlie Russell's favorite country is stunning: To the west are the Highwood Mountains and the nearby, smaller laccolith known as Round Butte; far to the north and east are the Bear's Paw and Little Rocky mountains; to the southeast and southwest are the Snowy Mountains and the Little Belts.

Best Annual Events

1. *C. M. Russell Auction of Original Western Art,* Great Falls; late March; (406) 761–6453

2. *Western Invitational AAU Basketball Tournament,* Lewistown; late March; (406) 538–7629

3. *Ice Breaker Road Race, Great Falls;* late April; (406) 771–2165

4. *Whoop–Up Days,* Conrad; mid–May; (406) 278–3623

5. *Fort Benton Summer Celebration,* Fort Benton; late June; (406) 622–3351

6. *Montana State Fair,* Great Falls; late July; (406) 727–8900

7. *Montana Cowboy Poetry Gathering,* Lewistown; mid–August; (406) 538–5436

8. *Chokecherry Festival,* Lewistown; early September; (406) 538–5436

The area is closed to the general public in the fall during hunting season. For maps or for more information call the Bureau of Land Management in Lewistown at 538–7461.

Fort Benton, 35 miles northwest of Square Butte on Highway 80, was once known as "Chicago of the Plains," "the world's most inland port," and less complimentary names such as "the home of cutthroats and horse thieves" and "the bloodiest block in the West." More recently it was nicknamed the "Birthplace of Montana." From the 1830s until the 1850s, steamboats ventured up the Missouri only as far as Fort Union, which straddles the present-day Montana-North Dakota border. But a new design of broad-bottom steamboats appeared in the 1850s, permitting travel into the treacherous upper reaches of the river. By the

Montana Trivia

*In 1991 the U.S. Coast
Guard established a
LORAN–C post north of
Havre, in as unlikely a
location as you'll ever find
Coast Guard personnel on
duty, 700 miles from the
West Coast.*

mid-1860s, Fort Benton was a primary port, controlling the trade between the eastern markets and the goldfields of southwest Montana.

There's much to be seen in the small town today. Fort Benton's main street, which fronts the river responsible for the town's very being, is the put-in for the float along the **Upper Missouri National Wild and Scenic River**, so designated in 1976. Most parties take seven days to cover the 150 river miles between here and the Fred Robinson Bridge on Highway 191. (For information on guided historic river tours, which can include overnights in restored homestead cabins, call the **Missouri River Canoe Company** in nearby Loma at 800–426–2926.) The swath of wild country traversed remains much as it was when Lewis and Clark passed through in 1805, minus a few grizzly bears and bison and a large share of its timber: In twenty-four hours of chugging, a steamboat burned as much as twenty-five cords of wood, which was cut and supplied by "woodhawks" working the banks of the river.

The intrepid explorers, along with their Shoshone Indian interpreter and ambassador, still stand sentinel over the river. The **Lewis and Clark State Memorial,** commissioned for the Bicentennial celebration in 1976, is one of the finest works by master western sculptor and Browning resident Bob Scriver. Cast larger than life, Clark, Lewis, and a sitting Sacajawea gaze out over the waterway they traced westward for so many hundreds of miles. (Incidentally, more statues of Sacajawea have been erected in the United States than of any other woman.)

Directly in front of Lewis and Clark State Memorial, mired in the river's mud, lie the sunken remains of the *Baby Rose*, one of the last steamboats to wend its way to Fort Benton. Also nearby, and more visible, is the full-scale replica of the keelboat *Mandan*, built for the filming of the movie based on A. B. Guthrie's *The Way West*. And just up Main Street a few hundred yards is the Bureau of Land Management's Lewis and Clark National Historic Trail headquarters. You can head onto those historic waters in Fort Benton by boarding the **Benton Belle** (622–2628), a 55-foot riverboat offering two- and three-hour cruises.

The **Fort Benton Museum** focuses on the early days of white settlement in the Fort Benton area, from the 1840s until the railroad pushed through toward the end of the century and effectively halted river trade. One museum highlight is an 1860s trapper's cabin, moved from its

Montana Trivia

A 2½–story house on Great Falls' lower south side recently acquired in a foreclosure sale by the Neighborhood Housing Services was originally procured from a Sears, Roebuck and Company catalog. The kit was purchased in the 1920s for approximately $1,500, with the pieces shipped to Great Falls from an Illinois lumberyard.

original site on the Teton River. Admission is $4.00 (a fee that will get you into a second museum, described below). It's open daily 10:00 A.M. to 5:00 P.M. from May through October.

The facility is situated at the edge of tree-canopied **Old Fort Park**, itself a museum of sorts, as the locations of the various structures of the original fort—first a fur-trading post and later an army garrison—are marked with interpretive signs. (Note: The fort is currently undergoing restoration.)

As you head out of Fort Benton and before passing the burial place of world-famous Shep the dog (you'll read there why he was world famous), stop in at the **Montana Agricultural Center and Museum of the Northern Great Plains**, the official state agricultural museum. Top-notch displays take up where the Fort Benton Museum leaves off—that is, after the railroad came through and the tough prairie sod began being ripped open by those attempting to scrape out a livelihood by farming the unforgiving land.

The museum focuses on the equipment, culture, and economy of the region from the time of the first homesteaders, around 1910, to the mid-1970s. In a new museum section are found the six bison mounted in 1886 by William T. Hornaday, then chief taxidermist for the U.S. National Museum in Washington, D.C. The sextet, which for years were displayed together at the Smithsonian, were recently refurbished by a Butte taxidermist; now, for the first time since 1956—when the display at the National Museum was dismantled—the six bison are together again. The big bull of this group is the most celebrated buffalo of all time: His likeness appears on the U.S. buffalo head nickel, the National Park Service ranger badge, on several postage stamps, and elsewhere.

The museum and adjacent Schwinden Library and Archives are open from 10:00 A.M. to 3:00 P.M. daily throughout the year. The complex is at Twentieth and St. Charles Streets, next to the high-school playing field (just watch for the colorful farming mural adorning the side of a long metal building). The $4.00 ticket will also get you into the Fort Benton Museum, described earlier. Call 622–5316 for more information.

The welcome sign on the outskirts of tiny Loma, 11 miles northeast of Fort Benton, reads, TAKE A BREAK: LEWIS & CLARK DID IN 1805. How could one pass up an invitation like that?

Turn south off the highway and you'll find a pair of surprising museums in which to take your break. The **Earth Science Museum** (739–4488) at 106 Main Street, is a collection of rocks, fossils, and minerals that will bring out the rock hound in anyone. The museum is open May 15 to September 30, daily from 9:00 A.M. to 7:00 P.M., and by appointment the rest of the year. A block south, at 106 First Street, is the **House of 10,000 Dolls** (739–4338), a collection of dolls from the early nineteenth century to the present. It's open June through September by appointment only.

The Big Sky

*P*ulitzer Prize–winning author A. B. "Bud" Guthrie, born in 1901, grew up in and around Choteau, Montana. After earning a degree in journalism in 1923 at the University of Montana, Guthrie launched a successful newspaper career that culminated in his being named executive editor of Kentucky's Lexington Leader. By the time the mid-1940s rolled around, Guthrie was serving as a Nieman Fellow at Harvard, where he wrote The Big Sky, his most famous work. The widely read novel's success gave him the means and impetus to move back to Montana, where he continued writing.

Guthrie became to Montana what Steinbeck is to California and what Faulkner is to Mississippi. Concerning The Big Sky, he wrote: "I had a theme, not original, that each man kills the thing he loves. If it had any originality at all, it was only that a band of men, the fur-hunters, killed the life they loved and killed it with a thoughtless prodigality perhaps unmatched." Although Guthrie's words make it sound as if The Big Sky is a depressing read, it is in fact an exultation: of the free trapper, of the Native American, and of the broad Montana landscape. His five books that followed, including The Way West,

(winner of the 1950 Pulitzer Prize for Fiction) and These Thousand Hills, continued the saga of the settling of Montana, whose nicknamed derived from Guthrie's most enduring story. (He once joked that he ought to receive royalties from the sale of Montana license plates, which are emblazoned with the words "Big Sky," just as he did from his books.) He also wrote screenplays for westerns, including Shane, considered by some critics the best of its genre.

In his later years, Guthrie, living outside Choteau—where he was surrounded by ranchers and mineral exploiters—was an outspoken conservationist, as he continued seeing evidence of the truth in the theme on which he based The Big Sky. "There are too many among us who think first and only of the immediate personal profit, not of the long-term and irreparable loss. They figure that posterity never did anything for them and to hell with it." Yet he also wrote that "not everything is lost. The air around my old home is still clean and tonic; Ear Mountain still stands and I imagine industrious boys can still find fish, and in the fall see a cottontail sitting."

Bud Guthrie passed away in 1991.

If you'd rather take an outdoor break, head down to the nearby confluence of the Marias and Missouri Rivers, where you can enjoy watching the proliferation of bird life at the **Richard E. Wood Watchable Wildlife Area**.

Hi-Line West

The territory north of the Missouri River and east of the Rocky Mountains in Montana is known as the *Hi-Line*, a term used variously to describe the Great Northern Railway, its route, and the surrounding countryside.

At the edge of Havre, the Hi-Line's version of a metropolis, is the 2,000-year-old **Wahkpa Chu'gn Archaeological Site**. The Indian words translate to something akin to "too close for comfort." Perhaps by this the Assiniboine Indians were describing their own position in relation to dozens of massive, charging bison.

The site, used throughout prehistory by at least three distinct cultures, includes a combination of a traditional buffalo jump, or pishkun, and a pound. Basically, pounds were traps—sometimes outfitted with sharpened, upward-pointing sticks for impaling the animals—which the Indians probably used to trap smaller herds. Tours to the site are hosted Tuesday through Sunday in the summer, leaving from the Holiday Village shopping center, just across Highway 2 from the **H. Earl Clack Memorial Museum**. The fee for a tour is $3.00 for adults and $1.00 for students.

On display at the museum are artifacts from Wahkpa Chu'gn, an exhibit on the Minnesota-Montana homesteading migration, details on the early Signal Corps Weather Station at Fort Assiniboine, and a brief history of the prohibition-era Bootlegger Trail chain, which connected the Havre area with Canada. The museum, located at 306 3rd Avenue in the Heritage Center, is open year-round Tuesday through Saturday from noon to 5:00 P.M. For information on tours to Wahkpa Chu'gn call the museum at 265–4000.

Not so much off the beaten path as *under* it: **Havre Beneath the Streets**. Some of the popular pursuits in a youthful Havre, when the turn-of-the-century town served as an important regional railroad and ranching center, took place underground, both literally and figuratively. Today a subterranean mall underlying a full city block of downtown features basements connected by walkways. In these dark depths thrived opium dens, bordellos, honky tonks, and other sorts of enterprises, both above and below the law. The rooms are packed with high-quality displays, vividly bringing those days to life. "People don't realize the magnitude of this project, nor did they expect to see what they saw," Havre resident Frank DeRosa, considered the father of Havre's underground movement, told a Spokane *Spokesman Review* travel editor. Havre's underground stands above those in other cities, wrote Graham Vink, because of its "quantity and quality—all authentic, all loaned and donated by residents of Havre and surrounding communities." Havre Beneath the Streets is open the year around, with hour-long tours available ($6.00 for adults, $4.00 for kids, and $5.00 for seniors; for children six and under the tour is free). Call 265–8888 to make reservations.

An unexpected find rising from the flat Hi-Line country is the weather-beaten volcanic Bear's Paw Mountains and *Beaver Creek Park* (395–4565). Beaver Creek begins 10 miles south of Havre on Highway 234 and runs south for 15 miles, encompassing some 10,000 acres. Hundreds of campsites await in the park, and good fishing and hiking abound.

Toward its southern end, Highway 234 enters the Rocky Boy's Indian Reservation and continues to the *Bear Paw Ski Bowl* (265–8404; www.skibearpaw.com), a low-key resort with low-priced lift tickets to match. The reservation, the smallest of the seven in Montana, was the last to be created. Two groups of Indians who had wandered down from Canada in the 1880s, Chief Rocky Boy's band of Chippewa and a group of Cree led by Little Bear, were still roaming the high plains of northern Montana well into the twentieth century. Determined lobbying by Charlie Russell and other concerned Montanans resulted in the federal government taking 55,000 acres of surplus land from the Fort Assiniboine Military Reserve and setting it aside as a home for these landless and destitute native people.

On October 5, 1877, one of the most valiant treks in American history ended at Snake Creek in the Bear's Paw Mountains, at the site known today as the *Bear's Paw Battlefield*. Chief Joseph of the Nez Perce had seen enough death and bloodshed, and it was here that he spoke the stirring words, "It is cold and we have no blankets. The little children are freezing to death. . . . Hear me, my chiefs! I am tired. My heart is sick and sad. From where the sun now stands, I will fight no more forever."

When the Nez Perce surrendered to Colonel Nelson A. Miles at Snake Creek, it ended a journey of nearly 1,200 miles, at times arduous, at times remarkable. The trek began in Oregon's Wallowa Valley, passed through northern Idaho, and then wound through Montana's Bitterroot and Big Hole valleys, into Yellowstone National Park and back into Montana. After failing to gain sanctuary from the Crow, a traditional ally of the Nez Perce, Chief Joseph continued north, intending ultimately to join Sitting Bull in Canada.

But they were caught in the Bear's Paw Mountains, 40 miles short of the border. After several days of fighting, the Indians were still holding off the soldiers, but the chiefs couldn't agree on their next move. Eventually, 300 Nez Perce followed Chief Looking Glass to Canada, and Chief Joseph surrendered for the rest.

Sixteen miles south of Chinook on Highway 240 you can visit the Bear's Paw Battlefield (357–3130), which looks much as it did in 1877: Snake Creek still twists across the swath of treeless prairie, cutting steep side coulees, and willow thickets crowd its banks. Until relatively recently the site was administered by the Montana Department of Fish, Wildlife and Parks, and therefore was the only one of four major Nez Perce War battle sites not included in the Nez Perce National Historic Park (NHP)—an unusual and intriguing "park," in that it encompasses some three dozen sites in Washington, Oregon, Idaho, and Montana. A movement to change the situation was successful, however, and the Bear's Paw Battlefield is now an official component of the Nez Perce NHP. (Technically, the state still owns the land, due to an old law prohibiting the state of

A Taste of Montana

*T*he Sweetgrass Hills, encompassing East Butte, Middle Butte, and West Butte, are a tiny mountain range rising against the skyline north of the highway between Chester and Shelby. Composed of 50-million-year-old igneous intrusions and the sedimentary rocks surrounding them, geologically the Sweetgrass Hills are closely related to the Judith and Moccasin Mountains outside Lewistown.

I'm not sure what it is the deer in that

country eat—other than farmers' grain crops—but the flavor of their venison is out of this world. Each fall our good friends from Missoula, Peggy, Robin, and son Ian, mount a hunting trip to the Sweetgrass Hills (Peggy grew up on a farm in nearby Rudyard), and Nancy and I are usually the lucky recipients of some of their bounty. The barbecued backstrap of a Sweetgrass Hills mule deer is a taste of Montana as sure as huckleberry hotcakes.

Montana from selling off its lands, but the National Park Service is the only bureaucratic presence you'll find there.)

The **Blaine County Museum** in Chinook offers tours to the site and also presents an outstanding multimedia show on the battle, entitled "40 Miles from Freedom." The free museum, located at 501 Indiana Street, is open year-round on a changing schedule; call 357–2590 for details.

Heading west from Havre along Highway 2, you'll pass through a string of Hi-Line wheat-farming towns: Kremlin, Gildford, Hingham, Rudyard, Inverness, Joplin. Classic T-shaped railroad towns, each has its own depot and set of grain elevators, creating the top of the T, and a business strip, forming the stem of the letter.

In Shelby, visit the **Marias Museum of History and Art,** where you'll learn about the Dempsey-Gibbons World Championship Heavyweight Fight. On July 4, 1923, nearly 25,000 spectators were in the small town to watch the match, in which Jack Dempsey outlasted Tommy Gibbons for fifteen rounds. The museum contains fight artifacts, photos, and displays, as well as exhibits on other Toole County historical happenings. It's open in summer Monday through Saturday, 1:00 to 5:00 P.M., and Monday through Friday, 1:00 to 5:00 P.M., the rest of the year. Call 434–2551 for further information.

High Central Plains

Stop first in Choteau at the **Old Trail Museum,** located along Highway 287 at the northern outskirts of town. Among the many displays of minerals and fossils in the museum's dinosaur grounds are photos and castings of the dinosaur nests for which nearby Egg Mountain has become renowned in dino-digging circles.

Museum of the Rockies and Montana State University paleontologist Jack Horner (who later served as a technical advisor for the film *Jurassic Park*) was first led to the Egg Mountain site in 1978 by rock-shop owners John and Marian Brandvold. In the mudstone of Egg Mountain, Horner located more than a dozen 6-foot-wide nests of duck-billed dinosaurs, with fossilized skeletons of baby dinosaurs still in them. The findings set the paleontological world on its ear: It had always been believed that dinosaurs were cold-blooded, solitary beasts with little intelligence. But here was proof, Jack Horner asserted, that these were warm-blooded, intelligent herd animals who cared for their young long after birth.

The species of duck-billed dinosaur first found by Marian Brandvold was named *Maiasaura peeblesorum*, or "Good Mother Lizard," and has since been named the Montana State Fossil.

For information on bus tours and on paleontology field classes, which range from two to ten days in duration, call the Old Trail Museum at 466–5332 or tap in to www.oldtrailmuseum.org. The museum, which also features exhibits on "homestead justice" and the Old North Trail, is open daily Memorial Day through Labor Day 9:00 A.M. to 6:00 P.M. (10:00 A.M. to 3:00 P.M. Tuesday through Saturday the rest of the year).

Egg Mountain is contained within the Nature Conservancy's unique, 18,000-acre **Pine Butte Swamp Preserve.** Also within the preserve is the 4,000-acre Pine Butte Swamp—a "boreal fen," technically—along with thousands of acres of foothills and rolling grassland. Part-time and year-round inhabitants include no fewer than forty-three species of mammals and 150 varieties of birds. Pine Butte, rising some 500 feet above its surroundings, is a fine place to hike to earn an overall view of the area.

To find the preserve entrance, go north on Highway 89 from Choteau for 5 miles and then turn west onto Teton Canyon Road. This is where the plains sweep up to marry the mountains; as you approach the stunning, hard-rock front, you'll notice pockets of ancient limber pine

Re-cycling Canal Paths

*A*s I discovered quite by accident one autumn day a few years ago, irrigation canal paths running across the prairies east of the Rocky Mountain Front offer great opportunities to those with mountain bicycles in tow. One such path parallels the Sun River Slope Canal, beginning on the southwestern shore of Pishkun Reservoir, which is found approximately 18 miles southwest of Choteau on county roads. The path encounters U.S. Highway 287 after twisting for some 12 miles to the southeast, amid rolling hills but at a steady, nearly imperceptible gradient.

Another path follows the Pishkun Canal, leading westerly from the west side of the same reservoir into Sun River Canyon, ending not far from a pleasant Lewis and Clark National Forest Campground. These little-used canal paths lead through areas visited by very few people, and the views earned from them are absolutely world class.

claiming more and more of the windswept plains. In 15 miles turn south and continue for about 4 miles until you see the information sign.

Access onto Pine Butte Swamp Preserve is limited in order to better protect its features and creatures. To obtain permission to hike in the swamp area or up onto the butte, call 466–5526. You also can use this phone number to request information on conservancy-guided summer tours originating daily at the restored Bellview School and on workshops conducted at the preserve.

No doubt the best way to see and learn about the preserve is to arrange a stay at the Nature Conservancy's nearby **Pine Butte Guest Ranch** (from 1930 until 1978 the privately owned Circle 8 Ranch). From May through September the ranch offers lodging for up to twenty-five guests in rustic, comfortable cabins set amidst stands of aspen, cottonwood, and fir. The cabins are constructed of native wood, each with a stone fireplace, private bath, and handmade furniture. Family-style meals, with an emphasis on fresh, healthy foods, are served in the main lodge.

The ranch combines a traditional dude-ranch atmosphere with an in-depth natural history program: Guests can enjoy horseback rides, naturalist-led hikes, wildlife-photography outings, and numerous other activities. Several special sessions are conducted as well, including "Montana Grizzly Bears," "Mammal Tracking," and "Dinosaur Digging."

From June through mid-September, guests are restricted to week-long stays, costing approximately $1,125 per adult and $875 per child. The rate includes cabin, all meals, horseback riding, participation in the natural-history program, and the use of all ranch facilities. During the shoulder seasons (May, late September, and October), the ranch offers less expensive weekly packages and special group and daily rates. All proceeds help to support the Nature Conservancy's good works in Montana. For reservations (a must) and more information, call 466–2158 or E-mail the establishment at pbuttegr@3rivers.net.

En route from Choteau to Great Falls, immediately after turning east onto Highway 200 from Highway 89 (15 miles southeast of Fairfield), you'll spot what is arguably Montana's most beautiful barn. The **J. C. Adams Stone Barn** isn't open to the public, but still the public can't miss seeing and being impressed by it.

Community dances and other events once were common on the hardwood floor of the barn's second story. Stock grower J. C. Adams built the 120-foot-by-40-foot structure in the early 1880s to serve as headquarters for his endeavor—selling livestock and goods to those traveling the Mullan Trail. The barn's sandstone blocks came from a nearby quarry, and Swedish stonecutters fashioned its unusual architectural details.

Great Falls, Montana's second largest city, was named for the Great Falls of the Missouri River, source of great trepidation for the Lewis and Clark expedition. Meriwether Lewis wrote, "The river was one continued sene of rappids and cascades. . . . The river appears here to have woarn a channel in the process of time through a solid rock."

Ornery Kid Russell

The name Russell is every bit as celebrated in and around Great Falls as are the names of Lewis and Clark. Charles Marion Russell, born in St. Louis in 1864, was sixteen when he set out for the Montana plains to sample the free life of a range cowboy. His parents thought the boy would quickly get the itch out of his pants and return home; little did they know, though, that when young Charlie lit out for Montana, he was going home: Russell fell in love with Big Sky Country, and he lived out his life there.

After cowboying for a decade in places like the Pigs Eye Basin in the Judith River country, in 1892 Russell moved to Great Falls, set up a studio, and commenced producing paintings and other works of art. Most depicted the open-range, cattle-growing period of Montana's history, and he quickly became known as "America's cowboy artist." He made the landscapes south and east of Great Falls familiar to people throughout the world; among his favorite backdrops were the territory surrounding the Missouri River, Square Butte, the Big Snowy Mountains, and the town of

Utica. Charlie Russell became very successful and incredibly popular—almost synonymous with wild Montana—because of his uncanny ability to recreate on canvas the things he'd seen and experienced, his down-to-earth and good-humored nature, and his wife, Nancy, who possessed the acumen for promotion and business matters that Russell himself apparently lacked.

Charlie Russell was a celebrity, no doubt about it, but he was the sort of celebrity that seems all too uncommon today: a modest one. Just before departing this earth for that wide-open, unfenced prairie in the sky he wrote: "To have talent is no credit to its owner; any man that can make a living doing what he likes is lucky, and I'm that. Any time I cash in now, I win."

A terrific, forty-page brochure, C. M. Russell Auto Tour, illustrated with color photos of Russell's paintings, is available to lead motorists through the heart of the country "Ornery Kid Russell" grew to love during his early years in Montana. To request a copy, call Russell Country at (800) 527–5348.

The party spent several days mapping their long portage route around the falls (now inundated by hydroelectric works) and then several weeks more traversing it. The route they eventually followed has been designated a national historic landmark and can be traced today by obtaining the self-guiding-tour brochure, *The Explorers at the Portage,* from the Great Falls Visitors Bureau (761–4434). (Another publication, covering the party's travels across all of Montana—*Lewis & Clark's Montana Journey: A Guide to Easy-to-Reach Sites and Fun Things To Do*—can be procured by calling Travel Montana at 800–847–4868.)

On June 18, 1805, Lewis's cohort, William Clark, wrote of another area feature, "We proceeded up on the river a little more than a mile to the largest fountain or spring I ever saw, and no doubt if it is not the largest in America known. . . . The water boils up from under the rocks near the edge of the river and falls imediately into the river 8 feet, and keeps its colour for ½ a mile emencely clear and of a bluish cast."

Today, picnickers, hikers, and fishermen enjoy the day-use state park at **Giant Springs**, located not far from the Montana Department of Fish, Wildlife and Parks' visitor center. The center holds outstanding displays on the rich bird and animal life of the region, including one of the most terrifying grizzly bear mounts you'd ever care to see.

As Clark suspected, Giant Springs is among the largest freshwater springs in the country, and 134,000 gallons of water per minute bubble from it. As if for contrast, the unimaginably clear waters of the spring's pool feed the Roe River, the shortest river in the world according to *The Guinness Book of World Records.*

This is one of the best urban birding areas in the Northwest, with bald eagles, loons, and other winged critters common in the winter, and more than one hundred species, including white pelicans, prairie falcons, and pheasants, present in the summer. Giant Springs State Park is located 3 miles east of Highway 87 on River Drive, between Black Eagle Dam and Rainbow Dam. In summer the visitor center is open from 8:00 A.M. to 7:00 P.M., Monday through Friday, and from 10:00 A.M. to 7:00 P.M. on weekends. Kids will enjoy feeding the ten-pound rainbow trout swimming about in the outdoor pond. Call Montana Fish, Wildlife and Parks at 454–5840 for more information.

So vital was the role the explorers played in the discovery and settlement of this region that Great Falls celebrates an annual *Lewis and Clark Festival* in late June and/or early July. The festival includes river tours, guided visits to expedition sites, buffalo-hump barbecues, running races, and performances of *Proceeding On*, a play based on the party's journals. For information on the festival, call 761–4434.

The Cascade County Historical Society (452–3462) offers guided tours to *Ulm Pishkun State Park*. Excavations taking place during the summer of 1992 resulted in new findings at this, one of the largest buffalo jumps in the United States. By following the short trail leading below the cliffs, you'll spot bison-bone fragments, some with obvious butcher marks, scattered about the ground where countless bison died.

To get to the park and its new visitor center, go 10 miles south of Great Falls on Interstate 15 to the Ulm exit, and then follow signs 6 miles on gravel to the northwest. The park, maintained by the Montana Department of Fish, Wildlife and Parks Optimists, is open April 15 through October 15. For more information, call 454–5840.

Hidden in the Smith River country, 55 miles south of Great Falls, is the *Heaven on Earth Ranch*, a working cattle ranch where Old West fans can come to enjoy wagon rides, cookouts, target shooting . . . and golf,

The Prairie Cathedral

*O*ften the only feature disrupting the rolling perfection of the central and northern Montana plains is the distant grain elevator, the ubiquitous "prairie cathedral." Abandoned, weathered, and leaning precariously with the prevailing winds, more and more of these historic grain-storing ghosts disappear every year.

During the homesteading boom in the early part of the twentieth century, thousands of new farms popped up on the face of the Montana prairies. At harvest, which usually occurred late in August, farmers were compelled to make dozens of trips to haul to the nearest elevator their bounties of

hundreds of bushels of grain. As a result, more and more railside elevators emerged throughout grain country. The structures, which typically held between 10,000 and 30,000 bushels, served not only as grain-collection sites at harvest time, but also in other seasons as gathering places, where far-removed neighbors would catch up with one another. Once the big grain companies came into the country, however, the small elevators could no longer compete, and they were rapidly abandoned by the score. But those who spent time in elevators say they can never forget the clamor, the dust, and the earthy essence of drying grain.

on what just may be the most isolated and underutilized nine-hole course in the country. Riverside cabins are also available to rent; call 866–3316 or 452–7365 to learn more.

Military and airplane buffs will fall all over themselves at the ***Malmstrom Air Force Base Museum and Air Park***. Called Great Falls Army Air Base when established during the months following the Japanese attack on Pearl Harbor, the base was renamed in 1955 to honor Colonel Einar Axel Malmstrom, a World War II hero who died nearby in a training accident.

The museum highlights the roles played by the base in the Cuban Missile Crisis, the Vietnam War, and the Gulf War. Included among the many flying machines displayed in the air park are an F-84F Thunderstreak fighter bomber, a Minuteman Intercontinental Ballistic Missile, a UH-1F Iroquois helicopter (the "Huey" of Vietnam fame), and a 1,200-mile-per-hour Voo Doo air-defense fighter.

Malmstrom Air Force Base Museum and Air Park, funded by donations and staffed by volunteers (not by the Air Force and your tax dollars, as they're quick to point out), is located at the east end of Second Avenue North in Great Falls. The air park is open during daylight hours, and the museum from 10:00 A.M. to 4:00 P.M. daily in summer (closed weekends the rest of the year). For information call 731–2705.

Fans of the lower tech machinery that prevailed before humans took to the skies can also be accommodated in the area, at the ***Mehmke Steam Museum***. Here, at a working farm set back from the highway in a protected draw, awaits one of the country's largest privately owned collections of operable steam-driven equipment. The museum is located 5 miles east of Great Falls on Highway 89 and is open year-round during daylight hours, weather permitting. Call 452–6571 for more information.

After witnessing how farmers did their duties early in the century, head for the ***MSU Central Agricultural Research Center***, where you can learn about modern techniques employed by the northern plains farmer. For decades the research center's goal has been to serve central Montana's farmers and ranchers by helping them produce and market their products in more profitable ways.

The center consists of several buildings, including a laboratory, a seed-cleaning plant, and a shop, and also works a diversified, 640-acre dry-land farm. The approximately 350 acres of tilled land are divided into thousands of tiny plots, no bigger than 3 feet by 20 feet. Among other purposes, these are used to test the relative performances of different seed varieties of wheat, barley, oats, and oil-producing crops, such as sunflowers.

The Central Agricultural Research Center has achieved a long list of accomplishments since its establishment in 1907, accomplishments largely responsible for the success of central Montana's dry-land farming industry. To learn more about past successes and ones in the works, you can visit the facility weekdays from 8:00 A.M. to 4:30 P.M. It's located 5 miles east of the Sod Busters Museum, or 2 miles west of Moccasin. For information on the annual visitors' field day, call 423–5421.

In Harlowton, stop at Fischer Park and tour the *E-57B Electric Train Engine*. The Chicago, Milwaukee, St. Paul & Pacific Railroad, better known as the Milwaukee Road, in 1917 completed the longest stretch of electrified railroad in the United States, spanning the distance between Harlowton and Avery, Idaho. The railroad saved a great deal of money along this line simply by taking advantage of gravity: On long mountain descents, electric motors became generators, driven by the train's momentum. Energy that otherwise would have been wasted was converted into electricity in a clever "regenerative braking system." On descents the engines could store about half the energy needed for getting up hills of equal length.

Still seen west of Harlowton are some utility poles that formerly carried electricity from the huge brick transformer stations that were positioned every 30 miles between Harlowton and Avery. One such station still stands on Highway 294 west of Martinsdale (and another near the Nimrod Tunnels, 30 miles east of Missoula).

Harlowton was a primary hub for the Milwaukee Road. Here, in roundhouses, eastbound trains swapped electric engines for steam engines, and westbound trains did the opposite. The three-story *Graves Hotel*, one of the flagship hotels along the Milwaukee Road line, has obviously seen better days, but fans of lavish architecture should drop by to have a look. As were several buildings in town, the hotel was constructed of massive sandstone blocks quarried from a nearby bluff.

Around fifty Hutterite colonies, claiming a total of more than 4,000 residents, are scattered throughout the northern plains of Montana.

(Another several hundred colonies, with a total of some 30,000 residents, are located in the adjacent northern states and Canadian provinces.) Many, like the **Martinsdale Colony** (572–3329), located just outside Martinsdale, sell meat and produce to the general public. Here, as elsewhere, telltale rows of neatly kept buildings—and an obviously successful farming operation—inform those passing by that this is a Hutterite colony.

Hutterites live spartan, communal lifestyles based on tenets of a sixteenth-century religious sect that emerged in Austria. Their predecessors escaped to North America in 1874 after living in Europe and Russia for more than three centuries. Hutterites, who speak a dialect of German, cannot own their own homes or cars and are not supposed to watch television or listen to radio; they dress in homemade clothes of Old-World style, and they are paid no money for their work, nor do they earn vacations.

So, why does their culture flourish? Perhaps it's because in their society harmony prevails; murder, mental illness, and divorce are said to be almost nonexistent. Hutterite families enjoy a closeness all but lost in twenty-first-century American culture, and the number of colonies in Montana continues to grow.

The **Charles M. Bair Family Museum Ranch**, opened to the general public in 1996, showcases the splendid home and stunning belongings of one of the state's foremost pioneer families.

Best of the Byways

*I*n April 1996, the American Recreation Coalition honored two Russell Country scenic drives by including them among just six 1996 "Best of the Byways." The **Kings Hill Scenic Byway**, a 71-mile stretch of U.S. Highway 89 passing through the Little Belt Mountains, links White Sulphur Springs with the town of Belt to the north. Highlights along the way include rugged ranchlands, steep-sided limestone canyons, a short side trip to Sluice Boxes State Park, and the Showdown Ski Area. The Great Falls cross-country ski club also grooms Nordic trails in the area.

The **Trail of the Great Bear**, the other honoree, is a 2,100-mile, international tourism corridor linking Yellowstone, Glacier-Waterton, Banff, and Jasper National Parks. A substantial portion of the trail runs through Russell Country, as well as through other tourism regions of Montana.

It wasn't until he had tried his hand at several careers that Charles M. Bair became a rich man. He arrived in Montana in 1883 as a conductor on the Northern Pacific Railroad, then entered the ranching business in 1893; finally, a few years later, he literally struck it rich in the gold fields of Alaska. During the ensuing years he invested in numerous interests, becoming the owner of one of the world's largest sheep herds in the process, running as many as 300,000 head of sheep at a time.

After moving permanently in 1934 to the ranch that they'd owned for two decades, the Bair family began adding to the existing ranch house, until it totaled twenty-six rooms. The daughters, Alberta and Marguerite, who became renowned Montana philanthropists and patrons of the arts (you may have happened across the Alberta Bair Theater in Billings), filled the house with paintings and antiques acquired during their numerous trips to Europe. The resultant mix of Old-World art, Old-West art, and memorabilia—the family was friends with, among other notables, Charlie Russell, Will Rogers, and Chief Plenty Coups—constitutes one of the West's most valuable and unforgettable family collections. It was the wish of the daughters that the home be retained as a museum for the people of the state they loved, and now it is. (Alberta, the last of the family, died in 1993.) For information on hours and tours, call the C. M. Russell Museum in Great Falls at 727–8787.

North of the settlement of Lennep, which is a few miles southwest of Martinsdale on Highway 294, along a bumpy back road known as the Lennep Route, you'll find the **Bonanza Creek Country** guest ranch. Here the Voldseth family works hard to ensure that a stay will be among their guests' most cherished memories, and a maximum of sixteen at a time enjoy the personal attention and beautiful countryside, where they're within view of half a dozen mighty Montana ranges, including the Crazy Mountains and the Castle Range. Working the cows on horseback (these folks aren't just playing cowboys and cowgirls; their herd numbers around 1,200), pedaling the back roads and trails on the ranch's mountain bikes, fishing, swimming, hayrides, and four-wheel-drive tours in the surrounding mountains are among the activities that'll keep you hopping. Accommodations range from private cedar log cabins to a re-created Plains Indian tipi (with indoor plumbing in all but the tipi!), and the wholesome food is reputed to be "the best home-cooking this side of the Crazies." A six-night stay goes for $1,200 per adult and $900 for each child twelve and under. For information, reservations, and

The Castle

precise directions, call (800) 476–6045, E-mail bonanza@3rivers.net, or go to the ranch's Web site at www.avicom.net/bonanza.

In White Sulphur Springs *The Castle*, home to the Meagher County Museum, sits high on a hill like . . . well, like a castle. The mansion was completed in 1892, for rancher-businessman B. R. Sherman, from granite blocks that were hand cut in the Castle Mountains, then hauled to town by oxen. Inside you'll find a varied collection of artifacts from area ghost towns and elsewhere in the county. The rich tones of the dark oak and cherrywood used in the woodwork lend the interior an air of dignity. The Castle, located at 310 Second Avenue Northeast, is open to visitors daily, 10:00 A.M. to 6:00 P.M., from May 15 to September 15. Admission is $3.00 for adults and $2.00 for children and seniors. For information on tours call 547–3666.

PLACES TO STAY
IN RUSSELL COUNTRY

LEWISTOWN
Yogo Inn of Lewistown,
211 East Main;
(800) 860-9646

Symmes-Wicks House
Bed & Breakfast,
220 West Boulevard;
(406) 538-9068

Lewistown Super 8,
102 Wendell Avenue;
(800) 800-8000

Trail's End Motel,
216 Northeast Main;
(406) 538-5468

FORT BENTON
Pioneer Lodge,
1700 Front Street;
(406) 622-5441

Fort Motel,
1809 St. Charles Street;
(406) 622-3312

HAVRE
Duck Inn,
1300 1st Street;
(406) 265-9615

Park Hotel,
335 1st Street;
(406) 265-7891

Havre Super 8,
166 9th Avenue West;
(800) 800-8000

TownHouse Inn,
601 West 1st Street;
(800) 442-4667

Our Home Bed & Breakfast,
66 65th Avenue Northwest;
(406) 265-1055

CHOTEAU
Best Western
Stage Stop Inn,
1005 North Main Avenue;
(888) 466-5900

Big Sky Motel,
209 South Main Avenue;
(406) 466-5318

Pine Butte Guest Ranch
(see p. 148 for directions);
(406) 466-2158

GREAT FALLS
Best Western Heritage Inn,
1700 Fox Farm Road;
(800) 548-0361

Holiday Inn Great Falls,
400 10th Avenue South;
(406) 727-7200

Fox Hollow Inn
Condominium Housing,
1700 10th Street Southwest;
(406) 727-0702

Comfort Inn,
1120 9th Street South;
(800) 228-5150

Collins Mansion Bed &
Breakfast, 1003 2nd Avenue
Northwest;
(406) 452-6798

WHITE SULPHUR SPRINGS
Spa Hot Springs Motel,
202 West Main;
(406) 547-3366

The Columns Bed
& Breakfast,
19 East Wright Street;
(406) 547-3666

PLACES TO EAT
IN RUSSELL COUNTRY

LEWISTOWN
Yogo Restaurant,
211 East Main;
(406) 538-8721

The Whole Famdamily,
206 West Main;
(406) 538-5161

Poor Man's Books
and Coffee,
413 West Main;
(406) 538-4277

Eddie's Corner,
17 miles west of town;
(406) 374-2471

HAVRE
Duck Inn,
1300 1st Street;
(406) 265-9615

Park Hotel,
335 1st Street;
(406) 265-7891

4-Bs,
604 1st Street West;
(406) 265-9721

Canton Chinese Restaurant,
439 1st Street West;
(406) 265-6666

CHOTEAU
Log Cabin Cafe,
U.S. Highway 89;
(406) 466-2888

Circle N,
925 North Main;
(406) 466-5531

Outpost Deli,
North Main Street;
(406) 466-5330

GREAT FALLS
Bert and Ernie's,
301 1st Avenue South;
(406) 453-0601

Best Western Heritage Inn,
1700 Fox Farm Road;
(406) 761-1900

Philly's,
400 10th Avenue South (at
the Holiday Inn);
(406) 727-7200

WHITE SULPHUR SPRINGS
Stockman Bar
& Restaurant,
117 East Main Street;
(406) 547-9985

Truck Stop Cafe, 511 East
Main Street;
(406) 547-3825

Index

A

A & S Tribal Industries, 127
Absaroka Range, 93
Afterbay Reservoir, 113
American Computer Museum, 81
Anaconda, 61
Anaconda Smelter Stack, 61
Anaconda Visitor Center Complex, 61
Anatosaurus, 119
Ant Flat Natural Resource Education
    Center and Historic Site, 3
Archie Bray Foundation for
    the Ceramic Arts, 67
Arts Chateau, 59
Augusta, 69

B

Bair Family Museum, 160
Baker, 119
Bannack, 45
Beartooth National Scenic Byway, 98
Bear's Paw Battlefield, 150
Bear's Paw Mountains, 150
Beaver Creek Park, 150
Beaverhead County, 41
Beaverhead County Museum, 47
Bellview School, 154
Bench Ranch, 95
Berkeley Pit, 56
Bigfork, 13
Bigfork Summer Playhouse, 13
Bighorn Canyon National
    Recreation Area, 111
Big Horn County Historical
    Museum and Visitor Center, 113
Big Montana Sheep Drive, 94
Big Mountain Environmental
    Education Center, 18
Big Open, 123

Big Sheep Creek Back
    Country Byway, 48
Big Spring State Hatchery, 142
Big Timber, 93
Billings, 106
Blaine County Museum, 152
Bob Marshall Wilderness Area, 25
Bohart Ranch, 83
Boiling River, 88
Boulder, 56
Bozeman, 73, 81
Bozeman Trail, 113
Browning, 24
Bull River Ranger Station, 7
Burlington Northern Depot, 19
Butte, 56

C

Carbon County Historical
    Museum, 98
Carousel for Missoula, 32
Carter County Museum, 119
Cassidy, Butch, 129
Castle, 162
Centennial Valley, 49
C. M. Russell National Wildlife
    Refuge, 133
Charles Waters Nature Trail, 35
Charlie Russell Chew Choo, 143
Chatham Fine Art gallery, 91
Cheyenne Indian Museum, 115
Chief Joseph, 150
Chief Plenty Coups
    Memorial Park, 110
Child Kleffner Ranch, 67
Chinook, 151
Choteau, 152
Church Universal and
    Triumphant, 89

Circle, 124
Clearwater Canoe Trail, 26
Clearwater Lake, 25
Cody, Buffalo Bill, 6, 91
Colstrip, 115
Colter, John, 75
Columbus, 95
Conover's Trading Post, 43
Corwin Springs, 89
Creston, 15
Creston Fish Hatchery, 16
Crow Agency, 113
Crow Fair, 113
Crow Indians, 88, 113–15
Crystal Park, 44
Culbertson, 127
Custer, General George
    Armstrong, 112

D

Daly, Marcus, 59
Daniels County, 130
Danny On Memorial Trail, 19
Darby, 35
Dell, 47
Dempsey-Gibbons world
    championship heavyweight
    fight, 152
Depot Center, 91
Dillon, 47
Dirty Shame Saloon, 2
Drummond, 63
Dumas Brothel Museum, 58

E

E-57B Electric Train Engine, 159
Earthquake Lake, 50
Earth Science Museum, 148
Egg Mountain, 152
Ekalaka, 119
Elkhorn, 56
Elkhorn Hot Springs, 44

Ennis, 51
Ennis National Fish Hatchery, 52
Eureka, 3
Eva Gates Homemade Preserves, 14
Evelyn Cameron Gallery, 122

F

Fairfield, 154
Festival of Nations, 97
Fishtail, 95
Flathead Indians, 8
Fort Benton, 145
Fort Benton Museum, 146
Fort Benton Park, 146
Fort Keough, 116
Fort Peck Dam, 132
Fort Peck Lake, 133
Fort Peck Theatre, 133
Fort Union Trading Post National
    Historic Site, 126
Four Winds Indian Trading
    Post, 9
Free Enterprise Health Mine, 55
Frontier Montana Museum, 63

G

Gallatin City, 73
Gallatin National Forest
    rental cabins, 81
Gallatin Petrified Forest, 89
Garfield County, 124
Garfield County Museum, 124
Garnet, 28
Garnet Ghost Town, 28
Gatiss Gardens, 1
Ghost Town Hall of Fame, 62
Giant Springs State Park, 156
Gigantic Warm Spring, 144
Glacier National Park, 19
Glasgow, 131
Glendive, 119
Going-to-the-Sun Sun Tours, 24

Granite Mountain Mine
    Memorial, 60
Granruds' Lefse Shack, 131
Graves Hotel, 160
Great Centennial Cattle Drive, 110
Great Falls, 154

H

H. Earl Clack Memorial
    Museum, 149
Hardin, 113
Harlowton, 159
Havre, 149
Headwaters Heritage
    Museum, 76
Headwaters State Park, 73
Hearst Free Library, 61
Helena, 64
Hell Creek State Park
    and Marina, 124
Hi Country Trading Post, 68
High Altitude Sports Center, 59
Historic Darby Ranger
    Station, 37
Historical Museum at
    Fort Missoula, 31
Hi-Line, 149
Hogan Cabin, 43
Homesteader Days, 109
Horner, Jack, 152
Hornet Peak Fire Lookout, 20
House of 10,000 Dolls, 148
Humbug Spires, 60
Hungry Horse Dam Visitor
    Center, 21
Huntley Project Museum of
    Irrigated Agriculture, 109
Hutterites, 160

I

Ingomar, 116
Inventors Hall of Fame, 84

J

J. C. Adams Stone Barn, 154
Jackson Hot Springs, 45
James Kipp Park, 141
Jardine, 88
Jewel Basin Hiking Area, 15
John Colter Run, 76
John L. Clarke Western
    Art Gallery and Memorial
    Museum, 23
Jordan, 123
Judith Mountains, 143

K

Kibler and Kirch, 97
Kintla Lake, 21
Kirk Hill Nature Center, 81
Knievel, Evel, 53
Knievel, Robbie, 134
Kootenai Falls, 6

L

Lake County, 9
Lake Mason National
    Wildlife Refuge, 110
Lakeview, 51
Lame Deer, 115
Last Chance Gulch, 64
Laurin, 53
Les Mason Park, 19
Lewis & Clark National
    Historic Trail, 146
Lewis and Clark, 32, 75, 109, 139, 156
Lewis and Clark Festival, 157
Lewis and Clark State
    Memorial, 146
Lewistown, 139, 141
Libby, 5
Libby Logger Days, 5
Lil' Joe, 63
Lincoln, 68
Lincoln County, 5

Livingston, 91
Logan, 79
Lolo Pass Winter Sports
   Area, 32
Loma, 147
Lost Creek State Park, 61

M

M & S Meats, 13
Madison Buffalo Jump
   State Park, 79
Madison Canyon Earthquake
   Area, 50
Magpie Toymakers, 98
Maiden, 143
Makoshika State Park, 119
Malmstrom Air Force Base Museum
   and Air Park, 158
Malta, 134
Manhattan Potato Festival, 81
Marias Museum of History
   and Art, 152
Martinsdale Colony, 160
McCone County, 124
McCone County Museum, 124
McLeod, 95
Medicine Lake National Wildlife
   Refuge, 123
Medicine Rocks State Park, 119
Mehmke Steam Museum, 158
Miles City, 116
Miles, General Nelson A., 116, 151
Milwaukee Road, 116, 159
Miracle of America
   Museum, 10
Mission Mountains, 8
Mission Mountain Winery, 13
Missoula, 30
Missouri Coteau, 129
Missoula Farmers' Market, 32
Missouri Breaks Back Country
   Byway, 139

Moccasin, 158
MonDak Heritage Center, 125
Monida, 48
Montana Agricultural Center and
   Museum of the Northern Great
   Plains, 147
Montana Candy Emporium, 98
Montana Cowboy Poetry
   Gathering, 142
Montana Law Enforcement
   Museum, 63
Montana Mule Days, 63
Montana Sheepherders
   Hall of Fame, 124
Montana Valley Bookstore, 34
Montana Woolen Shop, 84
Moss Mansion, 105
MSU Central Agricultural
   Research Center, 158
Museum of the Montana Historical
   Society, 66
Museum of the Plains Indian, 24
Museum of the Rockies, 81
Museum of the Yellowstone, 87
Myrna Loy Center for the
   Performing Arts, 67

N

Nashua, 132
Natural Bridge State
   Monument, 95
Nature Conservancy, 154
Nelson Reservoir, 134
Ninemile Remount Depot and
   Ranger Station, 29, 33
Ninepipes Museum of
   Early Montana, 10
Norris, 54
North American Indian Days, 24
Northern Cheyenne Indian
   Reservation, 115
Northwest Peak Scenic Area, 3

O

O'Fallon Historical Museum, 119
Old Fort Park, 147
Old Jail Museum, 7
Old Log Schoolhouse, 8
Old Montana Prison, 63
Old Number One, 58
Old Prison Players, 63
Old Trail Museum, 152
Old Works Golf Course, 61
Opheim, 131
Original Governor's Mansion, 65
Osprey Nest Antiques, 13
Our Lady of the Rockies, 60
Outlaw Trail, 129
Out to Lunch, 31
O'Fallon Historical Museum, 119

P

Paddlefish Spawning Run, 121
Paradise, 8
Patagonia Outlet, 47
People's Center, 10
Philipsburg, 62
Phillips County, 133
Pictograph Cave State
    Historic Site, 107
Pine Butte Swamp Preserve, 153
Pioneer Mountains National
    Scenic Byway, 44
Pioneer Town and Museum, 130
Plains, 7
Plentywood, 128
Plummer, Henry, 46, 53
Polebridge Mercantile, 20
Polson, 10
Pompeys Pillar National Historic
    Landmark, 109
Pony, 54
Poplar, 127
Prairie Drive In Theatre, 122
Pryor, 110

Pryor Mountain Wild
    Horse Range, 99

R

Range Riders Museum and
    Memorial Hall, 116
Red Lodge, 97
Red Rock Lakes National
    Wildlife Refuge, 49
Reedpoint, 95
Rendezvous Ski Trails, 87
Richard E. Wood Watchable
    Wildlife Area, 149
Riverfront Park, 107
Robber's Roost, 53
Rock Creek Testicle Festival, 25
Rocky Boy's Indian Reservation, 150
Rocky Mountain Elk
    Foundation, 30
Rolling Hills Llamas and
    Exotics, 129
Roosevelt, Teddy, 119
Roscoe, 96
Rosebud Battlefield
    State Monument, 112
Rosebud County Courthouse, 115
Rosebud County Pioneer
    Museum, 115
Ross Creek Scenic Area, 6
Roundup, 110
Russell, Charles M., 133

S

Sacajawea, 109
Saco, 133
Saint Xavier, 111
Seeley Lake, 23
Shelby, 152
Sheridan County Museum, 128
Sidney, 125
Sitting Bull, 128
Smokejumpers Visitor Center, 30

INDEX

Square Butte, 144
St. Helena Cathedral, 67
St. Ignatius Mission, 9
St. Labre Mission, 115
St. Mary of the Assumption
    Catholic Church, 53
St. Mary's Mission, 34
Stan Kalinski Collection, 132
Stevensville, 35
Stringed Instrument Division, 31
Sun River Wildlife Management
    Area, 69
Sweet Pea Festival, 83

T

Terry, 122
Thompson Falls, 7
Three Dog Down, 11
Three Forks, 73
Three Forks Saddlery, 77
Tipi Hills, 128
Tobacco Valley Historical
    Village, 3
Towe Ford Museum, 63
Trout Creek Huckleberry
    Festival, 7
Troy, 5
Twin Bridges, 53

U

Ulm Pishkun State Park, 157

V

Valley County Pioneer Museum, 131

Virginia City, 52

W

Wahkpa Chu'gn Archaeological
    Site, 149
Warren, 100
Watchable Wildlife Triangle, 35
Westby, 129
West Fork Falls, 3
West Yellowstone, 50, 83
Whitefish, 20
White Sulphur Springs, 162
Wildest One Day Show
    on Earth, 69
Wildhorse Island State Park, 12
Wild Horse Stampede, 127
Wildlife Visitor Center, 30
Willoughby Environmental
    Education Area, 35
Willow Creek, 78
Willow Creek Tool, 79
Winston Rod Company, 53
Wolf Creek Wild Game Feed, 69
Wolf Point, 127
World Famous Bucking
    Horse Sale, 117
World Museum of Mining on Hell
    Roarin' Gulch, 57

Y

Yaak, 4
Yellowstone Kelly's Grave, 105
Yellowtail Dam Visitor Center, 112
Yesterday's Playthings, 63

About the Author

Michael McCoy, a former eighteen-year resident of Montana, lives in Teton Valley, Idaho, where on a clear day, he can still see Montana. His outdoor and travel writing has appeared in *Snow Country, Men's Journal, Bicycling, Montana,* and other national and regional publications, and he serves as managing editor of *Jackson Hole* magazine. McCoy holds degrees in anthropology from the University of Wyoming and zoology from The University of Montana. His other Globe Pequot books include *The Wild West* and *Journey to the Northern Rockies.*

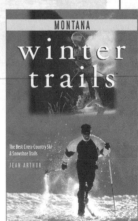